PIUS X

PIUS X

THE LIFE-STORY OF THE BEATUS

THE NEW ITALIAN LIFE OF PIUS X

By

FR. HIERONYMO DAL-GAL

TRANSLATED AND ADAPTED

By

THOMAS F. MURRAY, M.A.

DUBLIN

M. H. GILL AND SON LTD.

50 UPPER O'CONNELL STREET

1954

First Published, December, 1953.
Reprinted, February, 1954, May, 1954.

Nihil Obstat :
WILFRIDUS HILL,
Censor Deputatus.

Imprimatur :
✠ HENRICUS VINCENTIUS,
Epus Salfordiensis.

SALFORDII, *die* 29° *Junii, anno* 1953.

*Printed and Bound in the Republic of Ireland at the Press
of the Publishers.*

CONTENTS

ILLUSTRATIONS

TRANSLATOR'S PREFACE

THE new life of Pius X by Father Hieronymo Dal Gal is a valuable historical work based on the evidence of the witnesses consulted at the Diocesan and Apostolic Processes for the Beatification and Canonization and on the other sources enumerated in the list of documents. In 1951, on the occasion of the Beatification, Father Dal Gal published a work entitled *Beato Pio X*. This work has been translated into French and German but an English translation was never attempted, possibly because the Italian work is much in the nature of a compilation of facts with copious footnote references to sources only available in Italian. For the ordinary English reader such footnotes would be of little use, but without them the work would lose much of its purpose and might appear unduly repetitive, for in many places several witnesses are quoted for the same event.

The new life by Father Dal Gal, though shorter, presents the translator with the same difficulty, and this deterred me for some time from complying with the author's request to translate his work into English. It was only when he assured me that I was perfectly free to make omissions and abbreviations and to mould the material in any way which seemed suitable for an English reading public, that I braced myself for the effort, encouraged by such learned and competent judges as the Rt. Rev. Mgr. C. L. H. Duchemin, M.A., Rector of the Pontifical Beda College, and the Rev. Dr. Murphy, Procurator General of the Holy Ghost Fathers; to these eminent men I am sincerely grateful.

I owe a particular debt of gratitude to the many students of the Pontifical Beda College who helped me in a variety of ways, but especially to Mr. E. G. Riley, M.A., for his useful suggestions and for the care with which he corrected the manuscript and assisted me with the reading of the proofs.

Finally I must express my thanks to the Catholic Truth Society for their kind permission to quote directly from their English translation of the encyclical *Pascendi Dominici Gregis* in the chapter entitled " Instaurare omnia in Christo."

DOCUMENTS

1. Acta Pii X. P.M. (1903-1908), v. I-V. Romæ 1905-1914.
2. Acta Apostolicæ Sedis (1909-1914), v. I-VI. Romæ 1909-1914.
3. Pastoral Letters of the Bishop of Mantua (1885-1894).
4. Pastoral Letters of the Patriarch of Venice (1894-1903).
5. Private Letters of the Beatus.
6. Diocesan and Apostolic Processes for the Cause of Beatification and Canonization:

    Rome: Dioc. (1923-1931); Ap. (1943-1946).
    Venice: Dioc. (1924-1930); Ap. (1944-1946).
    Mantua: Dioc. (1924-1927); Ap. (1945-1946).
    Treviso: Dioc. (1923-1926); Ap. (1944-1946).

    Of the 240 witnesses who were interrogated in these Processes we have confined ourselves to the most authoritative, giving preference to those who were in daily contact with Pius X, beginning with his relations and friends and those who knew him in his infancy and youth, *e.g.*, the peasants of Riese, Tombolo and Salzano, the clergy and people of Treviso, Mantua and Venice, and the Prelates and Cardinals of the Roman Curia.

7. The Acts for the Introduction and Prosecution of the Cause of Beatification and Canonization:

    (*a*) Romana: Beatificationis et Canonizationis S. D. Pii Papæ X:
    Positio super Introductione Causæ. Romæ 1942.

    (*b*) Romana: Beatificationis et Canonizationis S. D. Pii Papæ X:
    Positio super Virtutibus. Romæ 1949.

    (*c*) Romana: Beatificationis et Canonizationis S. D. Pii Papæ X:
    Nova Positio super Virtutibus. Romæ 1950.

    (*d*) Romana: Beatificationis et Canonizationis S. D. Pii Papæ X:
    Positio super Miraculis. Romæ 1949-1951.

8. Monsignor G. Bressan, who was Private Secretary of the Beatus from the time he became Bishop of Mantua till his death (1885-1914).

9. Monsignor G. Pescini, who worked with the Beatus when he was Patriarch of Venice and was a co-worker of Mgr. Bressan during the Pontificate (1903-1914).

PUBLICATIONS OF HISTORIC VALUE

1. Monsignor A. Marchesan: *Papa Pio X.* Rome, 1910.

2. Sac L. Ferrari: *Pio X: Dalle mie Memorie.* Vicenza, 1922.

3. Monsignor G. Milanese: *Cenni biografici di Pio X.* Treviso, 1903.

4. Monsignor E. Bacchion: *Pio X (Giuseppe Sarto, Arciprete di Salzano: 1867-1875.)* Padua, 1925.

5. Cardinal R. Merry del Val: *Pio X: Impressioni Ricordi.* Padua, 1949.

CHRONOLOGY OF THE LIFE OF THE BEATUS
(June 2nd, 1835—August 20th, 1914)

1835	June 2nd.	Birth at Riese.
	June 3rd.	Baptism.
1845	September 1st.	Confirmation.
1847	April 6th.	First Communion.
1850	September 19th.	Reception of clerical cassock.
	November.	Entrance to Seminary of Padua.
1851	September 20th.	Tonsure.
1856	November.	First two Minor Orders.
1857	June 6th.	Second two Minor Orders.
	September 19th.	Subdiaconate.
1858	February 27th.	Diaconate.
	September 18th.	Ordination.
	November 29th.	Curate of Tombolo.
1867	July 14th.	Parish priest of Salzano.
1875	November 28th.	Canon of Treviso.
1879	November 27th.	Vicar Capitular.
1884	November 16th.	Bishop of Mantua.
1893	June 12th.	Cardinal.
1893	June 15th.	Patriarch of Venice.
1903	August 4th.	Supreme Pontiff.
1903	August 9th.	Coronation.
1908	September 18th.	Jubilee of Priesthood.
1909	November 16th.	Jubilee of Episcopate.
1914	August 20th.	Death.

ELEVEN YEARS PONTIFICATE
(1903-1914)

1903   October 4th.   Programme of Pontificate, *E Supremi apostolatus cathedra*.

      November 22nd.   Motu Proprio on Church Music.

      December 18th.   Motu Proprio, *Tra le sollecitudini*, on Catholic Action.

1904   January 20th.   *Commissum Nobis*: Condemnation of *veto* in conclave.

      February 2nd.   Encyclical, *Ad diem illum*, fifty years after definition of dogma of Immaculate Conception.

      February 11th.   Pastoral, *Quum arcano*: Apostolic visitation of the city of Rome.

      March 7th.   Decree, *Constat apud omnes*: Apostolic visitation of the dioceses of Italy.

      March 12th.   Encyclical, *Iucunda sane*: 13th Centenary of Gregory the Great.

      March 19th.   Motu Proprio, *Arduum sane munus*: Codification of Canon Law.

1905   April 15th.   Encyclical, *Acerbo Nimis*: teaching of Catechism.

      May 14th.   Pastoral, *Acre nefariumque bellum*: against the laws persecuting the Church in the Republic of Ecuador.

      June 11th.   Encyclical, *Il fermo proposito*: Catholic Action in Italy.

      December 20th.   Decree, *Sacra Tridentina Synodus*: on frequent and daily Communion.

1906   January 16th.   Reform of the Italian Seminaries.

      February 11th.   Encyclical, *Vehementer*: Condemnation of the separation of Church and State in France.

      July 28th.   Encyclical, *Pieni l'animo*, on the education of young clerics.

December 26th.   Apostolic letter to the Bishops of the East on the union of Churches.

1911 May 24th.   Encyclical, *Jamdudum in Lusitania*: condemnation of the laws persecuting the Church in Portugal.

November 1st.   Apostolic Constitution, *Divino afflatu*, on the reform of the Roman Breviary.

1912 January 1st.   Apostolic Constitution, *Etsi Nos*: reform of the Roman Vicariate.

September 24th.   Encyclical, *Singulari quadam*: on the Unions in Germany.

1913 March 8th.   Apostolic Letter, *Universis Christifidelibus*: on the occasion of the 16th Centenary of Constantine.

1914 August 2nd.   Exhortation, *Dum Europa*: to the Catholics of the world to implore the cessation of the war.

BEATIFICATIONS AND CANONIZATIONS
PERFORMED BY BLESSED PIUS X

BEATIFICATIONS

1904   August 29th.   Gaspare del Bufalo, Founder of the Missionaries of the Most Precious Blood.

September 8th.   John Baptist Vianney, parish priest of Ars.

October 23rd.   Agatangelo da Vendôme and Cassiano da Nantes, of the Order of Friars Min. Cap., Martyrs in Abyssinia.

November 1st.   Stefano Bellesini of the Hermits of St. Augustine, parish priest of Genazzano.
Marco Stefano da Körös, Canon of Strigonia (Hungary).
Stefano Pongracz and Melchiore Grodecz, S.J., Martyrs of Cassovia (Hungary).

1906   March 19th.   Giulia Billiart, Foundress of the Congregation of the Sisters of Our Lady of Namur (Belgium).

April 15th.   Eight Martyrs of Tonchino.

May 13th.   The Carmelite Martyrs of Compiègne.

May 21st.   Bonaventure of Barcellona (Friars Minor).

1908   January 22nd.   Maria Maddalena Postel, Foundress of the Institute of the Sisters of the Christian Schools.

January 31st.   Maddalena Sofia Barat, Foundress of the Society of the Sacred Heart.

May 3rd.   Gabriel of Addolorata, Passionist.

1909 April 11th. Joan of Arc.
John Eudes, Founder of the
Congregation of Jesus and Mary.
The Chinese Martyrs.

CANONIZATIONS

1904 December 11th. Alexander Sauli Barnabita, Bishop
of Aleria and then of Pavia.
Gerard Majella.

1909 May 20th. Joseph Oriol, Canon of Barcelona.
Clement Hofbauer of the Congrega-
tion of the Holy Redeemer.

MARGHERITA SANSON

CHAPTER I

HUMBLE BEGINNINGS
(June 2nd, 1835—September 18th, 1858)

> "From the very beginning of his life he resembled his divine Master, by the poverty and humility of the surroundings in which he was born." (Cardinal W. O'Connell, Archbishop of Boston, October 10th, 1935).

TWO CHRISTIAN PARENTS

A SHORT distance off the road which runs through the valley at the foot of Mt. Grappa, leading from Castelfranco Veneto to the picturesque hills of Asolo, lies a little village called Riese. On the afternoon of June 3rd, 1835, a group of mothers and godparents came out of the whitewashed church in that village after the Baptismal ceremonies. One of them carried a baby boy in her arms under a shawl and made her way to a humble cottage on the outskirts of the village. Margherita Sanson, the child's mother, had chosen the name " Giuseppe " (Joseph) for her son, little realizing the full significance of her choice, for as his patron had been the guardian of the Word made Flesh in the village of Nazareth, he was destined to become the guardian of the Mystical Body of Christ on the chair of St. Peter—the future Pope Pius X.

His parents, Giovanni Battista Sarto and Margherita Sanson, were simple, pious, hard-working country folk. His father was the local " Cursore "—a sort of Process Server combined with the menial function of messenger for the local municipality—and worked for about three shillings a day, and his mother supplemented the family income by her work as a seamstress.

They had not a great deal of the goods of this world—a small cottage completely destitute of anything that savoured of luxury, to which was attached a tiny plot of not very fertile land—but their wealth consisted of their profound faith, which they handed down to their children. In that

I

household a truly Christian spirit prevailed. The mother and father worked hard from early morning till late at night, endeavouring to provide for their ten children the necessaries of life. The will of God was their rule of life; they did not envy those who were rich, because they possessed the inestimable treasure of happiness, which could not be found in the possession of temporal things.

Giuseppe Sarto began to attend the elementary school of the village at a very early age. He was a happy little fellow and threw himself whole-heartedly into every one of the school activities. At games he was a leader and was always ready to take a beating; at study he showed an extraordinary ability for a child of his age, and at play-time he was ever ready to play pranks and take the consequences.

"He was the best boy in the school," writes one of his classmates; and "he was so good," affirms another, "that when the teacher was absent, no better prefect could be found than little Sarto."

Giuseppe had a sprightly nature which had to be kept in check, but his good mother took special care to curb but not suppress this natural exuberance, with tenderness or severity, as the occasion demanded. Françesco Gecherle, his school master, played his part, too, not failing to make generous use of the cane, which in those days was considered the most effective means of education. But if Giuseppe gave full play to the liveliness of his nature at play-time, he was no less whole-hearted about his studies at school; he would not go out to play until all his exercises were finished and all his lessons thoroughly learnt, and his recollection at times of prayer showed that he had a deep appreciation of the things of God. After an energetic game in the evening he would leave his companions and make for the little Church, where he would spend ten minutes or so in front of the Blessed Sacrament in fervent prayer, before returning home to help his mother, eat his supper and retire to his wooden bed.

Don Tito Fusarini, the parish priest, taught Giuseppe to serve Mass while he was still very young, and as soon as he had reached perfection in this elementary liturgical ceremony he eagerly awaited his turn and considered no punishment worse than to be deprived of it. Being dressed up in cassock and cotta, leading the priest to the altar, and bringing the heads of the whole congregation to a posture of adoration with a mere stroke of the bell naturally appealed to his childish instincts, but the fervour with which he recited the prayers, of which he understood not a word, and the regularity and alacrity with which he turned up daily for Mass showed that his attraction to the altar was much deeper.

At the Sunday school service Giuseppe always raced to take up a prominent place in the front row. He listened carefully to every word that fell from the lips of the parish priest as he explained the catechism and prescribed the portion to be learnt by heart for the next week. Don Tito Fusarini had a system of monthly examinations; the marks of each pupil were noted down and preserved not only in the church, but in every cottage in the village. It was these examinations which first brought Giuseppe into close relation with his pastor, for month by month his name took a leading place on the marks' sheet. Don Tito quickly realized that he had qualities quite unusual in a boy of his age and grew to love him and hold him up as an example to the other children.

One day while explaining the catechism Don Fusarini said, "I will give an apple to anyone who can tell me where God is." A deadly silence came over the pensive congregation for a moment or so, until Giuseppe jumped to his feet and declared, "And I will give two apples to anyone who can tell me where God isn't." This solidly theological reply, so spontaneously given, left the parish priest speechless. In future every time he spoke to his parishioners about the Cursore's little boy, he concluded with immense satisfaction: "You don't know what a great youngster little Sarto is. . . He has a brilliant intelligence."

"I WANT TO BE A PRIEST"

The little school of Riese had only two classes. When a child had finished those, he had either to go to Castelfranco Veneto to the grammar school or bring his school days to a hasty conclusion. When Giuseppe Sarto had finished his two years elementary schooling he began to take lessons in the rudiments of Latin grammar from Don Luigi Orazio, the curate, while the parish priest prepared him for the Sacrament of Confirmation, which he received on September 1st, 1845, in the cathedral of Asolo from the hands of Mgr. Giovanni Battista Sartori-Canova, Titular Bishop of Mindo.

The sanctuary was the centre of little Giuseppe's life. Day by day as he served Mass, paid frequent visits to the Blessed Sacrament and took lessons in Latin and Christian doctrine, the idea of becoming a priest developed in his mind. He could not give full vent to this ambition, as the obstacles which stood in his way were, humanly speaking, insuperable. But the divine whisper which he heard deep down in his heart would not be silenced by worldly persuasions.

Very often when alone with his mother, Giuseppe would whisper in her ear: "Mother, I would like so much to be a priest." And at such moments instead of considering the absurdity of the project in view of their poverty, Margherita Sanson's heart would swell with pride at the thought of seeing her "Bepi "[1] celebrating the Divine Mysteries at the altar of God.

But to Giovanni Battista Sarto the proposition appeared in different colours. The family was increasing, the struggle of life was becoming more difficult, and many new uses had been found for his three shillings a day. Furthermore, drought and constant use did not improve the fertility of the soil in the little plot of land. His son a priest! He a priest on whom he counted to supplement the family resources. Impossible! At first he was gravely tempted to refuse flatly, but his faith and the persuasive words of Margherita and the parish priest were forces before which his worldly prudence must yield. The subtle tongue of Don Tito Fusarini found a ready answer for his every objection, and kept up the fight until finally Giovanni bowed his head submissively and concluded: "If God wills it . . . if God wills it."

---

[1] A colloquial contraction of Giuseppe.

"Bravo, Battista!" exclaimed the parish priest, much gratified with his victory, and he lost no time in getting Giuseppe started at the senior elementary school at Castelfranco Veneto.

ELEMENTARY STUDIES

Every morning for the next four years Giuseppe had to rise at a very early hour. He attended the first Mass in the parish church, hurried home to his breakfast—a cup of coffee and a little dry bread—and then walked four miles to Castelfranco Veneto with his satchel of books on his back and very often with his sandals slung across his shoulder to prolong their life. As he walked through the village of Riese he saluted everyone he met, for the son of the Cursore was well known to them all. Besides books in the satchel, there were a few pieces of bread with some meat or a little cheese for his lunch. It was wholly inadequate to satisfy the appetite of a growing boy, and he was often forced to ask his companions for something to relieve his hunger.

The long journey on foot in the severe cold and thick mists of the winter and the enervating heat of the summer, the poverty of his clothing and the insufficiency of his diet, served only to harden his spirit for the life of sacrifice and labour which he was to lead as priest, bishop and pope.

He was poor indeed, but the best marks in the school were his. Even amongst the most assiduous of his fellow-students he had an easy first place. Count Louro Quirini who was at school with Giuseppe tells us: "I was a boarder, Sarto was a day boy. I remember him distinctly. I remember his shabby clothing which provided us with no little amusement; I remember seeing him pull his 'lunch' out of his satchel and consume it ravenously. But he was dear to us all; he never complained of his poverty, was always cheerful, and was the best boy in the school." Another contemporary of his, Mgr. Pellizzari, testifies: "He was goodness itself, an angel of purity, and a great lover of studies. He took a first place in all school subjects and meticulously observed all disciplinary regulations."

His teachers admired him and never tired of pointing him out to the whole class as an example of willingness, diligence and virtue.

At the mid-day break Giuseppe generally went to the house of Giovanni Battista Finazzi, a tax collector, who was a friend of the Cursore of Riese. Here he ate the meagre lunch which he had carried in his satchel. Sometimes Finazzi's wife was moved to pity and added a little to his morsel. It frequently happened during the winter that the walk from Riese to Castelfranco Veneto became impossible, and Giuseppe would be obliged to spend several days with the Finazzi family. Then the good woman of the house would prepare a little altar for him, because she knew it gave him great pleasure to perform, in his own childish way, the ceremonies of the Mass. This was a kindness he appreciated very much, and to show his gratitude he used to help her son Francesco, who was in the same class, with his Latin.

When he returned to Riese in the evening after his long walk and day of hard study he did not waste his time; he did his exercises, learned his lessons, ran messages for his father and helped his mother in whatever way he could. Knowing the sacrifices his parents were making to provide for their large family he tried to earn a little money by giving lessons to the children of the well-to-do families of the neighbourhood.

During the holidays he served Mass nearly every morning for both the parish priest and the curate. After breakfast he would set off with a band of youngsters of his own age to the sanctuary of the Madonna of Cendrole, a short distance outside the town. There the little party would recite the *Litany of Our Lady* and sing hymns in her honour. Giuseppe was always regarded as the leader and was loved and respected by the other children and their parents.

AN ANXIOUS WAIT

When Giuseppe Sarto had completed his fourth year at the senior school in 1850 he was classified " excellent " in every one of the subjects he presented for the final examination. There was nothing now to prevent his continuing his studies and even realizing the dearest wish of his life—to serve his Lord as a priest in one of the parishes of the Diocese of Treviso.

But what could the poor Cursore do? He still had the same large family and the same small income. Night and morning he was preoccupied with the problem of its upkeep. Even had he known that one day his " Bepi " would sit on the chair of St. Peter, it was just impossible for him to pay the seminary fees.

Was the divine whisper in Giuseppe's heart to be hushed? Must he suppress the desire he cherished most on earth? Must he kill the germ of priestly vocation and be content to succeed his father in the capacity of Cursore? Divine Providence was watching over this predestined boy, in whose heart lay the secret of a great calling.

By an ancient privilege the Patriarch of Venice had the right of assigning a few free places in the seminary of Padua to poor boys of the diocese who were aspiring to the priesthood. The Patriarch at that time was Cardinal Jacopo Monico, son of a blacksmith of Riese. Don Tito Fusarini was fully convinced that no case was more deserving than that of Giuseppe. Determined not to leave anything to chance at this crucial moment, he set off to see the Vicar Capitular at Treviso, Mgr. Casagrande, and presented Giuseppe's case with all the persuasion at his command.

In the meantime there was prayer day and night in the Sarto household. Giuseppe prayed more fervently than ever before, because he realized that his whole future hung in the balance. Kneeling before the picture of Our Lady in his bedroom each night, he recited the Rosary, pausing each time he came to the phrase, " Pray for us sinners now," for apart from the moment of death, what hour could be more important than this?

After a month of prayer and anxiety the answer finally came. Mgr. Casagrande, on August 28th, 1850, wrote to Giovanni Battista Sarto thus:

" It gives me great pleasure to inform you that His Eminence the Cardinal Patriarch of Venice has deigned to grant your son, Giuseppe, a free place in the seminary at Padua. I should like to point out that His Eminence took cognisance of the recommendation of His Lordship the Bishop, and graciously vouchsafed his consent."

Giuseppe could not contain himself for joy. There was untold rejoicing in that household, and Margherita Sanson began to feel that he was already ordained, and made the other children show him great respect.

IN THE SEMINARY AT PADUA

November 13th, 1850, was a cold, wintry morning, but it was the morning on which Giuseppe Sarto took the first major step towards the priesthood when he entered the seminary at Padua.

His new mode of life was vastly different from what he had been accustomed to: he had his own cubicle, a strict routine, long hours of study and prayer and, what appealed to him most of all, community life. Far from thinking this curriculum exacting, Giuseppe found here a haven of peace—the manner of life most suited to his nature. By his extraordinary application to study, his fervour at prayer and his cheerfulness at recreation he made full use of all the seminary had to offer him and quickly won the esteem of his professors and the affection of his companions.

"I get on well with all, both superiors and companions," he wrote a month after his entrance to the seminary to the curate of Riese, Don Pietro Jacuzzi. He got on well because his love for study and his priestly vocation had at last found the atmosphere in which they could flourish. He fully merited the splendid report of his professors at the end of the first term; he had first place among fifty-six students. At the end of the scholastic year, 1850-1851, he was honoured with this enviable eulogy: "Disciplinæ nemini secundus—ingenii maximi—memoriæ summæ—spei maximæ." [1]

This magnificent report was repeated invariably from year to year until the son of the Cursore departed from the

---

[1] "In discipline second to none, of the greatest ability, (blest) with a very great memory, and (giving) the highest promise."

THE COTTAGE AT RIESE

seminary, no longer a seminarian, but a priest. He received the Tonsure on September 20th, 1851, from the hands of his Bishop in the Cathedral of Asolo.

A GRAVE SORROW

The second year of the seminary course, which began under the most joyful auspices, was to be darkened by a most sorrowful event for the young cleric.

One morning at the end of April, 1852, Giuseppe Sarto entered the Rector's room and, with tears in his eyes, requested permission to go home.

"But why?" enquired the Rector, sympathetically.

"Because my father is gravely ill," replied Giuseppe, although it is highly probable, as Mgr. G. B. Rosa asserted, that no human voice had told him so.

On May 4th, 1852, the Cursore of Riese, after a short illness, went to his reward. The death of Giovanni Battista Sarto was a great shock to poor Margherita and left her without support for her eight young children. But she was a woman of admirable faith and knew how to accept this heavy cross from the hands of God with courage and Christian resignation.

And for young Giuseppe it was no less a calamity. His mind, which had formerly devoted all its energy to study and prayer, was now preoccupied with the thought of his poor mother left alone in the world, deprived of all resources and faced with a life of suffering, misery and want. He showed no signs of despondency but accepted the bitter trial from the hands of his Lord, flatly rejecting the suggestion of one of his paternal uncles that he, as eldest son, should succeed his father as Cursore, in order to help his mother in the upbringing of her large family. His manliness and resignation merited for him yet another title to the praise of his professors.

His brilliant success at study and the continual praise he received from all did not make him proud; he was always humble and modest, docile and prompt to obey every suggestion of his superiors, whose authority and prestige he carefully defended amongst his fellow students. " Eminent in study, in diligence and piety," wrote Mgr. P. Zamburlini, Archbishop of Udine, " he was a model for all in the Seminary."

A SAD HOLIDAY

First among the thirty-nine students, Giuseppe Sarto finished his second year of Philosophy with the usual report. Yet another sorrow, however, weighed down his heart, for he knew that when he went home for his Autumn holidays he would no longer find Don Tito Fusarini and Don Pietro Jacuzzi. Don Fusarini, on account of ill health, was forced to give up parish work, and Don Jacuzzi, to the great disappointment of the people of the parish, had been transferred to a little village in the neighbourhood of Treviso. Without the company of these two holy priests who had started him off in his studies and had given him considerable financial help, his life at Riese was no longer what it used to be. This painful situation was aggravated by the fact that the new parish priest was rather contrary, and tried to introduce systems that were strange, and which did not help to change the unfavourable attitude of the people towards him.

Parish affairs did not run smoothly as they had done for so long, and the great pain Giuseppe suffered on account of it is recorded in a letter which he wrote on September 9th, 1854, to his beloved and by no means forgotten Don Jacuzzi, who now seemed so far away.

He wrote: " Reading the other day your kind and ever welcome letter, I experienced within myself untold joy in the recollection of those pleasant days which I spent in your company. Now all joy has vanished. The presbytery is a place of solitude, and its occupants find their happiness in the pursuit of their own pastimes and not in the friendship of the people. Though I feel sorry to see the Autumn days pass away, it is my greatest consolation to know that soon I shall be going back to the Seminary where once again I shall find peace and happiness."

During the three summer months which the seminarians

spent with their families, Giuseppe showed how much he
appreciated his new state of life, and in what great esteem he
held a priestly vocation. His days were spent between home,
church and presbytery, attending the devotional exercises,
teaching Christian doctrine to the children and assisting
the priests in the religious functions of the parish. Sometimes
in the evening he would go to the house of his sister, Teresa,
and his brother-in-law, Giovanni Battista Parolin, who
owned a little inn called " The Two Swords." Now and again
he accompanied the parish priest and curate to the villa
of the Countess Marina Loredan-Gradenigo, a spirited old
lady who had at one time been at the court of Napoleon I.

But as the holidays came to a close another difficulty arose.
He was poor and needed pocket money for the coming year.
Don Jacuzzi from time to time would send him a small sum,
but not nearly sufficient to defray his many expenses. With
no little confusion and embarrassment he was forced to make
a door-to-door visitation of the parish like a beggar in order
to raise enough money to pay for books and the many other
things essential to a seminary life. The good people of Riese
gave generously, for they knew that he was a good boy, and
they felt certain that their donations would be used in the
training of a zealous priest.

In November, 1854, Giuseppe began the study of Theology.
With what great anxiety had he awaited this day! All the
time spent in the study of letters and philosophy had been
but a preparation for that divine science which it is the
priest's duty to preach to the people.

In the study of Theology and the many kindred subjects
Giuseppe was in his element. From the outset, he manifested
a speculative mind, a clear and ordered judgment, an ever-
increasing desire to learn and a virtue made steadfast by his
single intention of preparing himself to serve God and the
people as well as he could.

He had the unanimous approval of his superiors, who at the
end of his first year of Theology reported to the Bishop of
Treviso, Mgr. Antonio Farina, on July 28th, 1855: " Sarto
is a veritable angel and is far ahead of any other student in
the college."

At the beginning of the last year of his scholastic studies (1856-1857) he had asked to be permitted to live in a private room and to go out for walks accompanied only by his dear companion, Pietro Zamburlini, afterwards Bishop of Udine (1896). His superiors esteemed him highly and did not hesitate to grant this request. Giuseppe deeply appreciated the kindness. This is how he related the event to Don Pietro Jacuzzi:

"I have now spent six happy years in the Seminary, and I hope to spend this one more happily than all the others. My good Superiors have listened to my petition and have given me the silence and solitude I have so much longed for. They have assigned to me a room where the bell and the clock cannot be heard and where there is plenty of scope for recollection and prayer. On walks I no longer have to join the long black file which fills with pity all who look upon it, but now I am allowed to go out with my good companion. I am charmed with this liberty and could wish for nothing better. My superiors seem pleased with my efforts, for I willingly accept any little task they give me in gratitude for so great a favour."

One of the " little tasks " was to take charge of the church music in the college, for the superiors were aware of the love for music which he had learned from Don Pietro Jacuzzi.

" BEATI MUNDO CORDE "

Giuseppe was deeply impressed by the holiness of his vocation. That beautiful virtue which the Divine Master raised to the level of a Beatitude in the Sermon on the Mount—" Blessed are the clean of heart "—blossomed in the depths of his soul and was reflected in his every word and act.

Not only strangers but his friends and his own parents and sisters bear witness to the fact that no doubtful word ever crossed his lips and that he manifested in all his actions the most scrupulous reserve, as the following little episode will show.

At the end of the scholastic year 1856-1857, while Giuseppe

was preparing to return home for the summer vacation, Margherita asked the kind-hearted Giovanni Battista Parolin to go along to Padua with his little pony and trap to bring Giuseppe home. Giovanni lost no time in setting out accompanied by his wife Teresa, Giuseppe's sister. Giuseppe objected strongly to mounting the trap, and said that he wanted to see a few things in the town, thus obliging Giovanni to follow at some distance behind. It was only when outside the town that Giuseppe agreed to climb into the trap, and even then he took care to alight whenever he came in sight of any of the scattered cottages along the road. The embarrassment of his sister and brother-in-law can be well imagined.

As soon as he arrived home, Giuseppe described the journey to his mother and begged her that if at any time in the future she was sending a conveyance for him, to try and send one without a woman in it.

" But Teresa is your sister, isn't she? " observed his mother.

" Yes, she is my sister, but while you know this and I know it, other people don't! "

The good Teresa was so struck by this behaviour of her brother that every time she related the episode she would conclude in all simplicity: " Blessed Mother of God! Had I known what that journey would be like I should have kept far away from Padua."

ORDINATION TO THE PRIESTHOOD

On December 22nd, 1855, the future Pius X received the first two Minor Orders at Treviso and the second two Minors on June 6th, 1857. He received the Subdiaconate on September 19th, 1857, and the Diaconate on February 27th, 1858. Not many months now remained before he was to arrive at the goal of his eight year course—the Priesthood.

The Rector of his Seminary, writing to the Rector of the Seminary of Treviso thus testifies of him: " Sarto in all the eight years which he has passed in this Seminary has left nothing to be desired. He was a constant example of sincerity, piety and conduct. I often pray that God will multiply young men of this stamp in our seminaries."

On September 18th, 1858, his Bishop, Mgr. Antonio Farina, in the Cathedral of Castelfranco Veneto, ordained him priest. Filled with joy and radiant with the deepest faith, Margherita Sanson was present with her daughters, Teresa, Rosa and Maria, who were so happy at the thought of having a priest in the family that they felt as though they had suddenly become ladies of rank.

The next day the son of the poor Cursore celebrated his First Holy Mass in the parish church of Riese. Prominent in the congregation was the humble Margherita, reaping the fruits of a life of work, sacrifice, and faith. From the depths of her heart there issued forth a hymn of thanks to the "Father of Mercy and the God of all consolation" (*I Cor.* i. 3).

But what would it have been if instead of the "Tu es Sacerdos," [1] she were present to hear her "Bepi" proclaimed "Tu es Petrus" [2] and raised to the highest dignity on earth. That unforgettable day was for Don Giuseppe Sarto the beginning of a new life; the life of a man of God entirely dedicated to the salvation of souls.

---

[1] "Thou art a priest."   [2] "Thou art Peter."

CHAPTER II

CURATE OF TOMBOLO
(November 29th, 1858—July 13th, 1867)

"The Priest, elevated above all human beings, must himself keep above human interests." (Pius X to the Bishops of Italy, June, 1905).

CONSTANT ACTIVITY

" MOTHER, I have been appointed by His Lordship curate in the parish of Tombolo; I do not like the place because it is full of evil; but I must obey, and I shall go." Thus spoke Don Giuseppe Sarto, one evening in the late autumn of 1858, to Margherita Sanson.

Tombolo was a town composed mainly of cattle-dealers and brokers. They were a shrewd people, rough of manners and much attached to money; they were not over-particular about their morals, and what is worse, the habit of blasphemy was prevalent amongst them, but this was due more to ignorance than to malice.

It was a field overgrown with weeds, and needed to be tilled by an Apostle of God who was ready for every kind of fatigue. No better could have been found than the new curate, who did not need to be told that the life of a priest is a life of sacrifice, and whose Ordination had been the beginning of the road to Calvary. He himself pointed this out in a letter to a new priest whom he was to send to the Seminary later on. This letter shows the attitude which Don Giuseppe Sarto bore towards his life's work. It reads: " We live, alas! in times when the priest meets with contempt, hatred, and persecution; but it is in this very fact that we are to find our greatest comfort because there is in it a secret virtue and strength. If you put it into action you will be amazed at the results."

Don Sarto entered Tombolo on November 29th, 1858, the sacred chrism of Ordination, as it were, still fresh on his hands. It was the Vigil of the Feast of St. Andrew, the

15

patron of the town. Those who witnessed his arrival were astonished at the poverty of his clothing—shoes with wooden soles and a coat which could not but excite to sympathy all who looked upon it. He was poor, but he had come on an errand, simple and precise—the salvation of souls.

The parish priest, Don Constantini, was a priest of more than average common-sense and was well acquainted with the customs and habits of country people. He received Don Giuseppe with open arms because he knew instinctively that he had come with the interests of the people at heart, and he had been informed that the new curate was hardened to a life of poverty and sacrifice. Not many days had passed before parish priest and curate began to understand and even love each other with a mutual respect and esteem. They shared the same sentiments, the same aspirations, the same outlook, and were, of course, faced with the same problems.

Don Sarto set about his work as soon as he had received a few preliminary instructions from the parish priest. In the morning he rose at a very early hour, and frequently opened the church himself, so as not to disturb the sacristan. He said his morning prayers, made his meditation, and then, with an ever increasing joy, went to the altar to celebrate the Holy Sacrifice of the Mass. His recollection in this major work of the day was such as to justify expressions which escaped the natives of Tombolo, such as: "He strikes me as being a saint," or "I can't help thinking that I see Christ Himself at the altar."

He then set about the active part of his ministry. He was at the beck and call of everyone, and was never known to refuse anyone who summoned him, though at times he would have been justified in so doing. He never seemed to lose an instant, but was, as a niece of the parish priest testifies, in "constant activity."

Never wearied in the work of the Lord, he was often seen in his leisure moments on his knees before the Blessed Sacrament, or kneeling at the foot of Our Lady's statue, rapt in prayer. He studied, wrote his sermons, prepared his instructions on the Gospel text or the Catechism until

THE CURATE OF TOMBOLO

the early hours of the morning. "Often, in winter time," relates the niece of the parish priest, "though it was still dark when I was getting up in the morning, I would see a light in his windows.

"On one occasion when he came into the presbytery for his morning coffee, I asked him if he had forgotten to put the light out the previous night.

'Oh, no,' he replied, 'I had a little study to do!'

'But when do you sleep then?' I continued.

'Oh, a few hours are sufficient for me,' he returned, with a smile."

One day the curate of Galiera, Don Carminati, who was one of his intimate friends, put him a straightforward question: 'Tell me honestly, how many hours' sleep do you consider sufficient for yourself?"

"About four!" he replied unhesitatingly.

"It's well for you!" replied his friend. "You can live while the rest of us are dead asleep."

The young curate slept little, because his zeal for souls and his devotion to the work of God had a greater attraction for him than bodily comfort.

THE FIRST SERMONS

Don Sarto's style of preaching was easy, spontaneous and persuasive, his ideas clear and well ordered, and his words, simple but to the point, were spoken in a loud and sonorous voice. He preached with a warmth which penetrated the hearts of his listeners and awakened consciences often dulled by years of sin.

The parishioners of Tombolo willingly listened to what their new curate had to say to them, because they knew that he practised the Gospel he preached, and they felt instinctively that he lived in the presence of God.

Don Sarto did not rely entirely upon himself in the preparation of his sermons and instructions, but read them first to his parish priest. Don Constantini, eager to make his curate a good preacher, listened carefully and would comment at the end: "Look, Don Bepi, I don't like this part!" or, "I think it would be better if you said it like this!"

Don Giuseppe never disputed, but changed his sermon, cutting out or adding parts exactly as the parish priest suggested. One of the first sermons which he presented to Don Constantini for criticism provoked the remark: "This is not a sermon, it is utter rubbish! My dear Don Bepi, no more of this rubbish, please!"

Don Sarto smiled humbly and continued to study, work and preach. A few days later after much preparation the curate presented another sermon to Don Constantini. The parish priest listened to it attentively as usual, and was so amazed at the improvement that he commented with a smile: "Ah, beautiful, Don Bepi; but you must be careful, for it would never do to have the curate preaching better than the parish priest!"

Little by little Don Sarto, with the encouragement and guidance of Don Constantini, became so good at preaching that he was frequently invited to give sermons in the neighbouring parishes. It was not very long before he established such a reputation that parish priests vied with each other to get him to give the Sunday sermon in their churches, for they realised that his preaching always produced its effect in the confessional. One parish priest, having heard him preach, did not hesitate to say openly: "If you continue preaching like that, we shall very soon hear you preaching with a mitre on."

Don Constantini was so proud at the success of the young orator that he wrote one day to his dear friend Don Marcello Tossiti, parish priest of Quinto: "Don Bepi has now finished his course of Lenten Sermons at Godego 'laudabiliter.' His fame is spreading like wildfire. I am thrilled at his success, which in all humility I can call my own, because he took the first steps on the road to fame under my supervision and guidance. My dear Don Bepi! I am looking forward to embracing him and telling him that if further success is possible there is nothing I want more."

THE WHOLE BURDEN OF THE PARISH

Preaching was not the only thing Don Giuseppe had to do. Though his days were already full many new burdens fell upon his shoulders when, in 1863, Don Constantini, on account of a chest complaint, became so ill that he was forced to remain inactive for the greater part of the year.

The whole burden of the parish then fell upon the shoulders of the young curate. His only preoccupation was the salvation of the flock, to whom he administered the Sacraments with the greatest eagerness. On Feast-days and Sundays he heard Confessions without counting the hours; he explained the Catechism to the children and Christian Doctrine to the adults.

Much of his time was spent consoling the afflicted, calling people to their duties, settling disputes, making peace among families, and inciting all to do good and avoid evil. He did not neglect the choir which he himself had organized in order to add greater dignity to the liturgical functions of the Church. He taught Latin Grammar to young lads who had ideas of going for the priesthood. With boys he acted as a boy, that he might restrain them from evil. Quite frequently, when the local schoolmaster was absent, he took his classes, as though he had not enough to do with his own parochial duties.

The Eucharist was the centre of his life. A great deal of time was taken up preparing children to receive their first Holy Communion, arousing people to receive the Blessed Sacrament frequently, and inculcating a more lively devotion to the real presence of Jesus in the Sacrament of the Altar. He showed himself a continuous example of this, not only when he offered the Holy Sacrifice of the Mass, but whenever he exposed the Blessed Sacrament at Benediction. "At those moments," as one of the parishioners testifies, "he assumed an expression which seemed almost celestial. He kept his eyes constantly fixed upon the Host, and when he gave the Blessing the whole congregation was entranced by the intensity of his faith. There was something extraordinary about him."

This indefatigable curate could not rest while the sick, the infirm, and the dying were left unattended. He took great care that these should not be left in want. If they were poor he visited them many times a day, and should he be

sent for at night he rushed to their bedside without delay.
Want of the necessities of life, hard work, the inclemency
of the weather and long journeys along bad roads did not enter
into his calculations. He sacrificed himself to the exhaustion
of his strength. Not a few of the inhabitants of Tombolo
actually saw their curate faint through sheer weakness.

" Look here," he said one day to a little urchin, pointing
to his own shoes, " see how my shoes are worn out by
visiting your grandfather! "

With what great love and tenderness did he assist and
console the dying! He encouraged them for their passage
into Eternity with words of kindness and Christian resignation ;
he calmed their anxiety and consoled them with the hope
of the reward which was to come. He would not leave
their bedside until he had lightened their dying moments
with the prayers of Mother Church.

Though the whole burden of the parish rested upon him,
he never showed the slightest trace of discouragement or
sorrow. In his eyes shone a light of joy and contentment,
because he knew he was not working for an earthly crown,
but for the glory of God. The people of Tombolo were so
amazed at the stupendous activity of their curate that they
often asked each other how it was that he could stand up to
such continuous fatigue without ever seeming to rest. They
knew that he was of robust fibre, but they did not know
that the secret of his strength lay hidden in his heart, where
there was a well of divine energy the power of which was
only increased by the work he did.

KINDNESS TO THE SICK PARISH PRIEST

Don Constantini was very pleased with the activity of his
curate, but was more pleased with Don Sarto himself.
Don Sarto's sisters and the parishioners of Tombolo assure
us that they loved each other like brothers, and were of
one heart and one soul. The poor parish priest, constantly
ill, was often forced to remain in bed. It was at such
times that Don Giuseppe showed the kindness of his heart
in looking after him. Geniality and cheerfulness accompanied
him into the sick man's room, and selflessness and affection

marked the attention he showed him. Sometimes, when it was possible for the parish priest to get up, he would accompany him to the church, help him to vest, serve his Mass and return to the presbytery with him. Though Don Sarto did nearly all the work in the parish, Don Constantini was still the parish priest, and the humble curate would listen to and follow out the detailed instructions he received for his day's work.

The niece of the parish priest—whom we have mentioned before—relates: "In the morning Don Giuseppe would come to the Presbytery at an early hour, and with his usual willingness ask my uncle: 'How are you to-day? Is there anything I can do for you?' And if my uncle replied that he was not feeling well, and was unable to get up, Don Giuseppe was always ready with: 'Well, don't worry, take it easy! I can manage all right!' 'But haven't you a sermon to preach, a catechism class to take?' my uncle would sometimes add. 'Oh! that doesn't matter, I can manage that too,' would be the invariable answer of Don Giuseppe."

He always returned to work as the humble representative of the parish priest whose authority he respected—an attitude known only to the saints.

INITIATIVE IN WELL-DOING

Since Don Giuseppe was of very humble birth, and was born to a life of fatigue, it was little wonder that he was so popular with the people of Tombolo. He was often to be seen in the midst of a group of men or youths, taking a lively interest in their conversation. He understood them and listened now to one and now to another as they freely unfolded their ideas and difficulties. It was thus he learned to study their tendencies, observe their aspirations and appreciate their needs.

One evening a group of young lads lamented their utter incapacity to read or write. "Let us start evening classes then," suggested Don Giuseppe, who saw a possibility of waging war against the vice of blasphemy, which had assumed enormous proportions in Tombolo.

"Good idea! But how?" was the unanimous answer.

"How can it be done, when some of us know a little, and others nothing at all?" demanded a youngster, trying to pin-point the proposal.

"That is easily settled! Those who know something can be entrusted to the schoolmaster, and I myself will take those who know nothing," replied the curate.

"And how can we possibly pay you?" asked another of a more businesslike temperament.

"There will be no question of money! I want something much more valuable: that you stop blaspheming the Holy Name of God!" concluded Don Sarto emphatically.

The promise was universal and spontaneous, and the agreement was sealed by an enthusiastic handshaking. Those men and young boys went away assured of one thing, that the evening school was a campaign against the horrible vice of blasphemy, and that their curate was determined to see that vice obliterated. They had already seen in the past the holy indignation of the curate inflamed against the profane use of God's Holy Name. While he would never yield to impatience or temper, he would sometimes show a "just anger," but a very real anger, nevertheless, when he wished to correct someone who had become infected with this vice.

Don Sarto was just the man for the people of Tombolo. If they were a shrewd and cunning people, our curate had shrewdness and wit sufficient for every encounter.

There was an obnoxious custom at Tombolo. After Benediction the people would scurry out of the church without waiting for the priest to put the Blessed Sacrament back in the Tabernacle. In spite of his counsels, exhortations and reprimands, the parish priest had not succeeded in stamping out this irreverence. He was "wasting his sweetness on the desert air," and he knew it. One day, while the parish priest was lamenting this abuse, Don Giuseppe comforted him, saying: "Don't worry, Father, leave it to me, and I will put them in their place."

Don Sarto had observed that the people of Tombolo manifested a special devotion to the statue of the Madonna, which was venerated in the church. This devotion, decked out with a ritual of its own, bordered on the superstitious; by local law it was forbidden to lift the veil which covered the statue, without first lighting four candles and kneeling in front of the covered image. The statue unveiled, no one dared remain standing—that would have been the height of profanity.

One Sunday, while the parish priest was giving Benediction, Don Giuseppe lit the four candles required by the " liturgy " and waited until the Blessed Sacrament was being replaced in the Tabernacle. As usual, by sheer force of habit, there was a general rush of Tombolians for the door. With a sharp flick of the wrist Don Sarto snatched off the veil. As though struck by lightning, the whole congregation fell to its knees. For the first time in years they remained in church till the end of Benediction. He repeated this action every time Benediction was given, until it became a habit for the people to remain in the church until the priest left the altar.

" THE CURATE OF CURATES "

The curates of the neighbouring parishes, aware of the prodigious activity of Don Sarto, found great amusement in the nickname they had put upon him, " curate of curates." Don Sarto, on account of his open and jovial nature, enjoyed the joke as much as any of them.

On one occasion when the curates were enjoying themselves with their usual freedom at his expense, he suddenly exclaimed, plunging his right fist into the palm of his left hand: " Fellow curates! the time will come when you will all kneel to me."

" What arrogance! We will become parish priests soon," interrupted the curate of Galliera, Don Carminati, one of the wittiest of them.

" But parish priests too must come," replied Don Giuseppe, repeating the gesture.

" Even bishops will have to come," added another sarcastically, midst the peals of uproarious laughter which ensued.

"Even bishops will be under the curate of curates," replied Don Sarto, with a quite perceptible strain of seriousness mixed with his pleasantry.

Was it a presage of what was to come? Was it a prophecy? That we cannot say; all we can say is that forty years later the humble curate of Tombolo mounted the Chair of Peter to wield his sovereign sceptre over the whole world.

UNMEASURED CHARITY

The memory of Don Sarto was handed down from father to son, and still lives on, especially among the people of Tombolo. His spirit of charity, which embraced all in misery and necessity, was characteristic of him as curate, as parish priest, as canon, bishop, patriarch and pope.

All had recourse to him; now it was the orphan, now the broker rendered penniless through want of business, now the peasant unable to support his family because frost or drought had destroyed his crops, now the widow who could not feed or clothe her unfortunate children, now the sick plunged in misery, without medicine, without sustenance.

Don Giuseppe could not say "No," because he lived and had ever on his lips the words: "We are not born to eat, but to work and suffer." He gave away all he had, and more than he had; his charity knew no limits, his generosity no bounds. He did not care about his own needs, but deprived himself of everything; he took the bread out of his own mouth and was forced at times to beg a little flour or cheese to stem his hunger and that of his sister.

Was it exaggeration? The curate of Tombolo had learned the exaggeration of the saints; he had learned to raise himself above the unstable possessions of this world to the eternal things of God. To those who advised more prudence and self-consideration he would reply simply: "What is the use of clinging to the things of this world, which we must leave sooner or later? Is it not better to give them in charity to the poor?"

The stipends for the sermons he delivered in other parishes had to be sent to his mother directly, for she still lived in the poor cottage at Riese with her large family, or otherwise they would, inevitably, be handed to the poor. The niece of the parish priest tells us that one day when he had received an unusually large stipend for preaching in a neighbouring parish, he returned home without a penny. The money had gone to the poor of Tombolo who with reason assert that their curate had a heart of gold.

On another occasion having delivered a discourse at the funeral of an outstanding benefactor of Tombolo, he returned to the presbytery delighted to break the news that they had given him a huge stipend (about £5).

"Now you will be able to buy some clothing for yourself," suggested the parish priest.

"But I have given it all away," replied the young curate, who had abandoned himself entirely into the hands of divine Providence.

Don Constantini looked at him fixedly and severely, and was about to reprimand him, but struck with admiration remained silent.

"Don Sarto's coat was so worn," testifies one of the inhabitants of Tombolo, "that the neighbouring curates jestingly declared that he had been to the war."

One day he was invited to preach a sermon at Castelfranco, and Don Constantini advised him not to lose the opportunity of buying himself a new coat. Don Giuseppe at first listened to the advice of his parish priest, but shortly after he had preached the sermon he met one of his uncles, who asked him for a little help to clear off the arrears of rent on his house. His nephew did not bestow words of pity merely, but without hesitation parted with the whole stipend (about £3), which he had received, and returned to Tombolo with the same coat.

Nothing was safe in the hands of Don Giuseppe. His sister Rosa had worked hard for a long time in order to save enough money to buy a pair of linen sheets which were badly needed in the house. Very imprudently she entrusted the money to her brother, asking him to make the purchase.

Don Giuseppe took the money, and with nimble step set out towards the town. Some time later he returned—no

sheets! no money! The hard-earned money had been
distributed among a few poor little boys who had begged for
something to relieve their hunger. They could wait for the
sheets, but could the children wait for their morsels of
food? With this consideration and with the usual " God
will provide," he quickly soothed the anger of his disappointed
sister who, although herself outstandingly big-hearted, found
it hard to check a silent tear.

Don Constantini and his curate, with one exception, saw
eye to eye on everything. The question of charity was the
root of the difference. The parish priest sometimes gently
reproved Don Bepi, admonishing him to take more care
of his mother. But with admirable faith he was ever ready
with the reply: " These poor children have greater need
than she; God will look after her for He abandons no one."

" HAVE YOU ANY MAIZE? "

The curacy of Tombolo provided but a scant income for
Don Sarto. He depended solely on the collection of maize
and corn—the two products of the district—which increased
or diminished according to the generosity of the people.
In his hands this meagre income became still more scanty,
because the little he had did not belong to himself, for he
would say to those in need: " As long as I have any, let us
eat together."

One day in the Spring of 1861, a year of famine, a beggar
came to the curate to beg a few pence in order that he
might go and search for work.

"Whatever you want you shall have, but money I have
none," replied Don Giuseppe.

" But you have a little maize? " continued the beggar.

" Maize I certainly have," replied Don Sarto, remembering
that in the granary there still remained a small heap since the
last collection. " Go, fetch a bag."

The poor man did not need to be told twice, but hastened
off to his house and returned presently with an empty sack.
Don Giuseppe led him into the granary and pointed out the
maize—little more than a bushel altogether—piled up in

the corner. "Let us divide it into two parts, one for you and one for me, will that do?"

"Splendid," replied the beggar, with tears in his eyes.

A PANEGYRIC: APPOINTMENT AS PARISH PRIEST

Because of their immense love for their curate, the Tombolians feared that one day, sooner or later, he would be taken away from them. They knew that it was impossible for a priest of such outstanding virtue to be left permanently in a small obscure village. Don Constantini, who had a genuine interest in his curate, was indignant that he should have been left almost forgotten by his Superiors. It would have given him great pleasure to see Don Giuseppe promoted. He had already thought of doing something about it when in the Spring of 1866 Mgr. Luigi Marangoni, a Canon of Treviso, arrived in Tombolo. Don Constantini thought to himself: "Here is Mgr. Marangoni, a professor of Theology, a great authority, and one highly esteemed by the Bishop; now he could do something; now is the chance to strike the blow!"

During the discussion, many words of praise about the curate's talents of mind and heart passed between canon and parish priest. The latter concluded the conversation with the judicious suggestion: "My dear canon, you must speak about him in the Curia! It does not seem right to keep a priest so outstanding and courageous confined here among merchants and cattle drovers."

"How right you are, Don Antonio, but what can you expect? He studied at Padua and is unknown to his Superiors."

"That is all the more reason why you should speak about him in the Curia," was the unhesitating reply of Don Constantini. "I consider it your duty to speak about him!"

There was a short pause, during which the parish priest thought of a new line of attack: "Wait a minute, Monsignor! You said the Superiors know nothing about him? I can assure you they know him very well. When he had finished his first four years as my curate, they began to appreciate the

work he was doing in organizing the study of classics and
sending boys for the Priesthood, and they offered him a
Chair in the Seminary. He refused this position because he
preferred to labour in a parish and bring souls to Christ
directly."

" But do you really think," replied the Canon doubtingly,
" that your curate could deliver a panegyric in the Cathedral
of Treviso, on the life of St. Antony of Padua? " Such a
panegyric is regarded as of the greatest importance, for not
only all the clerics of the town, but the members of the
Cathedral Chapter attend, and furthermore it is a task that
is usually reserved for an orator of some renown.

" Of course he would be capable of it," replied the parish
priest.

" Right, then," concluded the Monsignor, " the Superiors
will get to know him a little better—your curate is appointed
to deliver the panegyric at Treviso."

This panegyric was a great success for the young country
curate who had dreamt of an apostolate in the midst of the
humble and down-trodden, of a modest, obscure life full of
hardship and privation.

The Bishop, who in fact had been carefully watching
Don Sarto's activities for a long time, summoned him to
take competitive examination for a parish in the diocese.
Though he wanted nothing more than to remain hidden with
the poor of Tombolo, he could not ignore the request of
the Bishop, nor could he turn a deaf ear to the entreaties of
his parish priest, who in order to overcome the resistance
of his curate, would often facetiously insist: " If you don't
go, I shall go myself."

The ambition of Don Constantini and the desire of the
Bishop were fulfilled on May 21st, 1867, when the splendid
results of the examination which Don Giuseppe had taken,
were published, and he was appointed parish priest of Salzano,
one of the most important parishes in the diocese, situated
in the fertile plain which stretches as far as the lagoon of
Venice.

The Tombolians were very sad when they received the
news, because they felt that they were losing " a pearl of a

priest " and still more, " a saint."   Did they not play on the consonant in his name, saying that their curate was not to be called " Giuseppe Sarto " but " Giuseppe Santo "?

The " curate of curates " began to prepare himself for the great future which lay ahead, not knowing that he was fulfilling the prophecy which Don Constantini had made shortly before in a letter to his friend Don Tositti, parish priest of Quinto, saying: " Don Giuseppe is a saintly curate; mark my words, you will soon see him parish priest of an important parish; then, maybe, with red socks; and then— who knows? "

CHAPTER III

PARISH PRIEST OF SALZANO
(July 14th, 1867—September 15th, 1875)

"His memory endures and his name is evoked as the Saint who glorified the Diocese of Treviso." (Mgr. A. Longhin, Bishop of Treviso, July 9th, 1923).

AN UNPOPULAR APPOINTMENT

D ON SARTO was only thirty-two years old. Physically he was a well-made man of tremendous strength, and his dignified bearing and straightforward way of speaking showed him to have a determined will and a keen intellect. His kindness and forbearance reflected a single-minded intention of spending himself completely for the salvation of souls. But his nomination as parish priest of Salzano met with much misunderstanding and brought down an avalanche of bitter criticism and insult from the Salzanese themselves.

Salzano was accustomed to having parish priests of gentle birth who, as a matter of course, passed on to the title of Canon in the Cathedral chapter when they had finished their term of office in the aristocratic surroundings of Salzano. But now a peasant, the son of a Cursore, an obviously uneducated upstart rustic, and worst of all, the curate of Tombolo to be appointed parish priest of the illustrious Salzano! Why, the thing was impossible! Indignation spread like wildfire. His Lordship must be out of his mind! Why choose a mere curate when there were so many distinguished parish priests in the diocese? Admittedly this unknown Don Sarto had great merit. Admittedly the Tombolians think very highly of him, but for Salzano he simply will not do!

The significant nod of the head, the confidential whisper— on no account to be repeated—the occasional unequivocal hint at social gatherings, very quickly developed into public declarations of disapproval, enthusiastic suggestions for the well-being of the parish and open denunciations of the public enemy, and ultimately a representative body was formed to approach the Bishop and demand that justice should be done.

Monsignor Frederico Zenelli, the Bishop, was a learned, shrewd and prudent man and was as well aware of the choice he had made as he was thoroughly informed of the attitude of the people of Salzano. He said nothing and did nothing, but waited. Very soon, but no sooner than he had anticipated, the representative body approached, armed with their carefully formulated objections set out in carefully chosen words by their carefully appointed spokesman, no less than the town councillor, Paolo Bottacin.

In the presence of the Bishop they were lost for words; he, on the contrary, without reticence and without preamble simply and unconcernedly declared: "I am giving you the curate of Tombolo as parish priest; in this I am doing Salzano a great favour." The representatives were dumbfounded, while their spokesman, with gaping mouth and upturned eyes, could not speak a word. They would surely have turned and beat a hasty retreat had they not beheld at the Bishop's side a pale-faced, half-starved looking figure, known to be a priest only by the black rags in which he was clad, and known by his evident fatigue to have walked a long way—from Tombolo to Treviso!

Paolo Bottacin was beginning to recover his senses, and he whispered to a near-by companion sarcastically: "A favour to Salzano! What a beauty he is giving us!" But that ragged-looking figure was soon to change their opinions. If at Tombolo he had been the "curate of curates" he was soon to justify the Bishop's confidence in him and prove himself as truly worthy of the title of "pastor of pastors."

OPINIONS CHANGE

On a very warm Sunday morning, July 14th, 1867, a large congregation assembled in the church of Salzano; there were the gentry and the ladies in all their summer finery, labourers clad in their Sunday best, and there were also the poor, all equally anxious to see their new pastor and hear his first sermon. Don Sarto, unperturbed and without affectation, entered the sanctuary. Having finished the Gospel he mounted the pulpit. He did not say much, but with a few well-chosen words he outlined for them his plans for the parish. In a few rapid but effective strokes he scattered all their prejudices. Each and every one of them was confident that the priest descending from the pulpit was a friend, a man of God, a born pastor of souls.

The seeds of confidence which Don Sarto had sown at his first Sunday sermon sprang into flower a few days later when he made his first parish visitation. Every family was visited and felt him to be one of its members; every person was greeted and felt him to be an intimate friend; every sorrow, ambition and interest was disclosed to become the sorrow, ambition and interest of the new parish priest. He held the whole parish in his hand, for he had each of its members in his heart. Their affection for him increased from day to day.

Now that he knew his people, their outlook and their needs, Don Sarto lost no time in settling down to the steady, laborious routine of pastor of souls. The people came to know him too; they knew where to look for him at all times— among the poor, in the confessional, or on his knees in front of the Blessed Sacrament, absorbed in fervent prayer. Were he called to the bedside of the sick, even in the late hours of the cold, wintry nights, he would promptly leave whatever he was doing and hurry away, an angel of comfort, to soothe the heart, calm the sorrows and prepare the soul of the dying person to face its all-important journey from time to eternity. A heart inflamed with the tender love of God would encourage and quieten a heart terrified by the fear of His judgments, and fill with Christian resignation, not only the sick person, but all those who were destined to suffer, whether in body or soul, on account of the decree of the Almighty.

The Salzanese were not slow to appreciate the zeal of their pastor. In their difficulties and sorrows they were sure of his love and sympathy, but in their sin they were equally sure of such heart-felt reproach as was only possible to a soul that loved God intensely and that was determined to eradicate vice at any cost to self.

Don Sarto realised that the most effective weapon in his

hands for uprooting vice and implanting virtue in its stead was the constant, thorough and enthusiastic teaching of the Catechism, and that if this means were neglected the Faith of his people would languish and die. His insistence on this point was constant, and he was frequently heard saying: " I exhort you most earnestly to come to the Catechism classes ; I would prefer to see you omit Vespers rather than neglect this duty, which is of paramount importance." Fully persuaded that sin against God and ignorance of the things of God were inevitably correlated, he lost no opportunity of inviting his parishioners to attend the instructions. These were delivered with such fiery vehemence and profound conviction that his congregation very soon found it a pleasure to attend and always went away deeply impressed with the lessons their pastor had set forth.

Don Sarto introduced the system of dialogue instructions with the aid of a young priest from another parish, and by this means he imprinted the truths of the Faith more easily on the minds of his flock. Large crowds were attracted every Sunday evening, not only from the outlying districts of his own parish, but from other parishes as well. A few of the neighbouring parish priests, seeing that this novelty confronted them with the painful ordeal of preaching to empty benches in their churches, Sunday after Sunday, made a complaint to the Bishop. But His Lordship, who was keeping a vigilant eye on the prodigious activity of the pastor of Salzano, simply replied: " Go thou and do in like manner."

Don Sarto did not limit his activity to catechetical instructions. In order to enliven in his people the spirit of religion and to stir up their faith, he used the greatest initiative in decorating the church. Whatever related to the worship of God must be of the very best. He insisted that the liturgical functions be carried out with all the splendour and exactness that Mother Church intended ; for this purpose he organized a choir, composed of boys, young men and a few of the older ones who could sing, as he had done at Tombolo. To shield his parishioners from the dangers of materialism and to prevent them from becoming absorbed in the things of this life to the neglect of their eternal salvation was the constant preoccupation of this devoted pastor. Devotion to the Blessed Sacrament, the Forty Hours, the Confraternity of the Sacred Heart, colourful May Devotions, interesting sermons and the living voice of the Gospel rendered the onslaught of the Evil One ineffective to all within the Fold. He prepared the children to receive their First Holy Communion at an age notably less than was customary at the time; this was the seed of the great Eucharistic movement which was to grow and reach maturity under the care of Don Sarto, Bishop of Mantua, Patriarch of Venice, and Vicar of Christ.

THE WELL-BEING OF THE PEOPLE

But while the indefatigable pastor spent himself instilling into his people the practice of piety, implanting virtue in their lives, keeping the peace amongst them and guarding them from scandal, he did not neglect to take a personal interest in the material well-being of each and every one of them.

The social question at that time under pressure of increasing industrialism was beginning to present a serious problem. The serpent of Socialism was entwining itself secretly but perceptibly about the town. The parish priest could not be indifferent to this. Clad in the armour of Christ, unsheathed sword in hand, Don Sarto came to the attack. Had he not come to Salzano resolved to cling to his single purpose of ever looking to the well-being of the people, had he not come to the Altar of God, resigned to suffer all privations, not to weigh sacrifices and not to spare himself? Now he must mobilise the powers of his will!

In Salzano a Jew from Padua, Moses Vita-Jacur, had bought up vast tracts of land and had built an up-to-date factory in which were employed 300 young lads, not to mention the large number of older workmen. If they were subject to their Jewish employer, they were still the sheep of their pastor. Don Sarto did not find it difficult to make an entrance into the factory, and Jacur soon realized the power the priest had over his men and became subject to that power himself. He rapidly grew to esteem this Catholic priest, to appreciate his zeal, virtue and judgment and to offer him, as well as his friendship, large sums of money to be distributed among the poor of the town.

Don Sarto took a keen interest and played an active part in all the economic affairs of his parishioners. The sale of crops, the banking system, struggles with extortionate landlords, antagonism between employer and employee, were but a few of the intricacies in which he became involved. As a result one can well imagine the heap of correspondence daily increasing in the presbytery, which was open to all both day and night. The former parish priest had been more of a hermit than a pastor; whenever a knock came to the door of the presbytery a little window would open, a pensive face would appear and the intruder would be obliged to give full details of himself and his business.

" Good day, Father."

" Good day! Do you want anything? "

" I would like to speak to the parish priest."

" Speak, I am the parish priest."

And so the unfortunate visitor would be obliged to relate his business while standing on the street gazing up into the uninterested face. Very often they were misunderstood and were sent away cursing the priest and what he stood for.

With Don Sarto there were no little windows, no formalities, no dread in the heart of the visitor; there was an open door, a broad smile, a kind word and a hearty welcome for all, be they never so miserable, or he never so busy.

HEROIC CHARITY

If at Tombolo his charity appeared a marvel, at Salzano it reached the limits of human heroism. His heart was always open to every little sorrow, and while he was content to be in want himself the needs of the poor would cause him the greatest sadness. His sisters saw his clothing, wheat, flour, and even his own modest diet of beans gradually vanishing; if they wanted to keep anything in the house they had to hide it so that he could not get his hands on it. Don Giuseppe had a task to accomplish, and for him this alone counted; he was never bothered with the temptation to accumulate money; he was never troubled with the thought of making provision for to-morrow: while the poor were in need Don Sarto and his relations must go without. When his sister, Lucia, wanted to marry the sacristan of the church, Luigi Boschi, she received a present of about twenty-five shillings from her brother and thought she was dreaming. Should it happen that he was unable to help a family impoverished by some disaster, he would not hesitate to go as security himself, very often knowing quite well that he would be forced to pay the debts from his own pocket. What did it matter if he were deprived of everything? What did it matter if he had to take his own prized treasures, Ordination presents, to the pawn-shop of Venice?

On one occasion when his sisters complained that he had no socks, he replied with all simplicity: "Repair the old ones, the cassock covers everything." During the coldest part of winter his sister Maria often expressed her surprise at the fact that he went about without a coat; to her entreaties he would simply reply: "I have no money." He had no socks because the poor needed them more than he; he had no money because, as the people used to say, "he emptied himself," and he had no coat because he had given it away. He had deprived himself of everything, even shirt and shoes, and kept for himself but the barest necessaries. His greatest joy in life was the joy of giving, his only sorrow that he could not give more.

One morning his sister Rosa hurried into the kitchen to see to the stew which she had put down to cook an hour or so before. It was gone! She turned her steps towards her brother's room, and prepared a fiery speech in the short passage between the kitchen and his room. But her outburst was greeted with a broad smile, a kindly gesture and the humble but unanswerable excuse: "A poor man came a short time ago whose wife was ill and whose four children were hungry; I hadn't anything else to give so I gave him the pot of stew; but don't worry, my dear, God will provide for us."

"That's all very fine, but what will we eat now?" demanded his sister, refusing to be calmed down.

" Bread and cheese! " came the none too pacifying answer.
Poor Rosa! She needed great virtue to make that silent but
very necessary retreat, but she realized that the next statement
would be the usual: " Are you afraid of dying of hunger? "
which at the moment would have been utterly intolerable.

The Salzanese contributed generously at the seasonal
collections with large amounts of grain, knowing full well
that the grain would end up in the hands of the poor, as
their pastor " always kept an open granary." The year 1860
was one of famine, and the misery and hunger of the poor
were extreme; in Don Sarto's granary there remained but
a bag of very inferior beans; all the rest had been distributed
among the poor.

The pestilence of famine raged once again in 1868; this
time, however, owing to an exceptionally long and severe
winter there was the additional hardship of lack of firewood;
the people were both cold and hungry. In the presbytery
there was a heap of wood but it rapidly diminished from day
to day. A priest, who was assisting with the parish work
during Lent, asked a servant one day: " How is it that so
much wood is used here? " " What can you expect? " came
the unhesitating reply, " Here the door is always open." The
supplying priest understood that the good pastor, wishing
to conceal his very great charity, had simply left his doors
open and his stock at the disposal of all; nevertheless he
wanted to confirm this fact and he put the question directly
to Don Sarto:

" How is it that the fuel in the yard is vanishing so quickly? "

" There are many poor people suffering from cold here."

" And yourself? "

" I am able to put up with it," was the heroic reply.

In order to get about the parish more quickly, Don Sarto
used a horse and cart, but it looked so old and shaken
that it enkindled pity in the hearts of all who saw it. One
day he complained to a visiting priest of a noble family that
he was unable to pay his taxes, was badly in arrears with
the Seminary fees for the students he was supporting, and
did not know where to turn for help. He suggested the sale
of the horse and cart. " The horse I should willingly sell,

but the cart is so shattered that I should blush even to give it as a present," came the prompt reply from his visitor. The horse was sold forthwith, but the cart remained on at Salzano and was used by all who needed it.

"Oh, Don Carlo! How do you come to be in this part of the world?" exclaimed Rosa when she saw Don Carlo Carminati, the good-humoured parish priest of Galliera, and a former colleague of Don Sarto when he was at Tombolo.

"I have come to pay a quick visit to your hungry pastor," replied Don Carlo, with his usual wit sweetened by his friendly smile.

"Wonderful!" ejaculated Rosa, and she drew him aside, continuing: "Listen, Don Carlo, I've something to tell you in confidence; this morning a merchant came into the town who has some good cloth for sale, and I know that yesterday Don Giuseppe received a little money, you understand? Now you know my brother only too well; he hasn't a stitch of clothing of his own—try to persuade him to buy some of that cloth."

Promising at least to try this almost impossible task, the parish priest of Galliera lost no time in formulating Rosa's request into a forcible argument, adding several new complementary reasons and presenting the case to his old friend, Don Giuseppe, in a most persuasive manner. It was simply a waste of time; Don Giuseppe persisted in changing the subject with: "Leave the clothes alone, we shall see to them another time, but just now. . ."

The quick-witted, light-hearted visitor, realized that a stratagem was necessary, and the necessary stratagem was very quickly designed. The merchant was called, a few yards of suitable material were selected and cut off the roll, the price was fixed and the deal was closed by presenting merchant, cloth and bill to Don Giuseppe: "So many yards . . . such and such a price . . . now pay!" The humble pastor saw that he was in a trap; he shook his head, looked at Don Carlo, and with a tone of reproof exclaimed: "Even you come here betraying me and playing tricks on me!" But knowing that his good friend had so acted only for his good, without another word he pulled out the money, which fortunately had not taken another road, and paid. Don Sarto was never caught again.

CHOLERA OF 1873

We now come to 1873, the terrible year of cholera, which was to mark the apex of the heroism of charity of the parish priest of Salzano. What great sacrifices, what overwhelming labours, what extreme privations he was to suffer in the interest of his terror-stricken, sorely tried flock! Was there one dying with the disease and wanting confession? There was one who ran about day and night, at all moments, at all hours and ever at the disposal of all, because in the delicacy of his charity he did not want his curates to expose themselves to the danger of infection. Were there some for whom the necessaries of life were lacking? There was one who ever thought of them, provided for them and helped them in every way he could. Were there families in which the sick were left unattended? There was one who would suggest the best remedies, give the safest advice, who would console the heart cast in gloom, buttress the wavering will, and who would not hesitate to act as doctor and nurse should the need arise.

" Blessed be God! " said an old woman, " were it not for Don Sarto, our good pastor, I should be dead and my family sunk in misery." Were arms lacking to carry corpses to the cemetery? There was a pair of willing hands ready to help with this work of mercy. One day when he was conducting a burial service, he found that there were only three men to carry the coffin across a not too secure bridge; he sprinkled holy water, intoned the *De Profundis*, and in cotta and stole got his back under the coffin to supply the place of the missing bearer.

When the danger subsided he publicly intoned the *Te Deum*. But the heartfelt anguish, want of rest, the privations and fatigue, the sorrow and distress of the people he loved so dearly, all this so severely tried his strength as to wear down even that robust frame. He lost his appetite, he could not sleep, he was reduced to a skeleton. He would not rest, he would not even slacken his pace, but put his trust in God and continued his prodigious activity. Don Carminati was completely amazed and distressed at seeing him so haggard and thin, and said to him one day:

" You are not well! "

" Don't you think so? " was the unsatisfactory reply.

" And what's more you are positively a sick man," continued his friend.

" You may be right; as a matter of fact I have not felt as well as usual for the past few weeks. . ."

" He is the servant of all," interrupted his eldest sister, " just look at him, Don Carlo, mere skin and bone."

" Your sister is right," continued Don Carminati, assuming a tone of reproof, " you are working far too much, but remember, the bow that is kept bent too long often breaks, and certain bows when broken cannot be repaired . . . understand? "

" Beautiful! What an excellent orator you are becoming! " commented Don Sarto with a smile which itself said, " Keep your advice to yourself, I know what I am doing."

Without convalescence, without medicine, without human help, he very quickly returned to his normal state of health and to his normal but most extraordinary routine.

DIVINE TESTIMONY

It was not without reason that the Salzanese regarded their pastor not merely as the best they had ever had or the best they could ever hope for, but as something altogether outside the ordinary; in a word, as a saint.

One day while walking through the fields on the outskirts of his parish he heard screaming in the distance, and on mounting a small hill he saw flames rapidly consuming a rick of hay which had been stored uncomfortably near a small cottage some 500 yards away. He was soon on the scene and saw that it was quite impossible to extinguish the fire, as there was no water available, and worse still that the flames were beginning to lick the house. The family, threatened with homelessness, tried in vain to check the fire and shouted in vain for help. Moved with pity, full of faith and confidence Don Sarto shouted, "Don't be afraid, the fire will be put out and your house will be saved!" At that very moment, the flames, as though by a mysterious command, turned about in the other direction, leaving the cottage practically unharmed and the family on their knees in prayer, thanking God for the mercy he had shown them through his servant.

Dark clouds once again settled over the people of Salzano in the year when their crops were devastated by an insect, which is commonly known as the Sigaraio, or cigar-maker, due to the fact that it causes the leaves of the vines to roll up like a cigarette. Seeing the serious damage which was being done to the crops by this pest, Don Sarto announced from the pulpit one Sunday morning, "To-morrow I shall ring the bell at a certain hour, and when you hear it unite with me in prayer and have great confidence in God." He did as he promised. The effect of the prayer was miraculous, for the insect was banished and further damage was averted.

LOVE FOR THE PEOPLE

The great parish of Salzano had completely changed. It was now a model parish. The people were good-living, laborious, regular in their attendance at church, careful about saving and spending, generous to the poor, and consulted their pastor in all affairs, both spiritual and temporal. Not a person could be found among them who would not now agree with Bishop Zinelli in saying that the coming of the curate of Tombolo was a great favour to Salzano. After his parochial visitation, Bishop Zinelli made the following report: " A wonderful religious spirit flourishes in the parish; there is a happy, united community grouped around a holy, devoted pastor; attendance at the Sacraments is consoling; a great number of children at Communion; the greatest regularity in everything concerning the worship of God."

Salzano could well be proud of its parish priest. He was loved by all, but especially by the children, into whose pastimes he would enter whole-heartedly, secretly scattering about the seeds of vocations which in many cases bore fruit. He was keenly interested in the future of each one of them and would direct, advise and even finance the ambitious dreams of those childish hearts; he pointed out to them the paths of virtue, and warned them against the dangers of the world. He was loved by the fathers of families, who felt that there was one to whom they could go and entrust their difficulties, fears and misfortunes. Old and young, the sick, the infirm and the poor, all felt that there was a heart that would both sorrow and rejoice with them, would console and help them and would receive and welcome them at any time. The curates loved him because they admired in him a priest who was always at work, completely free from vainglory, worldly ambition and selfishness.

AN UNEXPECTED HONOUR

One day in 1875 Don Sarto was summoned to the Curia of Treviso. The call was urgent. Obediently the parish priest lost no time in presenting himself. The Bishop, who for a long time had been carefully watching him but saying nothing, now smiled and declared: "Don Sarto! I have need of you. I have a Seminary without a spiritual director, and a vacant place in my curia. I now appoint you to both these tasks. You shall be a Canon at the Cathedral and live in the Seminary."

For a moment this unexpected proposal robbed Don Sarto of all words. Then with prayers and tears he did all in his power to persuade the Bishop to select someone more suitable and to permit him to return to his parish. The Bishop let him speak but only pretended to listen, until Don Sarto, breathless, distressed and overwhelmed, admitted defeat and bowed his head as though lost in thought.

That evening he entered his presbytery a sorrowful man, about to be deprived of the parish he so loved, and to be separated from the affectionate care of his dear sisters. His sisters were naturally curious and wanted to know what it was all about. He simply replied: " The Bishop wants me to go to Treviso as a Canon. . . I am a priest and I must obey."

Early on the morning of September 17th, 1875, Don Sarto crept out of Salzano, taking care not to meet anyone, for his heart was full of grief. What a difference between his departure and arrival! Then the people had avoided him, now he had to avoid the people.

CHAPTER IV

THE CANON OF TREVISO

(November 28th, 1875—November 16th, 1884)

"A priest's first care must be the salvation of souls; his greatest means must be charity and counsel." (Pius X to the Catholic Clergy, 4th August, 1908).

HIS NEW DUTIES

ON November 28th, 1875, Monsignor Sarto took his place among the Canons of Treviso in the capacity of diocesan chancellor and spiritual director of the Seminary. Both these offices called for sound judgement intelligence and prudence, but His Lordship knew where to find one who could respond to his expectations.

Monsignor Sarto was now forty years of age; his wisdom had not been derived from books but from his long experience of pastoral life. His mind was directed by the science of facts, his character frank and resolute, and his soul tuned to sacrifice and labour. His only ambition, the salvation of souls, sprang from the spirit of priesthood. These were the qualities which enabled him to embrace, without trepidation, the responsibility of directing souls destined to bear the priestly character, and to give a sound moral formation to the boys of the adjoining school, while at the same time acting as the right arm of the Bishop in the government of the diocese.

THE POWER OF EXAMPLE

The canons of Treviso, enjoying a privilege granted by the Patriarch of Venice, were permitted to wear a violet cassock, made of silk and adorned with tassels and buttons of varying colours to mark the grades of their dignity. Some of them looked like a vase of flowers against a purple background, and thanks to the abuse of their privilege could have suggested designs to Parisian dressmakers.

Monsignor Sarto walked through the streets in a black cassock, not much better than the one he had thrown away before leaving Salzano, and the only sign of his dignity was the strip of purple under his collar. Reasons were not lacking to show why this was an abuse; efforts were made to "convert" him, and cutting remarks and sharp innuendoes were the order of the day. This did not last long, for one by one the Canons fell into line with the new Monsignor, as the Salzanese had done before.

SPIRITUAL DIRECTOR OF THE SEMINARY

Frowned upon, tolerated and finally loved, first by the Salzanese, then by the Canons, and now once again by the seminarians at Treviso, who chuckled at the idea of having a country priest as their spiritual director, Monsignor Sarto very quickly won his way into the hearts of them all and gained for himself the esteem, confidence and affection of both young and old. Though this was only one of his duties, it was by no means a minor one, and it took up a great deal of his time, for when the care of souls was in question nothing was regarded as unimportant, nothing was done perfunctorily. His round of duties was considerable; the reading of the meditation in the morning, the weekly conference, the explanation of the Gospel on Sundays, the conducting of the monthly day of recollection, confessions on Wednesdays and Saturdays for about 230 students and a continual readiness to receive any student who might wish to discuss the problems and difficulties of the spiritual life.

Imbued with the thought that the priest should be the light of the world and the salt of the earth, he was determined that the young men for whose training he was responsible, should leave the Seminary fully prepared and equipped to take up their place in the front line of the battle against the enemies of Christ. In his conferences and sermons he constantly insisted on the dignity of the priestly vocation, the importance of zeal for souls, the power of deep but unostentatious piety, love for study and obedience to superiors, but above all on detachment from the things of the world and readiness to sacrifice all, even life itself, in carrying out one's duties in the cause of Christ. He felt it his duty to persuade a materialistic world, through the instrumentality of these future priests, that in reality there is no such thing as a purely natural order, that God is the beginning and end not only of every man's life but of every action and detail of that life and that an attempt to live without God is a defiance of the very nature of man and of the universe. Unless this conviction were firmly implanted in the heart of the priest, what chance was there for an unbelieving world? Though kindness and sweetness characterized all he did and said, when he spoke about respect for the things of God there was fire in his words and a tremor in the hearts of his hearers.

He knew how to pity the shortcomings of the young seminarians, but he would not tolerate slothfulness or carelessness; the Sign of the Cross made in mid-air, the semi-dormant listener at his sermons, levity at times of prayer came under the surgeon's knife and were mercilessly cut out lest the whole body should be infected. One day these young men were to be spectacles to the world, ornaments of the diocese and the joy of their Bishop.

But the severity of Mgr. Sarto was always tempered with mildness and sympathy. He knew how to reprimand, but he also knew how to forgive; those who experienced the vehemence of his reproaches to-day could be sure of the warmth of his friendship to-morrow. However stern his corrections might be, no one ever felt hurt or bore a personal grudge against him on account of them; on the contrary, they helped to enkindle in the heart of the culprit the confidence that there was one watching over them whose only interest was their spiritual good.

Every student knew that Monsignor Sarto's room was ever open to them, that he was ever prepared to listen to their little troubles and perplexities and to show that he took a special interest in all affairs which were confided to him. On one occasion a poor student, pale and trembling, entered Mgr. Sarto's room relating the sad story of a disaster which had overtaken his family and concluding that to save the honour of his father he must procure about £10 at once. The spiritual director listened to the tale with compassion, but at the end said: "I am very sorry, my son, I have but little money, but have confidence in the Lord and he will provide; come and see me to-morrow." On the morrow the distressed student once again came to his room and this time was greeted with the words "Well, here it is!" and forthwith the borrowed money was produced, much to the amazement of the student.

EPISCOPAL CHANCELLOR

The precarious state of the Bishop's health, the advanced age and infirmity of the Vicar-General, and the almost continual illness of the other assistant threw practically the whole burden of diocesan affairs on the newly appointed chancellor. It was edifying to watch him seated at his desk in a large room on the ground floor of the episcopal palace, especially on Tuesdays, when a huge assemblage of parish priests and curates from all parts of the diocese waited for him to attend to their various affairs. Each one was sure to be received with that inimitable expression of kindness, listened to with that patience, simplicity and naturalness, and have their business disposed of with that efficiency, impartiality and prudence which had characterized Mgr. Sarto in all he had undertaken in the past and which made one think he had been an episcopal chancellor all his life. He enjoyed the respect and confidence of all the priests in the diocese and above all that of His Lordship, Mgr. Frederico Zinelli, who was so satisfied with him that he often repeated: "I have never known a chancellor so quick, able and discerning in dealing with all kinds of people and all kinds of intricate problems, as Mgr. Sarto."

To the priests he was always friendly, and faithfully brought their complaints to the Bishop's notice, but at the same time he was always the stern guardian of the prestige of his Bishop, and when circumstances obliged him to reprimand or admonish, a cloud of melancholy descended on his brow, and then he spoke firmly. Woe betide any priest who showed resistance to that indomitable will of his or to the authority of the Bishop, for whom he had such profound respect!

On one occasion an intimate friend approached him to
plead for the promotion of a certain curate in whom he
was interested. Mgr. Sarto listened patiently to the verbose
apologies and reasonings, but then looked at his friend
fixedly and said, " You are pleading a lost cause; how do
you know that curate is worthy of promotion? " " Poor
fellow," unconsciously escaped the lips of the petitioner,
but immediately came the thunderous words: " Poor fellow,
indeed, and not only poor, but mad, incapable and unworthy!
Pray for him, help him in private by all means, but in public
or officially, definitely no. It would not only be an injustice,
it would be a scandal. Be silent and let us not discuss this
affair any further."

THE WORK OF FOUR

The windows of the two small rooms which Mgr. Sarto
occupied at the Seminary looked out on to a pleasant little
garden watered by the Sile. The peace and tranquillity of
the scenery invited one to spend hours gazing upon the beauty
of nature, but Mgr. Sarto did not have hours to spend, nor
was his constitution tempered to idleness of any sort. Neither
Tombolo nor Salzano had ever seen him idle, and the curia
was to be no exception. Six busy hours of the day were
passed among the cares and perplexities of the varied affairs
of the curia; he did not leave his desk in the great hall until
late in the afternoon, and then he took his leave with a bundle
of papers under his arm to give him work for the night.
The afternoon was spent in choir, and in the evening he took
dinner at the Seminary with the professors. This was his
only recreation, the only time he could put out of his mind
the harassing thought of curial business, the only chance he
had of giving full play to the lighter side of his character
with jokes, quick repartee and general pleasantry.

VICAR-CAPITULAR

On June 12th, 1879, the Bishop, wishing to reward
the merits of Mgr. Sarto, promoted him to the honour of
provost of the Cathedral. The acknowledgment came just

in time, for four months later, after a long illness, His Lordship passed to his reward. The Cathedral Chapter met to appoint a Vicar-Capitular, who should rule the diocese until the election of the new Bishop. There was no hesitation. Unanimously all turned to Mgr. Sarto as the one most worthy to fill this office. The clergy of the diocese received the news with universal approval.

Mgr. Sarto undertook his heavy burden with his eyes ever fixed upon the supernatural horizon, and this gave him courage and firmness to lay the axe to the root wherever abuses appeared, and gentleness and kindness to console, encourage and lead his priests in their fight with the powers of evil. Because earthly ambition had no influence upon him and the thirst for the salvation of souls was always with him, he never tired of pointing out to his priests that their lives must be clothed in prayer and sacrifice. He himself pointed the way and he insisted that all should follow. Thus he wrote on December 1st, 1879: " The priest, living in a permanent state of war against the forces of evil, will find that the faithful exercise of his ministry will sustain him against a multitude of ruthless enemies. The individual is powerless, but bound together in unity of thought, unity of ambition and unity of work we shall be invincible as a fortified rock and paralyze the ranks of our foes."

A spirit of contentment settled over the diocese during the time in which Mgr. Sarto ruled. The priests felt that he was a man of God. They knew that his reproaches and praises were always well deserved and that whenever promotion was given, justice governed the choice that was made. Nepotism in any form whatever was the abomination which the Vicar-Capitular was determined to stamp out. Don Giacomo Sarto, a cousin of the Vicar-Capitular, was an excellent priest but was by no means outstanding for intelligence. One day while he was talking to a parish priest of the diocese the conversation turned upon the new appointment.

" Don Giacomo, your fortune is made, now that your cousin has been appointed Vicar-Capitular."

" Don't you believe it! Under Mgr. Zinelli I was Rector

5

of Villa di Bosco, but as soon as my cousin took over I had to step down and am now simple curate of Spresiano."

Don Giacomo was a good priest but lacked the necessary talent to accomplish the task to which the late Bishop had appointed him, and his being a cousin of Mgr. Sarto made no difference whatever.

TOWARDS THE BISHOPRIC

Mgr. Sarto ruled the diocese for seven months only, but that was more than sufficient to show that he possessed the learning, experience and firmness to rule any diocese. The new Bishop, His Excellency Giuseppe Callegari of Venice, reinstated Mgr. Sarto in his two offices of episcopal chancellor and spiritual director of the Seminary, to which he added the third of Pro Vicar-General. But no one thought that he would remain long in Treviso, while the only one fully convinced that he would not become a Bishop was himself, for there was not the slightest shade of vainglory in him. He wished to live ignored by the crowd, in a humble capacity, and to place all his glory and happiness in God alone. He often quoted the words: " All flesh is grass and the glory thereof is as the flower of the field." When his friends hinted that his remarkable talents were being wasted and that he was a candidate for the episcopacy, he would reply: " These are not the wishes of friends, for while the priest carries the cross under his dress it is a sweet burden, but when he is forced to wear it over his clothing, though it be made of pure gold, he has a chain around his neck."

To his friend at Venice who suggested that he should be appointed as auxiliary Bishop of Treviso on account of all he had done for the diocese, he wrote thus: " Tell all who make such a ridiculous suggestion that I am far too small to aspire to such heights; my experience during the four years I have spent in the curia has taught me to recognise the thorns and the dangers inherent in such responsibilities. The glory of the pastorate does not compensate for these; remember the words of St. Philip Neri who always used to ask those aspiring to earthly heights, ' And then what will happen?—and then?—

and then?' All earthly glory must necessarily vanish as smoke."

Like the saints, in his innate modesty, his deep-felt humility, he could not bring himself to be "someone"; he looked upon all who aspired to the glory of insignia with a smile of indulgent compassion. Voices telling of dignity and honour buzzed about him, conspiring to rob him of his peace, but for him they were but empty words; his heart beat solely for duty, for the glory of God and the salvation of souls. The only glory for which he longed was the glory of heaven. On June 2nd, 1884, he wrote to one of his friends: "It is a great consolation to me to have reached my fiftieth year, and to be drawing close to the *redde rationem*. . ."[1] He did not imagine that the day was drawing close when the Lord would judge him worthy to ascend to the highest position on earth, that he might restore all things in Christ.

EPISCOPAL INFULA

Any thoughts of promotion which crossed the mind of the humble Chancellor were painful to him. But the voices still buzzed, and distasteful though they might be he could not fail to appreciate that there was foundation for what they said. His work under Mgr. Giuseppe Apollonio (1883-1884) and previously under Mgr. Giuseppe Callegari (1880-1883), as well as the months in which he had acted as ruler of the diocese, had put him in the public eye. Mgr. Callegari had found him a faithful confidant and an affectionate friend and had referred to him as "his right arm." He was known, not only at Treviso, but at Rome. Pope Leo XIII, who was a shrewd judge of men and of merit, had already inscribed his name in the golden book of prospective candidates for the greater responsibilities of Church government.

One morning in September, 1884, Bishop Apollonio entered the office of Mgr. Sarto in the curia and beckoned his chancellor to accompany him to his private chapel. "Let us kneel here and pray together, my dear Monsignor, for

---

[1] "Render an account."

there is an important matter which concerns us both," said
His Lordship gravely. There was an atmosphere of mystery
about the Bishop's behaviour, but Mgr. Sarto did not at all
suspect what was to follow. His Lordship rose to his feet
after a few minutes of prayer, put his left hand on the shoulder
of the kneeling Monsignor and with his right presented to
him his letters of appointment to the episcopal office as Bishop
of Mantua. No criminal ever received the death penalty with
such terror as Mgr. Sarto experienced in the few minutes
that followed. His only answer was the flood of tears which
gushed from his eyes as he buried his face in his hands and
turned to his Lord in the Blessed Sacrament to beg for mercy.

"Accept," said the Bishop after a long silence, "accept,
it is the will of God."

"But it is impossible, the weight is far too great for me. . .
I have not the ability . . . there are so many others . . . I
could never rise to such an office." A series of disjointed,
passionate entreaties burst from the lips of the unhappy
Canon.

"It is the will of God, accept!" continued the Bishop,
consoling and pacifying him.

But it was no use. Mgr. Sarto would not commit himself
to a formal acceptance of so heavy a burden, which he was
thoroughly convinced was far too much for him. He lost
no time in sending a carefully worded letter off to Rome,
pointing out that such an appointment was an utter
impossibility and enlarging upon all his weaknesses and
shortcomings. At Rome very little notice was taken of the
letter, for the Chancellor of the episcopal curia of Treviso
was too well known; he was told to obey. He did obey,
but only comforted by the thought that it was the will of
God, Who had spoken through his superiors. Mgr. Sarto's
appointment was no surprise to the Trevisians. Everyone
expected it and rejoiced; only the poor Monsignor himself
was surprised and dejected.

After a few days, when the excitement had died down
and Mgr. Sarto was becoming more resigned to the
situation, he decided to pay a visit to Riese, so that he could
see his mother, sisters and the little cottage once again.

The whole village turned out for the occasion; there was joy in every heart at the elevation of the son of the poor Cursore, there was joy on every face but his. The maternal eye of Margherita Sanson was not slow to perceive this, nor was she slow to inquire how it was that he should be so sad when all the rest rejoiced. He simply replied: "Mother, you do not realize what it means to be a Bishop—I shall lose my soul if I neglect my duty." He measured earthly honour in the light of eternal glory; the higher the honour, the greater the responsibility and the more fearful the account to be rendered at the last judgment.

Two months later, on November 13th, 1884, he was kneeling humbly at the feet of the great Pontiff, Leo XIII. On that cold morning the will of God was not his only consolation—he saw that there was still a chance of withdrawing, and did not neglect any means that might further this. He begged, pleaded and wept, hoping that His Holiness would take compassion on him and save him from the burden of the episcopal infula. Leo XIII was kind, compassionate and understanding, but at the same time firm, and relentless in decisions he had made. His only answer to the distressed Monsignor was: "You have written a letter asking to be dispensed from the episcopate, but it is Our wish that you go to Mantua."

That evening the Bishop Elect wrote to Mgr. Callegari describing what had happened: "The Holy Father welcomed me with all the goodness of his heart and told me the motives which prompted him to refuse my petition. . . What a cross, Monsignor! What a Calvary! I can but say with Jesus, ' Not my will but Thine be done.' "

On the third Sunday of November in the Church of St. Apollinarius, Cardinal Lucido Maria Parocchi conferred upon him the fulness of the priesthood. On that day the Mantuans were celebrating a feast of Our Lady, under the title of " Queen of Mantua," and the Gospel read at Mass was that of the parable of the leaven. Prophetic Gospel! The zeal of the new Bishop was to be the leaven which would bring new life to the Church of Mantua.

When the new Bishop returned to Treviso he received a

warm welcome.   One and all wished to show their love for
him by joyous and enthusiastic demonstrations.   This did not
appeal, however, to his humble heart, and so he quickly
prepared himself for his final departure, anxious to lose no
time in starting his years of labour among the Mantuans.
Nine years spent in Treviso had produced many affections
which had taken deep root in his heart, and he knew that the
departure from the Seminary and the Curia would grieve him
deeply.   He wrote to the Rector of the Seminary, Don
Antonio Romanello, saying: " Read this to the students in
the refectory when I am not there, and tell both professors
and students that, though I am leaving, I have each of them
in my heart; ask them to pray for poor Monsignor Sarto."

On the day of his departure, he arranged to have a carriage
wait for him some distance down the road at an early hour
of the morning.   He wished no one to see him go.   He went
alone with grief in his heart and tears in his eyes, uniting his
sorrow with that of the Man of Sorrows.

CHAPTER V

BISHOP OF MANTUA
(April 18th, 1885—November 22nd, 1894)

" His great and noble spirit dwelt in the mind and heart of the clergy of the world as a living example of a model Pastor." (Mgr. James McGuigan, Archbishop of Toronto, February 10th, 1935).

UNCHANGEABLE PROGRAMME

THE day on which Mgr. Sarto arrived in the ancient town of the Gonzagas (April 18th, 1885) and blessed for the first time the huge assembly of people, who came to give him a triumphant welcome, marked the resurrection of the whole diocese of Mantua. A month before this he had written to the Vicar-General of Mantua making quite clear his intention of carrying out the mission assigned to him as a Bishop should, and the plans upon which he proposed to work. He stated: " It gives me great comfort to assure you that, knowing the mission which I have from God, I know also the duty of submission to lawfully constituted authority. The ministry of religion has peace for its standard and charity for its law, and I am so fully convinced that the influence of the priest is useless and even harmful unless concord prevails that I shall do everything in my power to maintain peace and harmony among the clergy, and I am ready to make any sacrifice, however great, to uproot the slightest trace of discord which is so injurious to the happiness of priests and the union of hearts."

With touching sincerity he thus concludes: " Your new Bishop, the poorest of all, has but one ambition—to see all the children under his care united into one large, happy family, in the shelter of which their souls will be safe. For the well-being of souls I shall consider no sacrifice too great, and have nothing more at heart than your salvation. I know that for the salvation of my little flock I shall have to undergo great fatigue, encounter dangers, suffer insults, and strive against the foe who seeks its ruin, but my people will ever find me firm at my post, always meek and full of charity."

With such an eminently supernatural plan of action, and with a heart so full of the charity of Christ, Bishop Sarto began the restoration of the diocese which in a short time was to become the splendour of Lombardy.

A GLANCE AT THE DIOCESE

Those were sad days for the Church in Mantua. There was a great shortage of priests, and, what was worse, the few who still fought under the banner of Christ were divided in the politico-religious struggle of the time; not a few parishes were left without pastors; the mention of a vocation to the priesthood drew down derision on any well-intentioned young man, and the vast harvest of souls was left to the mercy of a few poorly-equipped, half-hearted labourers. The faith of the working-class people was enfeebled by newborn Socialistic doctrines, while the so-called cultured and educated classes were no less a prey to Liberalism, a powerful and aggressive ally of Freemasonry. It must be borne in mind that Continental Socialism and Liberalism have always been strongly tainted with anti-clericalism. There were some good, zealous priests, but so few in number that they were over-burdened with work and faced with an apparently hopeless task. They seemed helpless against the numerous evils which encompassed them, and the torpor and indifference of the people paralysed all their efforts.

Bishop Pietro Rota (Bishop of Mantua, 1871-1879) had grappled with Masonry and had suffered a unique form of persecution at its hands by being held up for public ridicule in the square outside his own Cathedral; nor had Mgr. Berengo, his immediate successor, been any more fortunate. This was the condition of the diocese when Mgr. Sarto took over in 1885. He was not slow to appreciate what he had to face. It was an alarming situation even for one prepared to sweat on rough and stony ground, but vain fear and useless tears would not help matters; he must roll up his sleeves and get to work, trusting entirely, as only the saints know how, to the mercy of God.

RENOVATION OF THE SEMINARY

The crying need of the diocese of Mantua was for priests. " I need professors in the Seminary, I need priests in the town and country parishes . . . something desperate must be done! " lamented Mgr. Sarto, reflecting on the impossible state of affairs on June 2nd, 1885; and raising his hands as though in despair, as one abandoned on the sands of the desert and shouting in vain, he complained: " On the first Sunday of August I shall ordain the one and only priest for the diocese this year—the only fruit of the Seminary!—only one when I need at least forty! "

If the diocese were to be saved he had to gather about him an army of fervent, zealous, hard-working priests with hearts beating in unison with his own; plainly, then, the salvation of the diocese depended on the restoration of the Seminary. For more than ten years it had remained closed. This was due chiefly to the political revolution, but the anti-clerical feeling which had crept into the people had played a large part. Mgr. Berengo's attempt to re-open it had been strangled for want of funds and, worse still, for want of vocations. Maybe the people were not sufficiently interested! But the faith was not dead in them, for had they not often requested priests for their parishes, had they not felt the lack of priests keenly? Certainly, something could be done, if only the people could be made to realize that it was quite impossible to have priests without a Seminary and that the closed gates of the Seminary were, in fact, the root cause of all their trouble. No one could bring this home to them so well as their new Bishop, no one knew better than he how to touch their hearts. On July 5th, 1885, Mgr. Sarto addressed the following moving letter to his flock:

" My greatest anxiety since the Holy Father deigned to entrust to me the care of this diocese is the lamentable condition of the Seminary. What a great sorrow it will be for me to be forced to inform a few young men next

Autumn that there is no place for them in the Seminary,
that they must refuse the heaven-sent invitation to embrace
the Cross in the priestly life, and that I cannot avail myself
of their services to minister to the many thousands of souls
who are left without pastors.

"The Church cannot stand without priests, and the
priesthood cannot last unless provision is made for the
education of clerics. We must do all in our power to make
our Seminary flourish once again. I do not ask the impossible;
I know that your earnings are small, but I also know that
there are many of you . . . many grains make aheap and
many drops a shower!

"Have you yourselves not witnessed the unused church,
the abandoned altar, the empty confessional? Have you not
seen young men growing up ignorant of the things essential
for their salvation, the sick and dying without the consolations
of religion, the mystic Sion now solitary?

"Love the Seminary! This is the desire of your Bishop.
Let no one allege the scantiness of his income or the poverty
of his parish, for there is no one who cannot give a centime,
a fruit, a vegetable. Nothing is impossible to him who
loves.

"Love the Seminary! This is most necessary for the
diocese of Mantua at the moment. Your small offerings
will renew for you the prodigy of the widow of Sarephta, who,
for the morsel she gave to the Prophet Elias, received the
promise that the pot of meal should not waste nor the cruse
of oil be diminished.

"Love the Seminary! In this you will fulfil the great
desire of your Bishop and you will merit to see this dear
family, the apple of my eye, growing to its fulness."

To such passionate words and to so ardent an appeal the
whole diocese could not but respond. Clergy and people,
rich and poor replied immediately with such an abundance
of offerings that within a few years the Seminary was able
to accomodate 147 students.

.   .   .   .   .

Mgr. Sarto could once again breathe freely. But to ensure

the lasting security of his Seminary he had not done enough. He must now give it a firm grounding in the spiritual life by a strict discipline calculated to imprint on its members a profound sense of Christianity and to prepare them for the life of labour and sacrifice they were about to undertake. He instructed the Superiors to exercise great vigilance in accepting and rejecting candidates. He recommended parish priests to inculcate in the young men of their parishes great esteem for the priestly life. Whenever they saw a possible candidate they were to leave nothing undone which might encourage his vocation, while taking great care not to pay too much heed to the wishes of parents, which often arose from vanity or greed.

The subtle false doctrines of the day could not be studied too much, for a priest could not be too well equipped to battle with the enemy. Mgr. Sarto chose his professors carefully, making sure they were thoroughly capable and well versed in their subjects; he increased the Philosophy and Theology courses, laying special stress on the doctrine of Aquinas, which he himself knew well; nor did he neglect any of the subsidiary sciences best adapted to render the sacerdotal ministry efficacious among his people. He went further. He reserved to himself the teaching of the more important portions of the Theology course, took upon himself the grave responsibility of Rector and lost no opportunity of supplying for any professors who for good reasons were unable to hold their classes.

If during the course of a lesson a professor saw the door of the classroom open and the Bishop enter, nothing happened. Mgr. Sarto would take up his place among the students, listen to the lecture far more attentively, ask his questions at the end of the class much more searchingly and form an opinion of the professor much more critically than any of the students. He presided at all examinations and was ever ready to supplement the theoretical questions of the examiners with practical examples drawn from his own manifold experiences, and to offer solutions to the more complex problems with greater clearness than could be found in any text-book.

After seven years of serious study and strict discipline the ordained cleric was sent upon his mission. But his studies had not terminated. Mgr. Sarto stipulated that for the next four years the new priest should present himself annually before a board of examiners to be questioned on a prescribed syllabus. He was never absent from these examinations.

The great Mantuan Seminary had now been put on a solid, economic, scientific and spiritual basis, and could compete with any Seminary in Lombardy in the number of its students, the comprehensiveness and soundness of its teaching and the soberness of its piety. The great labours and silent, daily fatigue of Mgr. Sarto, making untold demands upon his time and depriving him of much necessary rest, produced abundant fruit when 175 newly-ordained priests set to work in what, a few years previously, had been a priest-starved diocese. The people had shown their love for the Seminary, and he had kept the promise he had made for such love.

HIS CLERICS

When the clerics had finished their course at the Seminary, or even when they had finished their four years of junior clergy examinations, they did not escape the vigilance of Mgr. Sarto. He visited them regularly, he knew each of them personally, their names, country and conditions, and they always looked forward to his visits, for he was always affable and had a lively wit. He was interested in their needs, he studied their characteristics and tendencies and kept himself minutely informed of their conduct, studies and piety. No virtue and certainly no defect escaped his penetrating eyes. While he knew how to sympathize with their weaknesses and to encourage them in their deficiencies, he was rigid in prescribing the greatest discipline and used severe chastisements, the most cruel of which was often his reproachful glance, in recalling them to their duties if he noticed that any trace of carelessness had crept into their lives.

Love for sacrifice, obedience to authority, the necessity of overcoming pride, negligence in their duties, tepidity in the service of God and especially the " amor sceleratus habendi," *i.e.*, attachment to money, so out of accord with the ministry of religion, were the usual themes of his discourses and exhortations. Once a month he organized a day of recollection, when he gathered his clerics about him and by the exercises of a retreat refreshed in their minds recollection of the duties of their high calling.

But it was at the time of Ordinations that the zeal of Mgr. Sarto reached its zenith. He himself prepared the candidates for the serious step they were about to take, and with the most appealing words begged them to examine their intention in taking upon themselves the grave responsibilities of the priesthood, and pointed out what a serious wound was inflicted on the hearts of the faithful and on the prestige of the Church by the apostasy of those who embraced the priestly life with base motives.

And how he loved his clerics! " Like a good father, he had them all written in his heart," affirms a parish priest who was a student in the Seminary at the time. If through poverty one of them could not afford the necessary outfit he supplied it; if they could not pay their fees he paid them; if they were delicate or needed extra food or medicine he procured it for them. Being aware of the dangers of the long summer vacation which the students spent with their parents, he opened a villa where they could pass the summer months and keep up the regular exercise of piety and study while enjoying healthy recreations and frequent excursions. He would often visit them himself, spreading among them that joy and peace which always accompanied his kind, jovial personality.

The seminarians had to do their part too. They had to show that they were making an effort to be solidly pious and diligent at their studies. They had to show undoubted signs of a vocation, otherwise—the door! In this there was no hesitation. He was inexorable because experience had shown him that priests who were always seeking material comfort were the scourge of the Church. Such decisions were made only after being long pondered over in the light and counsel of God; but, once made, they were utterly irrevocable.   Justice demanded that the unsuitable candidate be expelled, but Mgr. Sarto was always merciful towards such unfortunate individuals and took care that they were set up in life and given employment suitable to their talents.

THE FIRST PASTORAL VISITATION

From his first contact with the Mantuans, Mgr. Sarto was persuaded that they were a sincere people capable of great fidelity and fruitful activity.   In their ignorance they had been led astray by false doctrines, but he knew that they could easily be recalled to the fold if they could but catch a glimpse of their pastor.   He must approach each and every one of them.   He must show a keen interest in their difficulties and troubles and he must instil into their minds the confidence that he really was their spiritual shepherd.   He must know all his priests personally, their conditions, their needs.   He must control their activity and rouse them from their sluggishness, encouraging them to persevere in their life of sacrifice.

Now that he was assured of the firm re-establishment of the Seminary, he made it his duty to mobilize and unite the energy of his diocese by a visitation of all the parishes.   In mystical language he wrote on August 18th, 1885: " I seek to gather together my straying flock, and if in the searching I must pass through the briars of the forest, if I must seek in the most difficult places, if I must plough through hedge and marsh with labour and pain, I shall not spare myself nor take repose until I have done all in my power to bring back to the fold all who have strayed from it and to exhort those inside never to abandon the flock."

He did not want to be received into the parishes with pomp and ceremony but stated: " The most acceptable reception for me is to enter the parish early in the morning and find a large number of the faithful recollected in prayer in the church."

*   *   *   *   *

For the next two years Mgr. Sarto lived with his clergy and people, walking from parish to parish on his mission of charity and peace. It gave him great joy, when he visited those parishes which had long ago bidden farewell to their pastors and which now depended on the chance visit of a priest for the Sacraments, to be able to assure the people that they would not have long to wait before they enjoyed the fruits of his labours in the Seminary. The details of his work on this pastoral visitation we have from the testimony of those priests who shared with him the inevitable sacrifices and hardships of his wanderings.

As a rule he would enter the church in the morning and take up his place in one of the confessionals until the time came to celebrate Mass. He would then give a short discourse to the people, explaining to them the purpose of the visitation and the plan on which he intended to carry it out. He administered the Sacrament of Confirmation, made a thorough examination of the church, inspected the parish registers and then began his house-to-house visit of the parish, paying no attention to the distances he had to walk. While waiting for dinner, which was always modest and frugal, he would ramble into the study of the parish priest, and should his eye fall on liturgical or theological books whose covers showed any trace of dust, he would pick them up and put them before the embarrassed pastor, who dreaded the ensuing silence more than the most severe remark. In the afternoon he summoned the parish priest and curates one by one, and demanded from them detailed information as to the working of the parish. By this means he quickly became aware of any abuses or any discord which might have arisen, and he then set about extirpating anything inconsistent with the single purpose of a priest's life. He would listen to the suggestions of the parish priests attentively, for he knew that they were more familiar than himself with the particular needs of their own parishes. He would only interrupt them to offer counsel or correction, and they, pleased with the consideration he showed for their opinions, were willing to accept his views and proposals even if these clashed with their own. He then took a short rest, after which he returned to the church, heard confessions, examined the children in Christian Doctrine and closed the visitation by delivering a

fervent discourse from the pulpit. He then gave his blessing
and departed.

Deep traces of his passage remained on the parish. He
left behind him a people thinking in different terms, in terms
of charity. Marriages were regularised, families re-united,
adults baptized, sinners called back to their duties, scandals
removed and much poverty relieved. He could depart
from the parish content and singing in his heart the words
of God to the prophet Jeremiah: " I set thee this day over the
nations to root up and pull down, to waste, destroy, build,
plant."

THE SYNOD

In the Spring of 1888 the first pastoral visitation ended.
Mgr. Sarto had made personal contact with the 153 parishes
of the diocese and like the Divine Pastor could now say:
" I know mine and mine know me." But if he had found so
much to give him joy and consolation in the fidelity and
willingness of the people, he had also found much that had
fallen short of his expectation: parishes completely abandoned,
ignorance of the things of God, children without Baptism,
families at variance and all kinds of distress both moral and
physical. During the visitation he wrote to the Bishop of
Padua from Canneto on October 30th: " Can you imagine
that in a parish of 3,000 souls there were present at the
Bishop's Mass some days ago just 40 women, of whom only
8 received Holy Communion, and at the Christian Doctrine
instruction about 100 children with the same number of
curious onlookers? And the man who presides over the
parish expects me to believe that things are not as bad as I
paint them."

.   .   .   .   .   .

The visitation gave Mgr. Sarto a complete picture of the
diocese, its deficiencies and necessities. He was a practical
man, and it was natural for him to seek the most efficient
remedies. He conceived the idea of holding a diocesan
synod on February 16th, 1887, when the first half of the

MONSIGNOR GIUSEPPE SARTO
BISHOP OF MANTUA

visitation had been completed. He saw that it was necessary to draw up a compendium of statutes and establish constitutions adapted to the needs and evils of modern times— needs and evils which the previous Synod had not even visualized. He made known his wishes to his priests several months before the actual date of the visitation, because he wanted the Synod to be an expression of the sentiments, not of one man, but of the clergy as a whole. To each parish priest was assigned a certain theme, which he was to investigate carefully so as to find remedies in the shape of laws which could easily be obeyed in practice. He warned them that if laws and decrees are abrogated on the very day on which they are made by never being observed they cause disorder and disrespect for the authority which has made them. While advising them to fly from novelties and to deplore laxity, he pointed out that in some cases where a law would be too severe an exhortation would be most effective, but at the same time they should cancel from their vocabulary the expression "an incurable ill." With such sentiments of humility, kindness and wisdom, Mgr. Sarto disposed his priests for the task of restoring the spirit of the diocese.

．　　．　　．　　．　　．

The last synod in Mantua had taken place in 1679, two centuries previously. Since that time many changes had taken place in the world, both civil and religious. The conditions of the diocese had completely changed. Many new laws had been promulgated by the Church which were in conflict with the standing diocesan decrees. It can well be imagined what an enormous amount of work awaited Mgr. Sarto as he returned from his two years of toil in the pastoral visitation. On the very day of his return he began searching the archives, consulting the acts and decrees of his predecessors, studying the privileges and faculties given to the various offices of the diocese, and balancing all in the light of local custom. It was a tedious, strenuous task, but motivated by love it was accomplished with remarkable speed and efficiency. Days and even nights were consumed in drawing up the proposed decrees in clear Latin.

. . . . .

On September 10th, 1888, the joyous sound of all the bells in the city announced that in the Cathedral the diocesan Synod had begun. About 200 priests filed in procession from the episcopal palace to the Cathedral, where Mgr. Sarto explained to a vast assembly of people the purpose of the Synod, and besought them to pray fervently that God would grant success to a Synod so gloriously begun.

During the first three days of the conference Mgr. Sarto outlined the work which was to be done. He spoke of the abuses to be uprooted, and proposed what he considered the most suitable remedies. He listened carefully to all suggestions made, but concentrated chiefly on impressing upon the minds of all present the spirit in which the reforms were to be made. Vital problems in liturgy, faith and morals, the obligation of teaching the catechism, the discipline regarding Matrimony, the first Communion of children, decorum in the sacred functions, the inviolable rights of the Church, the attitude towards the civil authority and towards the Jews, who were very numerous in Mantua at that time— these were among the most important subjects to be discussed. In order to sustain the interest of the people in the proceedings a regular bulletin, drawn up in simple language, was placed at their disposal.

The final Magna Charta of the Mantuan Diocese was an epitome of the practical sanctity of its Bishop. On September 28th, at the conclusion of the Synod, he wrote to Mgr. Jacuzzi, Bishop of Treviso, thanking him for his congratulations: "It is a great consolation to have at last in my hand a constitution suited to the needs of the diocese. I have laboured hard, feared no sacrifices and spent much money for the purpose of uniting my priests. Great credit is due to all those pastors who have worked with me, so deeply imbued with the spirit of my cause. The people, too, rose to the occasion far more than I had expected. For all I thank God, ' to whom be honour and glory.' "

THE SECOND PASTORAL VISITATION

The formation of a constitution is one thing, but the application of its laws in particular cases is quite another. There were those, fortunately few in number, who began almost immediately to lament and criticize the severity with which the axe had been laid to the root of certain abuses, for they were much attached to them even though they were in open conflict with the decrees and the spirit of ecclesiastical discipline.

The pastoral letter of May 20th, 1889, shows how much this grieved Mgr. Sarto. He reminded his priests of the proceedings of the Synod with the kindly expression of a father but with the stern authority of a Bishop nevertheless. He writes: "Example is stronger than precept; it is better to teach with works than with words. Let those who consider the recent Synod as having been too severe in its attack on such abuses as walking out in secular dress, reading anti-Christian newspapers and neglecting religious instruction of the people, realize the damage they are doing to souls by such conduct."

It was this last complaint—the neglect of religious instruction—which prompted him finally five days later to announce the second pastoral visitation. To those who objected that it would be too great a strain on him to undertake the fatigue of another visitation so soon after the Synod he replied: "I do not deny that this will be for me and for you a wearisome labour, but reflect that we did not enter the priesthood to seek a life of comfort. We must work! this is our duty. To be obliged to labour constantly and to be a priest are the same thing. We have the example of the apostles and the saints, and the spirit of the Church is expressed for us in the IVth Provincial Council of Milan, which tells us: ' Illud autem unusquisque clericus saepe repetat: se non ad inertiam neque ignaviam, sed ad spiritualis et ecclesiasticæ militiæ labores vocatum esse,' *i.e.,* each cleric should often repeat to himself that he is not called to a life of ease and laziness but to the labours of a soldier of Christ. This council reflected the spirit of its President, St. Charles Borromeo, who when told that his health would fail under the arduous labours he had undertaken, replied: ' Quorsum mihi mihi valetudo, nisi ut laborem? ' (what use is my health if I don't work?)."

The second visitation multiplied the good work that had been initiated by the first and by the Synod.

THE BISHOP OF THE CATECHISM

Mgr. Sarto never tired of driving home to his priests the importance of giving the people a thorough grounding in the knowledge and spirit of their religion. In his conferences with his priests he constantly came back to this topic, for he considered that if this were done well many evils must necessarily vanish. He had already made this known to his priests in his letter of October 12th, 1885, in which he had laid down that in all parishes a school for Christian Doctrine should be set up; that on all Sundays and major feasts the parish priest should explain the catechism to both children and adults and that parents and guardians who habitually prevented their children and charges from attending these instructions should be refused absolution.

Now on May 25th, 1889, when announcing the second visitation, he once again came back to this topic: " It will be my greatest consolation to enter a parish and find the teaching of Christian Doctrine regular and systematic. I have already recommended this to you very strongly, and in this visitation it will be the point on which I shall most insist."

Those who helped in the organization of the teaching of Christian Doctrine he held most dear to his heart, while to animate his priests with a lively interest in the matter he offered generous rewards of money to those who suggested methods which he considered simple, efficacious and suited to the circumstances. Nothing gave him greater joy than to gather about him large groups of children or adults and to explain some point of Doctrine to them. No sacrifice was sweeter than to walk miles to a parish where there was no pastor, or where the pastor had been impeded by legitimate causes from giving the weekly instruction, in order to teach the less fortunate of his flock the essentials of their Faith. No

surprise was greater or more distasteful to the parish priests
than to see their Bishop suddenly appear at the back of the
church during the instructions they were giving or should
have been giving.

If there was any fault which made him angry and really
severe it was the neglect of these instructions.   In this he
admitted no excuses.   On one occasion he was informed
that the parish priest of a country church had left much to
be desired in the fulfilment of this duty.   Just after mid-day
one Sunday, Mgr. Sarto knocked at the presbytery door.
No answer!   The parish priest was absent.   He entered the
church, called the sacristan and ordered him to give the bell
a few loud tolls to summon the people to their Instruction.
At the sound of the bell the people ran—the parish priest
also ran, little imagining what had happened.   When he
arrived at the church the Bishop interrupted the Instruction
which had already started.

"Ah, here we are!" said the Bishop, "the parish priest
has arrived!" as if to say "Now that he has come, he will
continue the instruction."

"My Lord," returned the frightened pastor, "I'm afraid
I had to receive some guests. . ."

"Very good," concluded Mgr. Sarto, "next time you have
to receive guests, let me know, and I shall come and supply
for you."

Mgr. Sarto reminded another parish priest who had not
been very particular about his duties in this respect that the
pastor who in spite of the grave deliberation of the Synod
neglected his obligation of giving his people regular instructions in Christian Doctrine could not consider himself free
from mortal sin.

.   .   .   .   .

Lest the Catechetical Instruction should be omitted
Mgr. Sarto issued a prohibition against the giving of sermons
in other parishes even during Lent and Advent.   Some
objected that the scarcity of priests would make it very
difficult to procure Lenten preachers in view of the new
prohibition, but with shrewd practical sense he replied:

"I would much prefer to see the Lenten sermons omitted, for very often they prove absolutely fruitless, whereas people who are unable to absorb oratorical outpourings benefit much more from the simple explanation of the catechism."

To others who suggested that the explanation of the Gospel text would be more beneficial than the catechism, Mgr. Sarto said: "No! The explanation of the Gospel and the teaching of the catechism are two entirely distinct obligations. The explanation of, or commentary on the Gospel narrative always pre-supposes that the people are thoroughly grounded in the rudiments of their faith, whereas in explaining Christian Doctrine your object is to move the heart and to make it conform to the spirit of Christ, which you demonstrate with a few well chosen examples from Sacred Scripture. This is in keeping with the spirit of Trent, which tells us to explain doctrine ' with brevity and simplicity of speech.' With brevity because as St. Francis de Sales tells us, ' when there is too much leaf on the vine there is less fruit,' and with simplicity, in imitation of the apostles, who, as St. Gregory the Great tells us, ' took the greatest care of the unlearned ' and so avoided all high-flown speech."

A STANDARD CATECHISM

The first National Catechetical Congress was inaugurated on September 24th, 1889, and at it the whole Italian Episcopate was represented under the presidency of Cardinal Capecelatro. Although Mgr. Sarto was engaged in the Visitation and far away, he did not fail to make his contribution to the congress by a letter which was counted among the most valuable documents. He had always lamented the inconvenience of having such a variety of catechetical texts and firmly asserted the necessity for a standard work. The subject had already been raised at the Congress, but the opinion of the acting president, Mgr. Scalabrini, who upheld the right of a Bishop to impose a text suited to the needs of his own diocese, had so far prevailed.

The attitude of the future Pope Pius X in imposing his catechism on the Universal Church in the fullness of his authority was already expressed in the letter which Mgr. Sarto sent to the Congress. He wrote thus:

"I, the undersigned Bishop of Mantua, pay my respects to the first Catechetical Congress and herewith make a proposal which I think is worthy of discussion by the members of the said Council. Since there exists such a variety of texts of the Catechism, many of which lack not only form but even dogmatic exactitude, it is desirable that a standard text should be approved and imposed on all dioceses. I am fully aware that this is not a matter which can be treated of at a private Congress, because Bishops, masters of the Faith of those committed to their care, have the right of presenting, each in his own diocese, that form of the catechism which is considered most suited to the needs of the particular diocese. I do not therefore suggest that the Congress discuss this matter, but that a unanimous appeal be sent to the Holy See on this important subject. As the Holy See has in fact already unified the Catechism for parish priests it is my wish that there should be introduced without delay a popular Catechism of history, dogma and morals, with brief questions and answers, and that it should be taught in all schools and translated into all languages. It would be a great advantage, in these times of easy communication, when so many leave not only their diocese, but also their fatherland, to have the text so unified that in all places the teachings of the Church could be heard in the same words in which they were learnt at our mothers' knees. I therefore hereby propose that the first Catechetical Congress of Piacenza present a petition to the Holy Father for the drawing up of a Catechism simple and popular, with brief questions and answers, divided into sections and prescribed for the use of the whole Church."

✠ GIUSEPPE, Bishop.

This letter of the Bishop of Mantua was received with enthusiastic applause, and with a single stroke it united all the members, including Mgr. Scalabrini, in the same opinion as that of Mgr. Sarto. The President expressed the great pleasure it gave him to announce that the desired petition would be sent to the Holy See. But which of those present at Piacenza in that September of 1889 imagined that the actual carrying into effect of that petition would be the work of Mgr. Sarto as Pope Pius X?

WITH HIS PRIESTS

In the pastoral letter which Mgr. Sarto addressed to his clergy shortly after he had taken up office as Bishop, he pointed out the great fear which he experienced on being exalted to so high a position. "Believe me," he wrote, "if there is anything to calm this fear, it is the confidence that you will live up to my expectations."

In a subsequent letter he explained to them what he meant by this: "A priest must bring his every action, every step, every habit into harmony with the sublimity of his vocation. The priest, who at the altar celebrates eternal mysteries, assumes, as it were, a divine form; this he must not relinquish when he descends from the High Mount and departs from the Temple of the Lord. Wherever he is, or in whatever work he engages, he must never cease to be a priest, accompanied by the dignity, gravity and decorum of a priest. He must therefore be holy; he must be saintly, so that his words and his works express his love, impress his authority and command respect. Exterior dignity is more powerful than eloquent words. A priest who is ever mindful of his high calling inspires confidence and attracts the homage of all; while, on the other hand, if he forgets the dignity of his character, if he does not show in his exterior comportment more gravity than seculars, he incurs the displeasure of those very people who applaud his levity but are not slow to despise both him and what he stands for."

. . . . .

The priests of Mgr. Sarto had to be priests in their every thought, word and deed; they had to be devoted to labour, unselfish and docile to the commands of their Bishop. Giving an exact and detailed diagnosis of the evils of the time in his pastoral letter of September 5th, 1894, he thus addressed the clergy of the two dioceses of Venice and Mantua: "If a priest at ordinary times must be a paragon of virtue, how much more so in times like ours? Priests cannot live in solitude; it is their duty to go among the people in the very heart of the town, where passion and vice are not only permitted but flaunted. The virtue of our priests must be very strong that they may withstand the onslaught of deceitful lust and the scourge of bad example."

Just as the "Exhortation" which the future Pope Pius X addressed to the clergy of the whole world can be counted among the greatest documents of his Pontificate, so can this letter to the priests of Venice and Mantua be reckoned as amongst the most important of his Episcopate. The sanctification of his priests was the thing most dear to his heart.

. . . . .

First among the virtues which must distinguish a priest, according to Mgr. Sarto, was integrity of faith and courage in defending and professing it. The most formidable enemy of the Faith is not the open persecutor or the blasphemous tyrant, but the insidious, underhand serpent who seeks to reconcile light and darkness or form a truce between justice and iniquity.

"No type is more dangerous than this," continued this watchful Pastor, "and, to be persuaded of it, it is sufficient to consider the obstinacy with which so-called 'Liberal-Catholics' cling to their false doctrine, trying to lure the Church herself into their way of thinking. Priests must watch against that hypocrisy which attempts to enter into the fold of Christ preaching Charity and Prudence, as though it were Charity to let the wolf tear the sheep to pieces, or Virtue to practise that prudence of the flesh which is reproved by God, 'For it is written, I will destroy the wisdom of the wise and the prudence of the prudent I will reject' (*I Cor.* i. 9). Priests must watch, for the faith is threatened, less by open denial than by the subtlety and falsehood of those perfidious Liberal-Catholics who, stopping scarcely on the brink of condemned error, find their strength in the appearance of pure doctrine.

"Let priests take care not to accept from the Liberal any ideas which, under the mask of good, pretend to reconcile Justice with Iniquity. Liberal Catholics (he speaks plainly) are wolves in sheep's clothing. The priest must unveil to the people their perfidious plot, their iniquitous design. You will be called Papist, clerical, retrograde, intolerant, but pay no heed to the derision and mockery of the wicked. Have courage; you must never yield, nor is there any need to yield. You must go into the attack whole-heartedly, not in secret but in public, not behind barred doors but in the open, in the view of all."

.   .   .   .   .

So solemn and so grave a denunciation of Liberalism, the root of so many evils and dissensions, and so formal an appeal to the clergy to guard themselves against it, had never before been proclaimed so clearly. Against Liberalism, that hybrid of truth and falsehood, which doctrine must the clergy defend and preach? "That which comes from God and is proposed by the infallible teaching of the Church," replied the future Pius X without hesitation.

"Alas!" he continues, "when a certain doctrine is inconvenient, or the Law of God seems an obstacle to some work or ambition, ease and success are sought in the transgression of those principles which alone are secure. But what will remain of these buildings without foundation, built upon sand? The winds and rains will come and devastate the house not built on the solid rock of firm and unshakable doctrine. Many fail to understand the solicitude and minute care which must be taken to safeguard the purity of doctrine. The progress of Science and the development of modern thought seem to demand that the Church relinquish some part at least of her ancient principles, for it seems intolerant that she alone should stay immobile in the face of such progress; let those who think thus recall the words of the apostle: 'I adjure thee before the God Who gives life to all things, before Jesus Christ Who bore witness to that great claim when He stood before Pontius Pilate, to fulfil thy charge without stain of reproach until the day when Our Lord Jesus Christ appears ' (*I Tim*. vi. 13-14)."

. . . . .

But in the struggle against error, simple doctrine is not enough. Doctrine must be founded and sustained by a sincere piety which so turns the soul towards God that the smallest deviation from virtue or truth is considered a monstrous crime. Mgr. Sarto thus cautioned his priests: " So as not to be drawn into the snares of falsehood and in order to conserve the integrity of faith and doctrine, you must, above all, cultivate a solid piety. What St. Gregory Nazianzen said of his father should apply to every priest: " Although second in doctrine he was amongst the most learned in piety " (*Orat*. xviii).

There are many documents which could be cited to show the untiring solicitude of Mgr. Sarto to see his clergy increase in piety and to base all their activity on it. Nothing gave him greater joy than to find himself in the midst of his priests in the peace of a retreat. He wrote on July 29th, 1889, inviting his priests to the Spiritual Exercises: " I experience such consolation on those blessed days on which we open our hearts to God that He may fill us with His grace and enrich us with that fervour which alone can perform great things."

And on July 28th, 1887: " Give me the consolation of seeing you in large numbers joined together in the exercises of a retreat. In such circumstances the bounds of reciprocal affection are strengthened and the grace of God, awakening us from a false security, will arm us against the tempests which have by no means yet passed."

Surrounded by his priests in the exercises of a retreat, he sought no distinction or honour; he was simply one of them. In intimate colloquy rather than in formal sermon he would bring back to them the clear vision of their duties, touching their souls with the love of Christ which shone so gloriously in his own. His discourses were not long; few words, but sincere, sensible and full of affection. No rigour, no severity, no opprobrious remarks crossed his lips; but, compassionate and kind, he imitated his Divine Master Who

" did not break the bruised reed nor extinguish the smoking flax " (*Matt.* xii. 2o).

It is no wonder that impetuous decisions and rash measures were wholly excluded from his system of government, for he kept ever before his mind the words of the chief of the apostles: " Be shepherds to the flock God has given you. Carry out your charge as God would have it done; cordially, not like drudges; generously, not in the hope of sordid gain; not tyrannizing, each in his own sphere, but setting an example, as best you may, to the flock " (*I Pet.* v. 2-3). He preferred persuasion to compulsion, kindness to severity and circumspection of the heart to fear of supervision. It was rather the charm of his virtue than the strength of his authority which enabled him to hold his diocese in perfect submission. He was determined that the Episcopal Palace should not become a sort of police court and that the Bishop should be a master, a doctor and a father rather than a stern legislator and custodian of the laws. His priests must find in him not an inexorable judge or an implacable censor, but a friend, a confidant, a brother, one ready and willing to veil human misery, to stretch out a hand to those in danger and to lift up those who had fallen.

He always received them with affection and kindness at whatever time they visited him no matter how important or pressing the business in which he was occupied. He listened to their stories, giving the keenest attention to every detail and showing the great satisfaction which they gave him. With words of Christian hope he encouraged the doubtful, the uncertain and the anxious; to those in need he stretched out a beneficent hand, grieving only that he could not give as much as he would like; if they had come from afar he obliged them to dine at his own modest table; while with those who after falling into some fault had promised sincere amendment, he was so generous with pardon that they could not refrain from exclaiming: " What a Bishop! one cannot speak with him without being touched."

. . . . .

It often happened that his reproaches consisted not even

of a word, but merely a look, a gesture, a smile. A parish priest of a country parish had let himself fall into the bad habit of remaining in bed a little too long in the morning, so that many of his parishioners were left without confession before Mass, and no one knew for certain at what time the Mass was likely to begin. One morning Mgr. Sarto arrived in the parish at an early hour. He entered the church, took up his place in the confessional and began hearing the confessions of those whom he had seen waiting. Presently the parish priest, still not fully awake, arrived on the scene, and perceiving that a stranger had usurped his position he walked angrily across the church, pulled back the curtain of the confessional and found himself face to face with his Bishop. The fatherly smile which greeted the now fully awakened priest was sufficient reproach, and the lesson did not have to be repeated.

. . . . .

Another parish priest in the city was wont to grumble and complain when summoned to the bed-side of the sick at hours which were not too convenient. On one occasion he was called to administer the Last Sacraments to a person who was seriously ill and in grave danger. As usual the reply: " I am far too busy now, I shall come to-morrow," greeted the messenger. Mgr. Sarto got to know of the situation, and though it was late at night he immediately set out for the house of the dying man. He heard his confession, comforted and encouraged him. He then betook himself to the nearby presbytery. The pastor, hearing that his Bishop had arrived, hastened to meet him, profering all the usual signs of courtesy and giving the impression that nothing was too much trouble if it would make His Lordship comfortable—in the interests of religion of course! Mgr. Sarto was not anxious to be entertained and simply declared that he had heard the confession of the dying man and would be extremely grateful to the parish priest if it would not be too much inconvenience for him to go at once with the Viaticum.

. . . .

One morning in the antechamber of the Bishop's Palace,

two priests were waiting to be received in audience by His Lordship.

" Oh! You here too! " said one to the other.

" Yes, I have been summoned by the Bishop to appear to-day at this time, but why, I cannot imagine."

" Then we are both in the same position, for I, too, have been told to come here for no apparent reason."

At that moment the door opened and the Bishop entered: " Well done, Fathers! It's so nice to see people prompt about appointments," exclaimed His Lordship. " Now I'm afraid I have to go out. But come along with me and we can discuss the business on the way."

The Bishop, followed by the two mystified priests, went down the stairs, across the hall and out into the street, where a carriage was waiting for him. Mgr. Sarto told the coachman to drive to the Convent of Our Lady of Grace. There was great excitement and fuss in the Convent on the arrival of the Bishop, but he simply declared: " Nothing! Nothing! Nothing at all; just a little work of charity. I have here two good priests who are very anxious to do a thorough course of the Spiritual Exercises, and I commit them entirely into your hands." With that he blessed the Mother Superior and set out for the town alone.

. . . . .

Mgr. Sarto, who was a Bishop living up to the ideal of St. Paul, " In omni bonitate " (*Eph*. v. 9) was full of goodness, understanding and kindness in dealing with his priests, but this was precisely the reason why his severity was set in such relief and was feared so much by all, when irregularities or abuses called for it. One parish priest was not over cautious about giving scandal and had thoughtlessly accepted the invitation of a certain Don Rodrigo, one of his parishioners, to a dinner party. The party was arranged to take place on a Friday, and the family of Don Rodrigo had long ago ceased to take seriously the law of the Church about abstinence. Don Rodrigo overcame the objection of the parish priest by promising that a special dish without meat should be prepared for him. The priest found himself seated at a table with a plate of fish in front of him, while all about him his disobedient children fed sumptuously on the forbidden meat.

Next day the priest was summoned to the Bishop's house. Yes, it must be the party! There wasn't anything else. Anyway he had kept the law in its integrity and that in spite of temptation. With this trump card in hand the priest faced his Bishop fearlessly. To his amazement Mgr. Sarto rose to his feet, took off his biretta and straightened his face; this could only forebode a storm. The terrified priest played his trump.

"That's no excuse whatever," was the angry answer. "Next time there is a fancy dress ball in your parish I suppose you will dress up and go to it, making the excuse that you didn't dance."

Then from the bookshelf came one of those short sermons of Frederico Borromeo which Mgr. Sarto was so fond of. The interview terminated with the suggestion that a few days in the silence of retreat reflecting on the words of St. Paul: "In all things, show thyself an example of good works, in doctrine, in integrity, in gravity" (*Titus* ii. 7), would be the most practical remedy for such levity.

In making any important decision Mgr. Sarto moved very slowly; he prayed about it and often took counsel with the older and more prudent priests of his diocese, but once the decision was made he was absolutely adamant; nothing on earth could change him. If there was danger to souls because of the carelessness of a parish priest he was sometimes forced to make the hard decision of removing such a pastor from his office. This, however, he did only after all other means had been tried.

In one of the parishes the pastor was not giving a very good example to those under his care. Mgr. Sarto had spoken to him several times, suggesting that he resign from office. In spite of his repeated entreaties the parish priest not only continued in his careless ways but was quite obstinate in refusing to resign. The Bishop then told him to do a course of the Spiritual Exercises, during which he should pray very fervently and listen to the inspirations of the Holy Spirit.

Having finished the exercises the priest returned to the Bishop with the story that he felt positively inspired to mend his evil ways and with the grace of God to make a fresh start, but that the Will of God for him was to remain in office.

" What a coincidence! " exclaimed the Bishop, " I, too, have prayed much over this matter and feel that the Will of God for you is to resign from the parish and leave yourself entirely in the hands of your Bishop." Then he added, " Go and make another three days' retreat, and then come back and tell me what you think." At his next visit to the Bishop the parish priest had reconciled himself to the idea of resigning. The document was signed and presented to His Lordship.

After a short time the spirit of evil once again urged the priest to make yet another attempt to get his parish back. He had recourse to the Keeper of the Seals, Signore Zenardelli, presenting the facts as he would like them to have been. The Minister answered the letter with a telegram which read, " Nothing can be done. I know the Bishop of Mantua. He is a Bishop who acts with justice; obey him! "

.   .   .   .   .

With a Bishop like that the priests always felt secure, knowing that there was one to whom they could always have recourse and on whom they could always rely. The fact that personal influence bore no weight with him, but that all promotion and all praise was given strictly according to their merits, put new heart into their work and eradicated motives of that petty jealousy which is so destructive of the peaceful working of a diocese. His priests had to be devoted to work, lovers of self-sacrifice and untiring in their zeal for the salvation of souls. Who had more right to be exacting than he who had shown the way to labour by his example, never stooping to human calculation and always indifferent to the criticism of the unwilling and the easy-going?

Tombolo, Salzano, Treviso had admired his prodigious energy, but Mantua witnessed the full-grown giant in action. " He worked for the glory of God, both day and night," testifies one of his priests; and "he slept but four hours in the twenty-four," affirm those who were in close contact with him. Speed and efficiency were the hallmark of all he accomplished. "To work is to rejoice; the soul is a fire which is kindled with work," he wrote on November 15th, 1886.

In the nine years of his episcopate he was never seen idle for an instant. His holidays were spent in the midst of the young students at the villa, which he had founded for them. And as though the government of the diocese and the Seminary were not enough for him, he never let a day pass without entering the pulpit to preach to either the clergy, the people or the children.

. . . . .

He was full of zeal for the preaching of the divine word. In his ears constantly resounded the divine command: " Cry, cease not, lift up thy voice like a trumpet and show my people their wicked doings and the house of Jacob their sins " (*Isaias* lviii. 1), and the admonition of the apostle: " Preach the word, be instant in season, out of season; reprove, entreat, rebuke in all patience and doctrine " (*II Tim.* iv. 2).

There was no church from the Cathedral to that of the smallest village in the diocese but had heard him preach; he never lost an opportunity of preaching on special occasions, and no invitation was ever refused, for he loved to speak to the hearts of his sons. His language was simple, his style was easy and friendly; but his success was always extraordinary—confessions and Communions were the proof— because he did not seek earthly laurels but souls, not human glory but the glory of God. He was a living example of the ideal he so often put before his priests. He commanded them to explain the Gospel on Sundays and Feast-days; this was a novelty for the Mantuan diocese, but it was soon to be imitated in other dioceses. So great was the importance he attached to this duty of explaining the word of God that if a parish priest was, for some just cause, unable to do it, Mgr. Sarto would come and supply for him.

WITH HIS PEOPLE

The promise which Mgr. Sarto had so solemnly made to the Mantuans on coming into their city, of spending himself in quest of the erring sheep and in working with and for his people rather than lording it over them, was kept faithfully in all its detail. Where faith was cold and hope languished, the irresistible force of charity alone could extirpate the firmly established roots of evil. That charity was seen on the first Pastoral Visitation, when the Bishop came to know his people by personal contact, and the people learned to love and respect their Bishop, not through the solemnity of liturgical grandeur, but through heart speaking to heart.

All who came to visit him at any hour of the day came under the spell of his kindness, which attracted their hearts, thawed the ice of formality and kindled their love and reverence for him as a friend and as a master. He listened carefully to what they had to say to him and never gave the impression that their affair was trivial in comparison with the graver matters on his mind. Even those who did not share his views on some particular point went away deeply impressed by his incomparable sanctity. The Mantuans quickly learned that when they were in need of comfort, advice or guidance they could be sure of a frank and safe judgment when they had recourse to their Bishop.

But where his charity appeared warmest and where it was often most effective was amongst those who lived unmindful of their eternal destiny. These he sought out with the greatest enthusiasm, often repeating: "Poor little ones! they are worthy of the greatest compassion." And whenever one of them returned to the fold, showing signs of true repentance, he seemed transformed with joy. Who could recount the number of souls (tormented with doubt or burning with hatred, passion or remorse) who found the light of faith and the comfort of hope on coming into contact with such a saintly man?

A well-known professor from an academy in Mantua was on the point of death and had declared that he wished to die as he had lived, far from the Church and the Sacraments. Mgr. Sarto arrived at the hospital and sent word to the sick man that his friend " Sarto " was anxious to see him. The professor was deeply impressed by this act of delicate courtesy and sent back an equally courteous message saying that he was waiting to receive his friend " Sarto." The following morning the whole city knew that the professor had confessed, received the Viaticum and Extreme Unction from the hands of the Bishop and had died reconciled to the Church which he had so often attacked during his life.

.   .   .   .   .

What would he not do to save a soul? He regarded no obstacle as insuperable and no amount of difficulty could make him stop trying; while there was life there was hope. At that time there were many Jews in Mantua, and not a few of them were converted before they died. It was the Bishop who baptised them, despite the opposition of their friends and in the face of insult, rudeness and even threats. One afternoon while walking past the Jewish cemetery with a young priest who had just finished his course of studies at Rome, Mgr. Sarto halted and stood for some time gazing at the tombs, not saying a word, as though lost in thought. He then turned to his young companion and said: " Tell me! Would a *De Profundis* do these poor souls any good? What do you think? " Mgr. Sarto could see him poise on his lips an eloquent reply enhanced with texts from Scripture and the Fathers. But he did not let him reply. He took off his hat and began: " De profundis clamavi ad te Domine." They finished the prayer and then continued walking, and the Bishop admonished the young priest, saying: " See! Rome has crowned you with a theological degree, and indeed this sovereign science is most essential. But believe me God has His own Theology, and it is a special system. Now you will understand why I wanted to pray for these unfortunate people."

.   .   .   .   .

Having said so much about the zeal of the Bishop for the preaching of the word of God and the catechetical instruction

of both children and adults, there is no need to insist further
on his action for the re-birth of the faith in Mantua. But we
cannot pass over his unquenchable eagerness to revive the
ancient splendour of the sacred liturgical functions. In this
respect he was most insistent on the introduction of the
Gregorian Chant, which inspires all classes of people with a
deep sense of prayer and reverence for the House of God.
There was nothing which pleased him more than to see a
multitude of worshippers in the Presence of Christ in the
Blessed Sacrament united in fervent prayer. To bring this
about he was untiring in his zeal for the organization of
societies and confraternities which would serve as an efficient
means for attracting people into the presence of their
Eucharistic Lord, Who could then speak to their hearts
directly. He brought back into flower the Company of the
Most Blessed Sacrament, and ordered that the sick and dying
receive the Viaticum, not in private, but in the midst of a
crowd of praying onlookers. The fundamental note of his
episcopate and the forerunner of those inspired " Eucharistic
Decrees " which would constitute one of the outstanding
characteristics of his Pontificate, was his desire that all
should receive Communion frequently, especially children.

Every form of pious Association received a vigorous impulse
from him, and above all the Third Order of St. Francis, of
which he himself was a member. His frequent pilgrimages
to the shrine of " Our Lady of Grace," and the feasts which he
ordained to be celebrated with unusual pomp on the occasion
of the more memorable events in the life of the reigning
Pontiff, Leo XIII, were but some of the means used by him
to instil into the minds of his people a deep sense of their
Faith, and to establish in their hearts a stout bond of loyalty
and affection for the Holy See.

The eloquence of Mgr. Sarto reached its summit when he
spoke of the Church and the Holy Father. " When speaking
of the Vicar of Christ," he wrote in his pastoral letter of
September 5th, 1894, " there is no need to examine the
commands, but to obey them; there is no need to cavil
over the precise meaning of the words, but to seek the spirit
behind them; there is no need to study the wisdom of the

orders given, but to avoid a direct insult to Christ Himself by such an attitude."

There was nothing on which Mgr. Sarto insisted more strongly than obedience to the Church and the Pope, because he saw clearly the danger of the new-born errors. These he attacked with all the vehemence of his fiery soul, for he was determined not to let them cloud the minds, or poison the hearts of his children. In his pastoral letter of February 7th, 1887, he thus affirms: "Not a few, having but a superficial knowledge of religion and knowing less of its practice, dare to take upon themselves the office of teachers, declaring that the Church must now adapt itself to the needs of the times; that it is absolutely impossible for her to preserve her laws in their ancient integrity; that from now on those shall be wisest and most practical who are condescending and tolerant, *i.e.*, those who are ready to sacrifice some of their ancient principles that the rest may stand. In this modern Christianity the folly of the Cross is forgotten and the dogmas of Faith are twisted to fit in with the ideas of a new philosophy. The moral code, now considered too severe, must adapt itself to the self-indulgence of the times, and all forms of discipline which run counter to human nature must be abolished, so as to assist the glorious progress of the laws of liberty! "

This advice of Mgr. Sarto to the people of his diocese, by which he tried to safeguard them against the danger of deviating from the beaten track of Christian teaching, was given on February 7th, 1887. Let us here note this date carefully.

Heresies are not born in a day, nor do they develop overnight. They establish their roots through a series of movements and events. Little by little they begin to show their heads, but like a cancer, when they become visible it is generally too late, for the strength of the organ is undermined.

In fixing a date for the first manifestations of " Modernism," one rarely goes back as far as 1890. Mgr. Sarto, however, even at that time was fully conscious of its doctrines and intentions. The heresy had not yet been given the name which

it was to bear in history, but was simply term e " Modern
Christianity," to distinguish it from, and to show its opposition
to, ancient Christianity, to the Christianity faithful to Christ
and His Church.

Mgr. Sarto was one of the first Bishops in Italy to raise his
voice against this " Modern Christianity," to point out its
characteristics clearly and to denounce its insidiousness
vehemently. Therefore, whoever writes the history of
" Modernism " cannot fail to record the name of the Bishop
of Mantua as one of the most powerful, if not one of the
first initiators—though he confined his activity to his own
diocese—of that providential anti-Modernist movement,
which was to reach its apogee during the reign of Pius X
in the unforgettable encyclical of September 8th, 1907.

The " Pascendi dominici gregis " throws light upon the
logical concatenation and development of the false principles
and errors of the " New Philosophy " which had been
denounced in the Pastoral Letter of September 7th, 1887.
Mgr. Sarto did not use the term " New Philosophy," nor did
he dwell upon its arguments, for he was speaking to
intelligences little versed in philosophic reasoning, but he
made quite clear the lines upon which it was working and its
disastrous consequences in faith, morals, authority and
discipline.

He certainly had no intention of declaring himself " Prime
Initiator " of the anti-Modernist movement. For him it
was enough to guard his people against the danger which
faced them and to strengthen the bonds of their fidelity to
the Church and the Pope, to whom alone is entrusted the
guardianship of truth among men. Hence his insistence on
absolute obedience and firm loyalty to the Church and his
efforts to develop as much as possible the full meaning of
" Pontificate " and " Pope " in the minds of his people.

But if the love he felt for the Pope excited his warmest
enthusiasm, making him eager to assemble his Mantuans
about him on every important occasion in order to give
the august Vicar of Christ convincing proofs of their veneration
and affection, his love became still more ardent when, in
accordance with the wishes of the Pope, he exhorted his

people to join in the recitation of the Rosary during the month of October. The very great confidence which Leo XIII had in this devotion was expressed in one of his most famous encyclicals. Mgr. Sarto shared this spirit of confidence in the Rosary, and the month of October was for him not only an occasion for giving vent to his sentiments of love for Mary, but a most favourable opportunity for exhorting his people to pray for the Church that she might be defended from the evils of the insidious party which was secretly persecuting her. The more this heresy raged, the more must Christians seek in fervent prayer the intercession of her whom they invoke as " Queen of Victories."

" Say the Rosary, my dear children," wrote the Bishop on September 21st, 1885, " for, if in our times intellectual pride which scoffs at submission, corrupts the heart and undermines Christian morality, lamentably prevails, there is no more secure means for the triumph of Faith than meditation on the mysteries of the Most Holy Rosary.

" Say the Rosary, because if piety is becoming tepid and is extinguished in the hearts of many, nothing can rekindle its flame better than the prayer which Jesus taught, the one with which the angel saluted Mary and the one which is continually chanted around the throne of God in heaven.

" Say the Rosary, for this is an exercise of piety which unites the faithful in prayer and cannot fail to inspire sentiments of concord which bring unity to families and peace to society.

" Say the Rosary; this will be the spring of untold blessings, the safeguard of the city and its people, for it is impossible that God should turn a deaf ear to the invocation of so many of His children and that Mary should not answer the prayer with which the Church implores her patronage."

The words of Mgr. Sarto were an eloquent commentary on the words of Pope Leo XIII.

THE FIRMNESS OF THE BISHOP

Mgr. Sarto did not allow anything to lower the prestige of his sacred office. His authority was seldom flouted while he was Bishop, but when it was he knew how to make it respected. "To be conciliatory, but without a shadow of weakness," was his rule in relation to civil authorities. He distinguished between the person and the principle; with the person he was all indulgence and kindness, but on matters of principle he was absolutely uncompromising, for with him duty must overcome all human consideration and must not sacrifice its liberty of word or action to the detriment of justice or truth. Thus when there was question of the law of God, the liberty of the Church, the importance of Christian Doctrine or the salvation of souls, Mgr. Sarto would admit of no discussion; he was inflexible.

There was a custom at Mantua that on March 14th each year, the birthday of King Umberto, the civil authorities chanted the *Te Deum* in the Cathedral, and immediately after went in procession with the same trumpets, the same swallow-tailed coats and the same tri-coloured flags to the Synagogue for a similar service. Putting the Synagogue on the same level as the Catholic Cathedral could not but be offensive to Mgr. Sarto, and in 1889, a few days before March 14th, he decided to put an end to it. He sent the usual invitation to the Municipal authorities, but added politely but clearly the dilemma: "It must be either the Cathedral or the Synagogue, the Bishop or the Rabbi."

Disconcerted with this ultimatum of the Bishop, the Town Prefect asked advice from Signore Crispi, who was then president of the Council of Ministers. He was an old soldier and a fervent Mason and cared as little for religion as he knew about the *Te Deum*. He sent the reply: " Neither in the Cathedral nor in the Synagogue! " Mgr. Sarto, relating this curious episode, always added that Signore Crispi had helped him to put a stop to what might otherwise have become a lasting scandal.

.   .   .   .   .

It is impossible to imagine Mgr. Sarto bending before the pressure or caprices of any town council. The Council of Cavriana—one of the towns in the diocese—used to solemnize

September 20th, a day dear to Italian Liberalism and Masonry, in remembrance of September 20th, 1870, when the Piedmontese army broke through the Porta Pia and entered Rome. The parish priest of Cavriana was not sufficiently courageous to refuse permission to the Council to ring the church bell as part of their celebrations.

But one day Mgr. Sarto arrived in the town and forbade the bell to be rung as long as he was there. In the evening, when he had finished the visitation, he explained to the people from the pulpit why he had not allowed the ringing of the bell. " The bell," he said, " must not be used to commemorate events that have caused the Vicar of Christ to weep, have offended the Church and have filled with sorrow the hearts of Catholics throughout the world. The use of the bell is not subject to the whims of civil authority; it is subject only to the authority of the Church." The Commemoration of September 20th with the ringing of the bell was very quickly forgotten.

.   .   .   .

The Bishop had nominated a very worthy priest as pastor of Pozzolo. Some of the élite of the parish, however, were not satisfied with the nomination and sent a delegation to the Bishop to point out to him his error of judgment, and to persuade him to make another appointment. Mgr. Sarto could not tolerate interference with his authority, and when he had listened to them patiently for some time, he sprang to his feet, made no attempt at argument or reasoning, and dismissed the delegation with the words: " I will send to Pozzolo the parish priest that I want, and when I want! "

.   .   .   .

The Bishop of Mantua sternly refused to allow any kind of custom which was not in keeping with the spirit of Church discipline. The diocesan Synod had forbidden the use of concert-hall instruments or bands in the sacred functions and processions of the Church. In one parish the custom had sprung up of celebrating the feast of their patron by introducing a band into the Church. Although the parish priest had been told that this was wrong, he feared the people and so let the custom continue. The Bishop considered it his duty to endorse the authority of the pastor. On the feast-day he secretly entered the church just at the time when the band, followed by a crowd of people, was taking up its position before the altar. The conductor was just about to raise his baton for the band to strike up when the Bishop appeared in the pulpit, and the words " Laudetur Jesus Christus " echoed through the church. At this apparition and salutation the whole congregation was mesmerized and instead of the musical notes of the band, the solemn tones of the Bishop were heard, outlining the reverence due to the house of God, the praise that is acceptable to God and the honour which is most pleasing to the saints. The band was heard no more in that church.

.   .   .   .   .

On account of the ruling of the Synod, the Bishop was most rigid in exacting that women and girls should not carry the statue of Our Lady in processions. One parish priest did not see eye to eye with this ruling and had the audacity to approach the Bishop and request that an exception be made of his parish. Mgr. Sarto let him speak, but after listening patiently to many well-reasoned and clearly presented arguments, he jumped up and without saying a word pointed to the door.

.   .   .   .   .

At Poggio Rusco, a stronghold of Socialism, only about half the children had been baptized. The people wished to celebrate the anniversary of the death of Garibaldi by holding a Baptismal ceremony at which eighteen children should be baptized, among them the son of the Lord Mayor. The ceremony was to be marked by the singing of the Garibaldian hymn to the accompaniment of a variety of instruments played in the church. The parish priest agreed to baptize the children but absolutely forbade both the hymn and the music. The Socialists promised to respect the sacred function. As soon as the ceremony had started, however, they burst into the church and began singing the hymn while the band played. The parish priest immediately interrupted the ceremony and telegraphed the Bishop.

The next day Mgr. Sarto arrived at Poggio Rusco and ordered the bell to be rung. The whole population of the place, out of curiosity, poured into the church. The Bishop mounted the pulpit and declared: " From now on I am your parish priest and I shall remain here as long as there are any unbaptized children in the town." He came down from the pulpit and exposed the Blessed Sacrament; the people joined with him in prayer of reparation for the offence that had been offered to God on the previous day. During the following day many parents had the comfort of seeing the regenerating water of Baptism poured upon their children by the Servant of God himself.

.   .   .   .   .

But what was it that gave him such authority? What was it that enabled him to act with such a sense of sureness and with such remarkable success in the midst of a people alienated from the Church by false doctrines? It was the sanctity shown in his extraordinary kindness and charity which inspired respect and veneration. He had not spent long among the Mantuans before his people, observing his life, were charmed by his meekness and won by his charity. They considered him a saint and were proud to have him in their midst. Sentiments such as " Our Bishop is a saint," " He is an angel of charity," or " He is more of heaven than of earth " were constantly on the lips of all. Even the Jews, convinced that no one had a heart so big and so generous as his, felt themselves obliged to hand over to him large sums of money to be distributed in charity to the poor.

WITH THE POOR

The Mantuans were unanimous in asserting that charity to
the poor was the characteristic note of the Episcopate of
Mgr. Sarto.   He regarded the poor as " his dear friends "
and, more than that, " as his favourites."   He was ready and
willing to receive them at all hours of the day, because with
the penetrating eye of living faith he perceived beneath their
rags the person of Him " Who emptied Himself."   His
happiness seemed complete when on Holy Thursday in the
liturgical service, it was his privilege to wash the feet of a
group of poor men; kneeling on the ground he felt himself
to be kissing the feet of the Master.   For the poor he was
willing to forget himself; for them he would go without the
necessaries of life, leaving himself on many occasions penniless
and in want of clothing.

His motto was: " Little for self and all for the poor,"
and this he carried into practice with an inexhaustible
generosity which excluded no one, not even his own
adversaries or the enemies of the Church to whom he often
handed, together with a loaf of bread, the light of Christian
faith long forgotten.   The indigent, uncertain of to-morrow;
the miserable, living a life void of hope; the sick, deprived
of necessary comfort; families, born in poverty, or fallen
into it from wealth, all were ever sure of finding in Mgr. Sarto
succour, ready and generous.   No one ever had recourse
to him and went away empty-handed.   Whoever entered
the Bishop's Palace on Fridays would see renewed the charity
of Charles Borromeo at Milan or of Laurence Justinian at
Venice.

.   .   .   .   .

There lived at Mantua a singer who had once been famous
but had now fallen into the most squalid misery.   In spite
of the shame of her state, and still more of her conduct, she
made her appearance one morning at the Bishop's house.
The Bishop received her with respect, listened to the story
of her evil life with compassion and showed her the charity
and kindness of a saint.   He then slipped some money into

her hand in such a way as to diminish as much as possible the humiliation for her. She was seen leaving the room by a person who risked telling His Lordship that she ought not to have been allowed in and that she did not deserve such kindness. But Mgr. Sarto simply answered, " What she received is not from me, but from God."

.   .   .   .   .

When Mgr. Sarto was nominated Bishop of Mantua, the mother of the Jew, Leone Romanin-Jacur of Salzano, whom we have mentioned before, presented him with a beautiful episcopal ring in which was set a stone of great value. One day when the good woman had come to Mantua for the sake of visiting the Bishop, she saw the ring glittering on his right hand with no small satisfaction. This complacency did not escape the notice of the Bishop who remarked: " Oh! please do not look at that, Signora, for though you presented me with the ring, the stone has been changed for one of glass."

The Bishop had disposed of his valuable stone in order to relieve in some measure the needs of the poor.

.   :   .   .   .

Alcibiade Moneta, a Socialist of Mantua, had written and widely distributed a venomous libel against the Bishop, but had hidden behind a mask of anonymity. The name of the author was discovered, and Mgr. Sarto was strongly advised to denounce him to the civil authorities in order to preserve the honour of the Lombardian Episcopate.

" But do you not see," said Mgr. Sarto to his adviser, " that the unhappy man has more need of prayer than of chastisement? " Some time passed. Reverse of fortune threw the calumniator into the most extreme poverty. His creditors, who were embittered against him, accused him of fraudulent bankruptcy. For him all was lost; but a beneficent hand, also anonymous, stretched out, bringing him unexpected relief. The Bishop, knowing of his miserable state, had summoned a pious young lady and instructed her

to take a certain sum of money to the wife of the unfortunate
man, but on no account to mention the name of the donor.
He added that if it became necessary to say who sent the
money she could attribute it to a very pious Lady, known as
" Comfort of the afflicted."

Without distinction of party, of social condition or of
faith, all at Mantua looked upon Mgr. Sarto with admiration
and deep love, and regarded him as a Bishop whose like
they had never before known.   His Eminence Cardinal
Parocchi, Vicar of Leo XIII, declared a great truth every
time he spoke of Mgr. Sarto, for he always concluded: " He
is by far the best of the Lombardian Bishops."

CARDINAL AND PATRIARCH OF VENICE

The life of Bishop Giuseppe Sarto was like a mountain
stream gushing limpidly over the rocks, never stopping,
never becoming turbid, but ever tending through diverse
regions towards the main stream into which it flows unsullied.
He kept before his mind the ideal of Cardinal Frederico
Borromeo, whose life he seemed to re-live.

It was his ambition that his whole life should be spent
among the Mantuans, but Pope Leo XIII had for long been
watching his untiring and whole-hearted activity, resplendent
with heroic virtues, and had destined him for greater honours.
In the Secret Consistory of June 12th, 1893, he created
him Cardinal, and three days later promoted him to the
Patriarchate of Venice.   It was the Pope's intention that the
dignity of the Purple should precede the Office of the
Patriarchate so that all might know that he had been made a
Prince of the Church more on account of the greatness of
his merits as Bishop of Mantua than for the glory of the city
of St. Mark.

.   .   .   .   .

The news ran like a knife through Mgr. Sarto's heart.
" Anxious, terrified and humiliated," as he himself wrote,
on account of the dignity that had been conferred on him,
a dignity which had been so foreign to his thoughts and so

opposed to his ambitions, he prayed and attempted every possible means to withdraw from the honour which he dreaded as a plague. " I have sent a letter," he wrote to the Bishop of Padua, Mgr. Callegari on May 9th, 1893, " putting forth every conceivable motive in the hope of moving the Holy Father to dispense me from the honour of the Roman Purple, and I am now suspended between hope and fear, more depressed by the fear than strengthened by the hope. But may the Holy Will of God be done."

When His Eminence Cardinal Rampolla, in a private letter, informed him that his refusal would cause the Holy Father grave displeasure and that the Holy Father loved and esteemed him very highly, he accepted the dignity with tears in his eyes. In his profound humility he could not understand how it was that the Pope had created him Cardinal. " A thing," he wrote, " which must seem incredible to all, for it is most incredible to myself."

Mantua, the scene of his most recent labours, Venice, the famous city of St. Mark, the renowned Treviso, the little Tombolo, the populous Salzano and the humble Riese rejoiced and exulted, but Mgr. Sarto wept and feared both the honour and the responsibilities that went with it.

.   .   .   .   .

On the afternoon of June 23rd, 1893, Mgr. Sarto returned from Rome, clad in the splendour of the Purple. On his arrival at the station of Mantua the jubilant ringing of all the bells in the city could scarcely be heard above the applause of the enthusiastic crowd which spontaneously assembled to greet him. The richly decorated, festooned carriage of the Marquis of Bagno was put at the disposal of the eminent Bishop, but some were so carried away with excitement that they unharnessed the horses and pulled the carriage themselves through crowded streets from the station to the Bishop's Palace.

There was but a very small group of anti-clericals who tried to show their hatred for the newly created prince of the Church. They acted like madmen, shouting anti-Christian slogans and waving banners on which were written un-complimentary remarks. Their leader was a man who had many times experienced the charity of the Cardinal; but eaten bread is soon forgotten. Some days later this man, not knowing where to turn as the result of an unforeseen mishap, was seen writing a letter to the Cardinal imploring his assistance. His unforgivable misbehaviour of a few days before had been pointed out to him, but he replied: " I know I am a wretch, but the Bishop has a heart so good and so generous that I can feel sure not only of pardon, but of charity."

The Bishop sent for him. When he entered the Cardinal's apartment he was greeted with the usual smile and the words: " Take this: it is a greater alms than usual, but since you tired yourself more than all the others shouting against me, it is only right that you should need greater relief to recover your strength." This magnificent gesture threw into relief the tremendous charity of the Bishop of the Mantuans.

.   .   .   .   .

HIS MOTHER'S LAST KISS

Never had the jubilation of the Mantuans been so great as when the Bishop returned from Rome, their first Cardinal for three centuries. But the joy and enthusiasm of the little town of Riese surpassed all the rest. Riese!—the little mystical Nazareth of Giuseppe Sarto. In the poor little cottage where the prince of the Church was born and brought up as a child, his dear old mother waited. She was now infirm and well advanced in age. The sisters wrote a touching letter to the Cardinal, saying that his aged mother desired to see him for the last time. Margherita Sanson recognized his footsteps and threw her arms around him with great tenderness. This incomparable woman is an example for all Christian mothers, for she, throughout the rapid ascent of her Giuseppe, always kept herself in the obscurity of her little hearth. She now wept tears of joy as she pressed to her bosom her great son vested in the splendour of the

Purple. Her feeble voice, choked with tears, could utter but a few words: " My son, give your mother a last blessing." With a tremor in his voice, and with accents of filial love he found difficulty in voicing the words: " May God bless you, mother." He pressed his lips to her forehead, knowing that that kiss was the last farewell to his mother on earth.

THE QUESTION OF THE " EXEQUATUR " FOR VENICE

Cardinal Sarto could not leave for Venice immediately because the Italian government refused to recognize his appointment as Patriarch of Venice, maintaining that such appointments were their privilege. Signore Giolitti, Prime Minister at the time, based this claim on the right accorded to the government by Pius IV, *de mera liberalitate,* and on the confirmation of that right by Pius VII's concession to Austria. But since 1866 Venice had ceased to be under Austrian dominion and was now annexed to the kingdom of Italy, so that the claim the government was now making was completely groundless. Lawyers, politicians and historians were unanimous in asserting that the right of appointing the Patriarch of Venice had fallen back into the hands of the Church, but the obstinate government, which had promised to respect the freedom of the Church, seemed determined to regard Mgr. Sarto's appointment by the Church as an outrage.

" The affair of Venice," Mgr. Sarto writes on March 2nd, 1894, " is becoming more and more confused, as the government propose multifarious reasons to substantiate their claims. . . But I shall remain firm and shall not be false to the position to which I have been appointed. In this God will provide." What these words mean is not known. Perhaps it was that someone attempted to force the Cardinal to make some statement or perform some action in recognition of the government's right. If so, the tempter must have been ignorant of the unyielding strength of character of one who would rather die than bow before injustice.

It was impossible to forecast what the outcome of this dispute would be, but the only thing that troubled Cardinal

Sarto was the fact that Venice was left without a pastor. He begged the Holy Father to appoint another Bishop for the See of St. Mark, and to permit him to remain in Mantua, where he could do much good.

In the meantime the Municipal Council of Venice, composed of radical freemasons, did all in its power to keep out this pastor who was said to have " an iron hand in a velvet glove." But the Catholics of Venice did not remain idle; they held meetings, made demonstrations, plastered the walls with posters and littered the streets with leaflets. It was useless. The question of the " Exequatur " was only the ostensible concern of the government; its real interest lay in opposing the Church and limiting her liberty as much as possible. With a peaceful conscience, fully reconciled to the Will of God, Cardinal Sarto watched the various stages in the development of the dispute from his home in Mantua.

DURING THE WAIT

The months which Bishop Sarto passed while waiting for the " Exequatur " were by no means spent in idleness. Though he felt " like a bird without a nest," his zeal was not damped, for he accepted the situation as from above and continued working among his beloved Mantuans. Their affection he esteemed far higher than the honour of the Red Hat and the Venetian Patriarchate. He resented the injustice of the government less than he rejoiced at its happy consequence of keeping him where he wanted so much to be.

The humility which characterized little Giuseppe as he first departed from the poor cottage in Riese and entered the Vineyard of the Lord grew up with him, ever deepening its roots, and was not at all diminished by the honours of the Purple and the Mitre. Like any simple curate he celebrated his Mass each morning and then took up his place in the Confessional, remaining as long as there were any people waiting, and never asking anyone to make the sacrifice of returning at a more convenient time. He then went to the Bishop's Palace and began his day's work which was not interrupted until two o'clock in the afternoon when he ate a frugal lunch. In the afternoon he took a walk in the city accompanied by his secretary, but they inevitably ended up in a hospital or orphanage where he delighted to administer the Sacrament of Confirmation to sick and dying children. He often went out through the Porta di S. Giorgio to walk along the banks of the Mincio and chat familiarly with the fishermen. He never remained long, for time was always limited; hours and minutes had to be counted, for urgent, important work was always calling. On returning he made his visit to the Blessed Sacrament and went back to his office.

In the Bishop's Palace his sisters were responsible for the domestic affairs. While there was no shadow of luxury, necessaries were never wanting, for he always had to be prepared to offer hospitality to dignitaries of Church or State. He had but one secretary, one porter and one waiter; no cooks, no carriage and no horses. An atmosphere of simplicity and humility surrounded this Bishop. He was his own servant and would not permit anyone to render him personal services, even to the cleaning of his shoes.

With him there was no fixed time for interviewing people. An obsolete time-table hung on the wall about half-way up the big stairs, but no one took any notice of it and least of all the Bishop. Rich and poor alike would enter the house, make their way directly to his room and knock upon the door, which he himself would open. On entry there was no ceremony or ritual, but simply a friendly smile and a heart-to-heart conversation.

One day a young priest who had just taken his doctorate in the Ambrosiana of Milan came to Mantua. He said his Mass in the Basilica of S. Andrea and then asked the sacristan if it were possible to arrange an interview with the Bishop. "Go to the Bishop's house," replied the sacristan. "Go up the stairs until you come to the big hall on the second floor. On the left you will see a door; knock and you will meet His Lordship. There is no need for appointments with our Bishop, but go early, for later on the place will be crowded."

The young doctor followed out these unusual instructions

carefully. He entered the Palace, went up the stairs and knocked at the door which had been described to him. A voice from inside shouted " Come in! " The Lombard priest entered and found Bishop Sarto seated at his table engrossed in some important business. The Bishop sprang to his feet and greeted him cordially.

" Have you said your Mass? "

" Yes, my Lord, I have just finished."

" Then you will join me in a cup of coffee," said the Bishop, making for the door to call one of his sisters. But there was no answer to his call, for the sisters were still in church. The embarrassed young doctor very soon felt at his ease as he helped his host to prepare the coffee, for the Bishop chatted freely while in his apron he went through the kitchen routine of coffee-making.

The young priest was Don Achille Ratti, the future Pope Pius XI, and it gave him great pleasure to relate in future years the story of how two future Popes made a really splendid morning drink.

．　．　．　．　．

Bishop Sarto did not hesitate to prepare coffee for his guest, nor was he unwilling to perform the duties of altar-boy when the need arose. In September, 1894, while the question of the " Exequatur " was still being discussed, he had a visit from one of his old friends, a professor at the Seminary of Treviso. He spent a few days in this delightful company, but then the professor told him that he must leave the next morning, and that he would like to say an early Mass. " Say it at whatever time you wish," said Mgr. Sarto, " you will find everything ready. Remember that you are staying in a Bishop's house as the guest of a Cardinal."

The next morning Mgr. Agnoletti, as the professor was called, went to the Bishop's private chapel at an early hour. The Cardinal was already there. The professor hesitated for a while, a little puzzled at seeing the Bishop lighting candles, filling cruets, etc. He ventured the enquiry: " But who will serve? "

" I will, of course," replied the Cardinal.

" You, but. . .! "

" Don't you think a prelate in my position is capable of serving a simple low Mass ? " interrupted the Cardinal, as he proceeded to offer his friend the amice, assist him in putting on the alb, hold the girdle for him and tie his maniple. He then knelt down on the floor and made the responses to the verses of the " Introibo ad altare Dei," as he had done many years before at Riese.

THE " EXEQUATUR " FOR VENICE

On September 5th, 1894, the Italian Government, convinced that they could no longer pretend to justify their claims, granted His Eminence Cardinal Sarto the " Exequatur " for the Patriarchate of Venice. It was the feast of St. Laurence Justinian. This happy augury deeply impressed the people of Venice, and that impression was strengthened by the mysterious event which took place the previous night. The Archpriest of S. Pietro di Castello, the Church in which the remains of St. Laurence are kept, was suddenly awakened from his sleep by the ringing of the church bell. He got up, opened the window and shouted: " Who is ringing that bell? " The bell ceased ringing, but no reply came to break the silence which hung over the peaceful lagoon. In the morning the Archpriest described his experience to the sacristan and curates. All had heard the bell, but none could throw light on the mystery. Was it a sign from heaven? Who knows? But one hour later the newspapers published the news of the granting of the " Exequatur " to Cardinal Sarto.

. . . . . .

Words are inadequate to express the joy and enthusiasm of the Venetians, who had anxiously waited fifteen months for their pastor. Their delight was equalled only by the sorrow of the Mantuans, who mourned the loss of a Bishop who had loved them so much and whose Episcopate had seen the renovation of their diocese. Never before had such a crowd of people been seen on the steps of the Cathedral as in the last few days he spent amongst them. People were coming and going from early morning until the late hours of night, all wanting to see their beloved pastor for the last time. The poor were conspicuous in this crowd. They had been his special friends, to them he was most dear. They would feel his loss most of all.

A shabbily dressed old woman entered the ante-chamber of the Bishop and asked for an interview. The seminarian who was acting as secretary refused to admit her, saying that His Eminence had important affairs to attend to, and offering her an alms to pacify her. She sharply refused the alms and began to raise her voice in protest at being refused admittance. Cardinal Sarto heard the shouting, opened his door and immediately summed up the situation. He reprimanded the secretary, saying: " The poor must have free admission to me at all times; before I leave Mantua I want to see them all." He led the woman into his room, listened to her, gave her a blessing and a little present and then accompanied her to the door of the palace. The good woman was deeply moved at his kindness, but when he turned away she looked at the young seminarian scornfully and remarked: " Hum! It's easier to talk to the Cardinal than to a stupid greenhorn! "

On another occasion an old man, dressed in decent but well-worn clothes, walked up the steps of the palace carrying in his hand a basket. The same young secretary who had received and repelled the old woman rushed to meet him, offering him an alms. " Not at all, my boy," exclaimed the old man resentfully, " I haven't come to beg. I heard that the Bishop was leaving Mantua and have come all the way from Coreggioli to bid him farewell." He had walked the whole night, covering a distance of nearly twenty miles. As soon as he saw Bishop Sarto, he rushed to meet him and said, with touching simplicity: " Oh, Monsignor, is it true that you are going away. . . I often think of the wonderful work you did in our little town of Coreggioli," and, offering him the contents of his little basket (some flour, eggs and the other ingredients necessary to make a dish of pasta), continued: " I would like you to have this present before you go." This simple gift of the good old man was an expression of the love which all the people had for their Pastor.

FIRST PASTORAL LETTER TO THE DIOCESE OF VENICE

Although Cardinal Sarto had been rightful Pastor of the Patriarchate of Venice since the June of the previous year, a right which no earthly power could dispute, he considered it prudent to refrain from announcing his coming until the "Exequatur" had arrived. His first Pastoral Letter showed the deep insight he had into the evils of the time and the most urgent needs of the diocese.

The prevalent sin of the time was denial of the existence of God. There have been sins and heresies in every century, but it was not until the eighteenth century that the very root of all religion was attacked, that faith in God's very existence was denied by individuals, societies, governments, through the medium of science, art, economics and politics.

As in his first Pastoral Letter to the Mantuans in 1884, so now in this to the Venetians he exposed these fundamental errors, pointing out to clergy and people the only possible remedies. He wrote: "God is banished from politics through the separation of Church and State; from science in its attempt to attribute everything to material causes; from art by its appeal to the passions instead of the intellect; from law which is oriented to the will of the flesh; from the schools where religious instruction is no longer given to the children and from families whose hearths are desecrated and whose life-springs are choked for want of Sacramental Grace."

Cardinal Sarto wrote these lines shortly after the bill had been proposed in Parliament for the contracting of civil marriage before the Church ceremony. Such a law must necessarily open the front door to divorce. At the same time great efforts were being made to prevent religious instruction in schools. The obstinacy of the State in opposing the rights of the Church was evident from the refusal to grant the "Exequatur" for as long as was possible. The Government left nothing undone to hinder the Church in the free exercise of her mission, and to render open confession of the Faith impossible for Catholics.

Dealing with the social question Cardinal Sarto continued: " God is banished from the hearts of the poor, who refuse to ask help from those who alone can make their miserable life bearable. He is banished from the palaces of the rich, who no longer fear the Eternal Judge Who will ask them to render an account of the use they have made of their possessions. They fear Him not; they refuse to bow before Him; they think themselves sufficient without Him."

In the face of this deliberate blindness to truth, which was working such havoc on the faith of the people, what could be done? Cardinal Sarto gives the answer: " The force of our attack must be brought to bear on the principal crime of our time, the sacrilege of putting man in the place of God. All problems, education, family, rights and duties, property, can be solved only by the application of the precepts and counsels of the Gospel. Harmony between the different social classes must be re-established; peace must reign on earth. This is the task I intend to perform for you; this is the duty I promise to fulfil that all may once again be subject to the dominion of God, Jesus Christ and His Vicar on earth."

And how was the new Patriarch to fulfil this seemingly impossible task? What weapons was he to use? " Justice, piety, love, patience, meekness—these will be my arms in the fight for the defence of the faith, which I have confessed before men and which, with the grace of God, I shall continue to confess to my dying day in the teeth of the most frenzied opposition."

" GOOD-BYE MANTUA! "

On Sunday, November 11th, 1894, the Cardinal celebrated his last pontifical Mass as Bishop of Mantua. After the Gospel he preached as usual but made no mention of his departure. The much abused secretary took it upon himself to inform His Lordship that the people expected a word of farewell, but His Lordship answered: " And would you like to see your Bishop weeping in the pulpit? "

On the 19th he bade a formal farewell to the civil, military and Church dignitaries, as well as to the more important families in the town. On the 21st with tear-filled eyes he said good-bye to his secretary. Mantua would have liked so much to give him a ceremonious send-off, but he kept the time of his departure secret, for he knew that the emotion would have been too much for him. At four o'clock on the morning of the 22nd, accompanied by three priests, he departed from the city of the Gonzagas. He could take his leave with a peaceful conscience for the field he left was in full flower. Mantua did not forget its Bishop; even to this day there is a very special devotion in that city to the Beatus who stands before the throne of God interceding for the children of those thousands who, under God, owe their eternal salvation to the heroic efforts of their one-time Bishop.

Chapter VI

PATRIARCH OF VENICE
(November 24th, 1894—July 26th, 1903)

"BENEDICTUS QUI VENIT."

O N the afternoon of November 24th, 1894, a steamboat of the Royal Marine carried Cardinal Sarto over the peaceful waters of the Grand Canal, stopping in the close vicinity of the Golden Cathedral of St. Mark. All the bells in the city announced the joy and triumph of the multitudinous throngs lining the canals and crowding at the windows of the palaces. They waved their white flags beneath the rich marble balconies and shouted a prolonged chorus of jubilation as the Cardinal in his scarlet robes passed by, blessing them as a father does his children. In years to come many would look back in happy reminiscence of that day, and with Lord Byron, in a different context, exclaim:

"States fall, arts fade—but Nature doth not die,
Nor yet forget how Venice was once dear,
The pleasant place of all festivity,
The revel of the earth, the masque of Italy."
                    (*Childe Harold's Pilgrimage*)

Midst such festivity, flourish and magnificence did the humble Patriarch enter the city of the Doges; he who but a few days before had expressed his desire to enter locked up in a box, unseen, if such were possible. There was dead silence in one building only. In the Farsetti-Loredan Palace, the seat of the Masonic City Council, the windows were closed, the lights were out, the walls unadorned and the Patriarch unacknowledged. Far from damping the enthusiasm of the Venetians, this conduct on the part of their local Government, who did not see fit to give a public reception to the Patriarch, raised a storm of indignation and utterly defeated its own malicious purpose.

FIRST PASTORAL EXHORTATION

Cardinal Sarto's first real meeting with the Venetians took place the following morning when he celebrated Solemn High Mass in the Cathedral of St. Mark and addressed his first words to them from the pulpit. The Cathedral was brilliantly illuminated, and a huge crowd of people hastened to take a closer glance at their new Patriarch and listen to his words. He wished to express how deeply he responded to the love and affection they had shown to him, almost a stranger, the previous day. He began his sermon:

" It would ill-become me if I did not express my love for you; for as Jesus Christ demanded from Peter a threefold confession of his love before committing to his care the sheep so dear to Him, so, above all, it is required of a pastor of souls that love for those over whom he has charge should occupy a first place in his heart. It is my earnest wish to manifest my love for you in all that I undertake in this Patriarchate, and my greatest consolation will be to know that you return that love and realize that your pastor has no other ambition than the defence of the truth and the welfare of his flock.

" And should it happen that one day I fail in this promise which I now solemnly make, I pray that God will rather let me die. How I tremble to think that souls can be punished for all eternity on account of the negligence of their pastor, that innocent people can be led from the path of truth because the words of the Inspired Text were never preached to them, and that the spirit of the world, and of our time especially, should pour into ill-instructed minds for want of a firm hand to check its tide. I have a sacred duty to defend the truth openly, for God will ask me to render an account for all those souls who have strayed into the ways of perdition; even though they hate in me the Bishop and pastor, their fate is my responsibility."

THE BEGINNING OF HIS WORK IN VENICE

The first days which a Bishop spends in a new diocese are entirely taken up with receptions and visits from all classes of people. Cardinal Sarto very quickly made it evident to

all where his strongest affection lay—with the poor. Nearly
the whole population had a chance of seeing him: the sick
and infirm who were unable to leave their homes; the outcasts
from human society who languished in the prisons and work-
houses; those confined to their beds in the hospitals; all
were visited in person by the new Patriarch and made to
feel that here was one who really cared for them and made
their interests and sorrows his own. In every household
detailed enquiries were made about the spiritual and temporal
affairs of each and every member. In every house the
impression made was that a new member had entered the
family, and the family naturally reciprocated by focusing
its attention on the interests of that new member. This
was the beginning of his Patriarchate.

The Venetians have always been known to be loyal sons of
the Church, but three years without a pastor had not failed
to leave their mark. Many abuses had crept in, together
with a general negligence which endangered the Faith and
caused the decay of many of the ancient noble traditions.
Personal feeling guided many of the parish priests in their
work, so that they acted as little Bishops, each a law unto
himself. Such a state of affairs could not continue, especially
under Cardinal Sarto. His experience in Mantua had shown
him exactly where the root of the evil lay and exactly what
remedies to apply. The situation in Venice was bad, but
no worse than he had anticipated, and so without losing
time he rolled up his sleeves and set to work. First of all
he must examine the clergy, rekindle the zeal of the lukewarm
and encourage those of goodwill in the ways of sacrifice and
perfection.

" Every priest," he said, " must be ready to fulfil the duties
of the office which the Lord has laid upon him. In time of
war when every citizen is a soldier can the officers in the midst
of the battle remain idle? "

The most dangerous foe to the Faith, ignorance of eternal
truths, must take a first place on the list of reforms. Once
again the Cardinal turned his attention to the teaching of
the catechism in the schools and of Christian Doctrine in
the churches. Undoubtedly some instruction was being

given, but it fell far short of his high standards, especially
the instruction of lads who had just left school and were
passing through a dangerous period in their lives.

As in Mantua those were not wanting who considered
that the sermon on the Gospel was an adequate substitute
for the regular systematized teaching of the doctrine of the
Church.   These sermons had fallen into the spirit of the
times, having as their object style and eloquence more than
the instruction of the people.   As Cardinal Sarto put it:
" Preached from the lofty heights of the pulpit they were
nearer to the pipes of the organ than to the hearts of the
faithful." Preaching was plentiful, oratory was rich, but solid
instruction was rare.

On January 17th, 1895, scarcely two months after his
arrival, he issued a severe circular letter to the clergy of his
diocese, lamenting the pitiable condition into which the
teaching of the Faith had fallen.   He wrote: " We have far
too much preaching and far too little real instruction.   Have
done with these flowers of eloquence; preach to the people
with simplicity and piety; give them the truths of the Faith
and the precepts of the Church; tell them the meaning of
virtue and the danger of vice.   Even people who according
to the standards of the world are considered learned are
very often surprisingly ignorant of the most fundamental
truths of their religion, and in some cases are not so well
instructed as small childern.   The people thirst to know the
truth; give it to them; give them what they need for the
salvation of their souls.   The sermon should be constructed
according to the capacity of the people; it should be aimed to
touch the heart and not merely to charm the ear; its result
should not be the glory of the preacher but the repentance of
the sinner and an increase in the number of Communions.
Oratorical eloquence has nothing apostolic in itself; it is
purely profane and wholly lacking in supernatural influence.
The sermon might be pleasing to the people, but their hearts
are not touched; they leave the House of God as they
entered.   ' Mirabantur,' as St. Augustine would say, ' sed
non convertebantur.' " [1]

---

[1] " They were roused to wonder, but were not converted."

A thorough inspection of the way in which the catechism was taught in the schools followed immediately after this letter. For the next few months Cardinal Sarto could be expected in any church in the diocese at the time of the Instruction. These surprise visits had a wonderful effect and soon even the most careless parish priests were brought into line.

In order that his priests might understand clearly what he meant by preaching with simplicity he often went into the pulpit himself and, using the parables of the Master, drove home the most elementary truths to the people. In his simplicity there was a persuasiveness, a clarity and a power which rendered his words irresistible and his teaching within the grasp of even the most ignorant members of the congregation. What a change from the usual grandiloquent orations, academic hair-splitting and empty sound, which evoked nothing but vain praise from the few listeners who had succeeded in keeping awake throughout! Cardinal Sarto insisted that the pulpit was not to be used as a stage or the church as a theatre and that his preachers should refrain from seeking the applause of their learned listeners; for many of the others who were capable of absorbing a little of what the sermon was trying to express would find it but " sounding brass and tinkling cymbals."

A young priest was one day preaching in the Cathedral of St. Mark with the simplicity and devotion of a saint. After the sermon the Patriarch said to a group of seminarians who had been present, " This is what I call preaching—don't forget it! " What a novelty it was for the people of Venice to attend their weekly sermon feeling that the preacher was addressing them and understanding what he was saying! It was not long before the bombast of eloquence vanished from the pulpits of the Patriarchate.

SEMINARY AND CLERGY

The Venetian Seminary was in a far better condition than that of Mantua had been before the arrival of Bishop Sarto. There was, however, much to be desired in its discipline, organization and education. A few visits, a careful inspection of the building and a brief examination of the registers were sufficient to unfold to the Cardinal its condition and the steps which must be taken to bring it into line with his own high ideals. The certainty that he would meet with opposition, that he would come into conflict with traditional methods and give offence to the more sensitive did not move him from his constant purpose of attacking all evil at its roots.

First of all he ruthlessly suppressed the College for lay people which was being run in the Seminary buildings and causing the seminarians to come in contact with outsiders. The code of discipline was completely revised in accordance with the norms of the Council of Trent. The professorial staff was renewed, and additional lectures in Canon Law, Scriptural Exegesis, Church History, Christian Archaeology and the Economic and Social Sciences were introduced. These special courses were made obligatory, not only for the seminarians, but for all the priests of the diocese, so that, equipped with up-to-date knowledge, they could the more easily combat the errors of the time. These reforms were exceptionally rich in effect; the moral and spiritual formation of the students was put on a solid footing, the number of vocations began to rise almost at once, and the young priests leaving that Seminary were models of what priests should be.

Cardinal Sarto was not one of those who give commands and then take little heed as to their being obeyed. He seldom left the Bishop's Palace without paying a visit to the Seminary. He wanted to know his clerics more intimately, to have exact information as to their talents, their diligence in study and progress in piety, for he realized that the fruit of their future ministry depended very much on this. He would not confer Orders until he had taken the greatest care to ascertain that the candidate showed signs of having a genuine vocation; the smallest particulars were taken into account and pondered carefully before the Blessed Sacrament after the most searching enquiries had been made.

Nor were his priests forgotten. They needed help, sometimes in the form of money or clothing, but frequently comfort and encouragement were more important. Those

who had fallen victim to the calumnies of priest-haters had
to be defended and their honour vindicated. Cardinal Sarto
was the universal benefactor whatever their needs might be
or whatever demands were made upon his own personal
belongings, or even more precious, his time. He was ready
to interrupt any work to attend a dying priest and to give
him the all-important death-bed consolations. " He was all
love, all heart, and a pastor of souls in the truest sense of the
word," testify his fellow-workers.

The salvation of souls is the fruit of the priest's ministry,
and so the sanctification of the priest was his dearest interest.
It was for this reason Cardinal Sarto insisted that every priest
should make the Spiritual Exercises at least once a year, and
that the last Thursday of each month should be spent as a
day of recollection. He loved to join them in these retreats
and to speak to them during the Holy Hour. From every
priest he demanded the fidelity, zeal and blamelessness of a
son, a fellow-worker and a saint. Two things he would not
tolerate were disobedience and slovenliness.

To a young priest who could not be persuaded to move
to an outlying parish because he wanted to be near his
relatives and friends in the town he addressed the stern,
emphatic command: " Go! it would be a pity if you were not
allowed to officiate in the town any more." The priest
understood, packed his bags and made for his destination
without delay.

An old priest requested a dispensation from attending the
conferences on Moral Theology on the grounds that at his
age he did not need to learn any more. The Patriarch
replied: " Excellent! Come and let the others benefit by
your experience and learning." The priest, knowing that
Cardinal Sarto did not repeat his commands, struggled up
the steps in front of the Bishop's Palace for the next
conference and enlightened the others by his experience.

Cardinal Sarto only brought the weight of his authority to
bear on his priests when circumstances demanded it. Duty
and sympathy were at conflict in his heart on such occasions.
" When I am obliged to admonish a priest," he tells us, " it
makes me feel ill." The pressure of his authority rather lay

CARDINAL SARTO
PATRIARCH OF VENICE

in his gentle smile and fatherly kindness. A servant who was working in the Bishop's Palace at that time tells us that from the adjoining room he often heard priests putting forward substantial arguments and a multiplicity of reasons for declining some office or duty which the Patriarch had asked them to undertake. When the priest left the Bishop's study the servant always asked the same question: " How did you get on? " and invariably received the answer: " There is no arguing with the persuasive force of a smile."

Though his charity was not always appreciated and even if he received ingratitude for his kindness, he could not speak ill of any one. On one occasion a former fellow-worker from Mantua came to see him and in the course of the conversation reminded him of certain priests who had given him great trouble, commenting: " What a pity it was that they received such kindness from Your Eminence! " The Patriarch's face darkened as he replied reproachfully: " How cruel your words are! I never thought you would descend to this. Do we do good to be recompensed? Never say anything like that again."

PASTOR BONUS

Positions of responsibility were given in Venice only to those who were worthy and suited to them. Nominations were made with only the interests of God in view. He knew his priests and what they were capable of. He took into account the special peculiarities of the field of action and chose his workers after careful deliberation. He had a keen insight into the consequences of an appointment, and all were persuaded that his decisions were guided from above. His priests respected his decisions knowing that earthly influence bore no weight with him; they took his admonitions to heart seeing him day after day giving an example of devotion to souls by sitting for hours in the confessional of this or that church, and they did their best to return in some measure the love he showed them. He conducted the retreats of the seminarians, gave regular courses of lectures to men and women, taught the catechism to children, visited the homes of the poor and consoled the sick and the dying, leaving everywhere the impression of his boundless generosity. No opportunity of helping souls was ever lost, be it ever so unimportant, distasteful or inconvenient. In March, 1895, he went on foot from the Palace to the Church of the Redeemer—a distance of some miles—in a very bad thunderstorm to keep an appointment which he had made there. To a person who told him that he was imprudent and did not take sufficient care of his health he replied: "No one, least of all one of high rank, should keep others waiting. It shows want of consideration for other people."

A certain convert who had been a Freemason was dying and asked to see a priest. His relatives would not permit a priest to enter the house. When the Patriarch heard of this he went to his private oratory, prayed for a moment and then set out to comply with the wish of the dying man. The relatives tried at first to impede his entrance with groundless excuses; then, when these failed, they had recourse to protests and even threats, but the indomitable Cardinal made his way through their midst unperturbed. He comforted the dying man and gave him the last Rites of the Church. Returning to the relatives he shook hands with each of them and with a broad smile took his leave.

The famous poet Giacinto Gallina was prevented from receiving the Last Sacraments by the Freemasons. Cardinal Sarto raised a storm of public protests that a soul in its agony had been deprived of the consolations of religion.

THE REFORM OF CHURCH MUSIC

Cardinal Sarto lived in the spirit of the liturgy. He loved the solemn ceremonies of the Church, not because of the display of vestments or the beauty of the singing, but because he felt that these ceremonies were most efficacious in elevating the minds and hearts of the faithful to God. Already as curate of Tombolo and parish priest of Salzano he had attempted to direct all singing in church into its proper channel—liturgical prayer or the prayer which interiorly unites the hearts of the faithful to one another and to God by exteriorly uniting their voices in the beautiful chants of the Church. In Mantua he had made it his aim that Church music should express a truly religious and artistic sentiment, and that any form of music incompatible with the spirit of prayer should be ruthlessly expelled from the House of God. Music suitable only for the village square, the public-house or the theatre must be left in those places, and to introduce it into the church is a desecration of the Service of God.

In October, 1893, while the Patriarch was Bishop of Mantua, Mgr. Callegari, Bishop of Padua, had held a meeting in Thiene to discuss church music. Mgr. Sarto was unable to attend the meeting but took a keen interest in its progress and addressed the following letter to the president of the meeting. " Gregorian chant should be so encouraged that it will begin to appeal to the people. What a wonderful thing it would be if the faithful could be got to join in the singing of the *Kyrie, Gloria, Credo, Sanctus* and *Agnus Dei* in the same way as they sing the *Litany* and the *Tantum Ergo!* It is my opinion that Church music could receive no finer development, because then the faithful could play a real part in the liturgy, and piety and attention would be sustained. Sometimes at Benediction, when I hear hundreds of enthusiastic voices joining in the *Tantum Ergo* or *Te Deum,* l imagine hearing in a village church a thousand voices chanting the *Missa de Angelis* or the *Psalms of Vespers*. To my mind such choral singing is far more important and impressive than the complicated melodies of polyphony."

In Venice the Cardinal undertook the reform of Church music with still greater earnestness. Special courses in Gregorian chant were started in the Seminary, and the priests of the diocese were urged to attend so that, having a more thorough knowledge of the principles, they would have a keener interest in introducing the chant into their churches.

Under the dome of the Golden Cathedral of St. Mark the magnificent tones of the choral chant, worthy of the splendour of the building, the religious sentiment of the congregation, and the well-known musical genius of the Italian people, would in the future echo the praises of God in a manner well pleasing to Him. This Cathedral had one of the finest choirs in Italy, and it was fitting that the reform should start there. A most opportune time was the day of the Centenary celebrations. On that occasion only choral music was played in the Cathedral, and both the impression made on the people and the success of the initial stages of the reform were evident from the enthusiastic manner in which the thousands of voices blended, pouring forth the praises of the Lord from over-flowing hearts.

Liturgists and artists had long awaited this reform and had eagerly watched the tentative efforts of many Bishops in Italy to initiate it, but they now realized that to Cardinal Sarto alone could the merit of it be attributed. Observing the joy and interest with which the people took part in the Centenary festivities, the Patriarch decided to publish his famous pastoral letter of May 1st, 1895, the harbinger of the *Motu Proprio* for the reform of Church music throughout the world which Pius X was to issue on November 22nd, 1903.

In the short introduction to the letter he referred to the musical triumph which had been achieved at the Centenary celebrations of St. Mark's. He then directed the attention of the people to the purpose of singing in church, which was not entertainment or display of talent but, according to the mind of the liturgy, the worship of God and the elevation of the spirit. The melodies must move the people to fervent prayer, for prayer draws down the grace of God on the soul; that should be the fruit of the solemn services of the Church.

The Cardinal then went on to point out the efficacy of Church music for achieving this object: " Church music has a special power over the heart because of its close connection with the ceremonies of the altar and the words chanted. The music thus shares the sanctity, artistic value and universality of the time-honoured psalms, The Church has always frowned on music which has a tendency to the ludicrous, extravagant or stilted, and also on any form of composition more congruous with the stage performer than the suppliant in prayer. She has always stood by her principle: ' Sancta sancte,' in encouraging true art."

Guided by this principle the Church had constantly favoured

through the course of the centuries the Gregorian chant, which was nearly a thousand years old, and the classical Roman Polyphony originated by Palestrina in the sixteenth century. The abuses and decay of later centuries, however, did not leave sacred music unscathed. The ancient melodies which for centuries had been rich in the fruits of fervour and unity had now been pushed aside to give place to new-fangled interpretations which appeal only to the feet. To these Cardinal Sarto refers:

"Characteristic of modern theatrical church singing is the constant repetition of a theme, which goes on and on *ad nauseam* with regular beats which cause the toes to tap on the floor and the heart to thirst for distracting novelty rather than for the love of God. Otherwise there is some soothing melody which lulls to sleep or wafts the mind on its gentle breezes over a garden of delightful reminiscenses or sensuous desires. In place of the solemn chants of the Church, ballroom ditties are taken and twisted rather than adapted to the sacred words by some make-shift dabbler in the ' science ' of harmony, without art and in most cases without even intelligence. By this means the liturgical functions, rich in meaning and significance, are lowered to the level of worldly shows, and the mysteries of faith are so profaned as to deserve the reproach of Christ: ' My house shall be called the house of prayer to all nations, but you have made it a den of thieves ' (*Mark* xi. 17)."

The Patriarch was firmly resolved to uproot the prejudices of the lovers of frivolous music and the lamentable abuses which had set in, even at the cost of imposing the most severe commands and if necessary canonical penalties. All worldly music must vanish at once from the churches of the Patriarchate; the Gregorian chant was to be taught in schools and in parishes, and only men of blameless life were to be admitted into the choir, for it was their duty to sing the praises of the Lord.

Venice very quickly became aware once again of its splendid musical and artistic traditions, and the reform gathered strength day by day, until those who had been its most obdurate opponents at the start had to admit that the fervent prayer resulting from the choral singing of the Gregorian chant had its effect on the lives of the people.

A CLAMOROUS VICTORY

When Cardinal Sarto made his solemn entry into Venice on November 24th, 1894, the windows of but one house remained closed and unadorned, the Town Hall with its Freemason Council. The Venetians later expressed their displeasure and disgust at this unbecoming behaviour in the presence of the Patriarch, but he replied confidently: " Be without fear; if they shut the windows we will open them." He had in mind the coming local elections.

Many were of the opinion that the Catholics, on principle, would refrain from voting even in local elections, but that was by no means the attitude of the Holy See. The Church insisted again and again that Catholics should concern themselves with public administration so as not to surrender the government into the enemy's hands. Even in con- stituencies where Catholics were a minority it was their duty to try to make their voice heard on many vital issues such as the teaching of religion in the schools and the independence of charitable institutions.

Before the arrival of Cardinal Sarto, no one had seen the full implications of the political position and there was certainly no one with sufficient determination, fearlessness and popularity to stimulate the people to action, unite them in a common cause and act as their leader. The political life of Venice now received a new impetus. It was absurd to think that a clique of Freemason Church-haters should be allowed to attack the most sacred traditions, take every possible opportunity of making the practice of the Faith difficult and give free vent to the bitterness in their hearts towards everything Catholic, and that in the very Patriarchate of Cardinal Sarto.

The election in the Constituency of Venice was to take place in July, 1895. The Cardinal took it upon himself to rouse the people to action, not with long-winded speeches, but in simple persuasive language which they understood and knew to come from a leader convinced of his purpose and confident in the possibility of success. He gathered priests, men and youths about him and having instructed them carefully sent them to give sermons and lectures in all parts of the town. He organized committees and sub-committees for a variety of operations in the general task, but he himself supervised all.

In spite of his best efforts it was quite obvious to him that the Catholics, on their own, must inevitably fail. With great ability and prudence he approached the more important leaders of the unbiased Liberal Party and persuaded them to join hands with the Catholic Party against their common foe, the Freemasons. To substantiate this undertaking he wrote no less than three hundred letters within three days and three nights to priests, representative laymen, Catholic organizations and religious institutions. He was now really in the thick of the battle, with the war-cry: " Down with the enemies of St. Mark." The Venetians gradually began to realize that there was something worth fighting for and threw themselves whole-heartedly into the work, for they knew now that the freedom of their religion, the honour of their city and the preservation of their traditions were at stake.

July 28th, 1895, was the day for the election in Venice. The atmosphere of excitement was somewhat checked by the confidence which the Cardinal had instilled into the hearts of his children. That confidence was justified, for each and every Catholic played his part, the Liberals kept their promise faithfully and the Freemasons were overthrown, not to trouble the Venetians as governors again for many a long day.

Conte Filippo Grimani was the leader of the newly elected party. He was a brilliant statesman, a loyal son of the Church and a descendant of the Doges of that name. During the twenty-five years in which he was to shape the destinies of Venice, the magnificent past, which many thought dead and gone forever, was to come to life again in all its pristine strength. The former Government had forbidden the teaching of Christian Doctrine in the schools, had banned the crucifix from the classroom and rendered public festivities in honour of the Blessed Virgin and the saints quite impossible. It

was only when all these things were suddenly restored that
the Venetians gave serious thought to the importance of their
famous traditions and fully appreciated what Cardinal Sarto
had done for their fatherland. Religious instruction was
immediately restored, pictures of the crucifix adorned the
walls of classrooms and hospital wards, and in veneration and
gratitude the people clustered around their Patriarch as their
ancestors had around the Doges.

PATRIARCH SARTO AND LEO XIII

By this time rumours had reached Rome that Cardinal Sarto
had joined hands with the Liberals and that co-operation
between the Catholics and Liberals was a danger to the
principles of the Faith. Leo XIII sent for the Cardinal and
questioned him on this point. The Patriarch explained the
situation to the Pope and made it quite clear who these
Liberals were. " They are Liberals," he said, " who regularly
frequent the Sacraments, are present at Sunday Mass and
take an active part in the celebration of every feast, not
hesitating to carry the canopy in the Corpus Christi
Procession."

" Then," interrupted His Holiness, " they should be called
Catholics! "

The discerning Pontiff saw fit to direct a letter to the
Catholic Youth of Venice which silenced the evil tongues,
extolled the loyalty and devotion of their Patriarch, and
commended the Venetians for their heroic efforts in the
struggle for a Government worthy of their fatherland and
their Faith. " Rectum civitati regimen omni ope secundoque
exitu contendistis."

It is important to remember that the compact between
the Catholics and the Moderate Liberals was proposed by
the Catholic Party and that the programme of work common
to each of the parties dealt with such vital points as respect
for religious liberty, religious instruction in schools, public
celebration of feasts, civic spirit and the administration of
charitable institutions. Was the Faith endangered by forming
a block of honourable citizens ready and willing to renew the

glorious traditions of Venice and to blot out the memory of the anti-clerical Government which had ruled over this Christian and Catholic city?

A EUCHARISTIC CONGRESS

On April 6th, 1895, an iniquitous hand had seized the ciborium from the tabernacle in the church of the Discalced Carmelites and had scattered the consecrated hosts about the street. This villainous crime filled the whole of Venice, and especially the Patriarch, with horror. The Cardinal at once ordered that three days of prayer be devoted to making acts of reparation to God for the blasphemous act. On the last day the Patriarch himself carried the Blessed Sacrament through the streets in solemn procession. He stopped to give Benediction and address a few soul-stirring words to the people, impressing on them the meaning of love and gratitude for the great gift of the Holy Eucharist.

The love of Mgr. Sarto for Jesus in the Blessed Sacrament was notable in all his sermons and letters, and even in his private conversation. He never tired of recommending the frequent reception of Holy Communion. As at Salzano and Mantua he again insisted that children should make their First Holy Communion at an early age. To lead his people back to the living Faith of the first Christian centuries he realized that it was essential that they should have a burning love for the Eucharistic Saviour and feed upon the mystical bread of life which purifies, sanctifies and nourishes. The plan for a Eucharistic Congress gradually grew within him.

The first Eucharistic Congress had taken place in 1881. Its abundant fruit had affected not only the religious but also the social sphere, for the huge assemblies of people, gathered in praise and adoration of the Sacred Heart of Jesus in the Eucharist, felt united to one another more closely by the bonds of love which united each to his Master.

At the Bishops' Conference in 1896, Cardinal Sarto proposed to the suffragan Bishops present that a Eucharistic Congress should take place in Venice the following year. The proposal was sent to the Pope for his approval, which was immediately granted.

Cardinal Sarto set to work without delay on the initial
stages of preparation. He sent a circular letter to the people
of the Patriarchate announcing the date of the Congress and
appointed committees to take charge of the multitude of
details. Every decision had to be presented to the Patriarch
for approval, and every step was supervised and studied by
him with the greatest prudence, energy and practical common-
sense. This meant for him the sacrifice of many hours of
necessary sleep. He was present at all the important sessions
of the committees, gave many lectures instructing the leaders
in the true spirit of the Congress and above all stressed the
importance of prayer as the most essential part of the
preparation. Adoration of the Blessed Sacrament throughout
the night was organized in as many churches as possible.

On the morning of August 9th, 1897, His Eminence
Cardinal Sarto, in the largest church in Venice, the
monumental SS. John and Paul, opened the Venetian
Eucharistic Congress, in the presence of the Cardinal
Archbishops of Milan, Bologna and Ancona, twenty-nine
bishops, three abbots, the most prominent representatives
of the Italian clergy, laity and a huge throng of people. In
his address he explained that the Eucharistic Lord was to
be adored not only by the individual but also by the community
and that the Congress now beginning had as its purpose the
uniting of all hearts in praise and reverence for the Most
Holy Sacrament. Amongst many other things he said: " The
aim of this Congress is to honour Christ in His Eucharistic
presence, to make reparation for the blasphemies of the
world and to return in some measure His great love for us.
We are assembled here to make His thoughts our own,
His moral teaching our rule of life, His truth our faith,
His justice our law, His life our life. This has been very
clearly expressed in the pastoral letter. This and this alone
is the aim of the Congress, that Christ may be venerated
and in His veneration our hearts changed. I feel it my duty
to make this known clearly to our opponents, who try to
read into our activity an attack on public authority and
regard it as a disturbance of the peace. The guiding principle
of the Christian is found in the words of St. Paul: ' Render

therefore to all men their dues. Tribute, to whom tribute is due; custom, to whom custom; fear, to whom fear; honour, to whom honour ' (*Rom.* xiii. 7). We obey the Government, not through fear, but because our conscience demands that we should give everyone his due, whether taxes, customs, reverence or respect.

" Naples, Turin, Milan and Orvieto have each shown public veneration for the Eucharistic God, why not, then, Venice? Venice has preserved with noble pride the memory of so many famous men, saints, doges, patricians, artists. Will she not at least keep pace with her sister towns in the veneration of her God? We will pray for the conversion of those who, although our opponents, are also our brethren and as such called to share in the glories of that Kingdom which triumphantly resists the hostilities of men and the destructive work of time. Not only on the Piazza of St. Peter's but to the ends of the earth, in all places and at all times, let the cry resound: ' Christus vincit, Christus regnat, Christus imperat et regni ejus non erit finis.' " [1]

During the four days of the Congress, Venice seemed to have been transformed into one vast temple of God. In the church of SS. John and Paul crowds of people were present, day and night, in adoration of the Blessed Sacrament exposed on the altar. The best orators addressed the multitudes from the pulpit, keeping before the minds of the people the importance of fervour in prayer during the days of the Congress, that the life of faith might be renewed in them never again to wane. Cardinal Sarto was deeply moved by the fidelity of his people, as he saw them in large numbers, at all hours of the day and night, in silent adoration before their Eucharistic Lord. He himself was present for the night adoration, in spite of his great exertions during the day.

Leo XIII followed the progress of the Congress with great attention and interest. He received in audience, a few days later, a priest who had been at Venice during those memorable days. The words of the Pope, " Your Cardinal, indeed,

---

[1] " Christ conquers, Christ reigns, Christ rules, and of His kingdom there will be no end."

deserves great praise," voiced the sentiments of all the
Venetians, who felt that the Congress was a work of his
love—his love for Jesus in the Blessed Sacrament and his
love for his people.

ECONOMIC AND SOCIAL MOVEMENT

Cardinal Sarto had come from working-class people and
had spent his whole life in close contact with them, and
even as Patriarch he delighted to put himself on the same
level as the most humble workman by the simplicity of his
life. He more than anyone understood their needs, their
sacrifices and sufferings. Far from placing himself on an
eminence and barely condescending to take cognizance of
their existence or regarding that existence as a mere
instrument for his own homage, he felt himself one of them.
He was one of them, and the glory of the Roman Purple
far from elevating him above them, imposed on him a special
duty towards them and made him, more than ever, one of
them. He was more than a member of the working class,
he was a special member. It is only natural, therefore, to
expect that he would take a special interest in the moral
and social conditions of the people.

He was aware of the difficult problems which faced the
people of his time: work for purely material ends; forgetful-
ness of the sanctification of Sunday; the use of men as mere
parts of machines; the decay of the spirit of thrift; and
above all the blindness to truth and hatred of it which came
into being in the noise and bustle of the factory. What
hurt him most was the distinction made between the " great "
and the " small " in social circles. There was only one way
to unite the two classes—a renewal of the Christian spirit,
derived from a thorough understanding of the spirit of the
Gospel.

In August, 1901, the Socialists assembled the 2,000
workers from a tobacco factory and tried to win them over
to their own way of thinking. Mgr. Sarto left nothing to
chance but went into the factory, gathered the workers
around him and pointed out to them the frightful moral and

economic consequences of unemployment, which would be the logical outcome of their following the Socialists. He warned them that if they joined the Socialist trade unions, their peace was at an end and that their position would be far worse than it now was. He then proposed to make their interests his own and to be their leader. At this proposal a burst of applause resounded above the roar of machines. Venice was now thoroughly convinced that the Patriarch was the workers' Cardinal, and the Socialists were deprived of the great advantage this following would have been to them.

Workers' meetings were in future presided over by the Cardinal; the feasts of their patrons were once again celebrated; the drudgery of their work began to be coloured with spiritual significance; any form of injustice on the part of employers met the stern opposition of the Patriarch; savings banks were established and organized; mutual assistance societies, orphanages and free hospitals began to spring up, and the workers received a just wage for an honest day's work.

He was indeed the Bishop who sanctified with his blessing every activity beneficial to his people. He carried the name of God into human society for the triumph of Christian charity, for the glory of Christ and for the true greatness of Venice.

FATHER OF HIS PEOPLE

As a devoted Pastor of souls, Cardinal Sarto rarely left Venice. His prodigious programme of work took up all his time and very often deprived him of necessary sleep. He needed a few days of rest, especially during the summer, when an oppressive humid atmosphere hung over the lagoon, but the only relaxation he allowed himself was the few hours he spent at Crespano del Grappa. There he presided over the examinations of the members of the Institute of the Sisters of Charity of the Child Mary. Now and then he visited Possagno, where his nephew, Giovanni Battista Parolin, was parish priest. Once he said to him: " Giovanni, when I am too old to push my cart, I shall come to you as curate."

He seldom visited Rome. Leo XIII once said to him

"Your Eminence should come oftener; you are a welcome
visitor." The Pope loved and greatly esteemed him and used
to call him "The pearl of the Sacred College." He would
have liked to have him as Vicar General in Rome.

The Patriarch shared the joys and sorrows of Venice. He
knew that many were in need of him and he would not have
them search in vain. He knew that in spiritual matters hearts
are won by giving, by perpetual prayer and by tending the
needs of those who do not ask. His charity towards the poor
had never decreased. Even as Cardinal he was penniless at
times, and frequently in want of the bare necessaries of life.
He never hesitated to give, firmly convinced that Divine
Providence would not leave him without what was essential
for the carrying out of his duties. The money which he
received from the offerings of the people slipped like sand
through his fingers.

He was sometimes forced to borrow money in order to
pay the expenses of his own household. It was with complete
truth that he wrote to a parish priest in Mantua: "I am
ashamed to answer your request for help with this meagre
subscription, but I must confess that it is all I can do; when
I was in Mantua I was poor, but now I am a beggar."

The Patriarch had taken it upon himself to support the
orphan girls in a certain convent. One day a Canon of the
Cathedral went to the Bishop's Palace to collect his
contribution. The Canon tells us: "Great indeed was my
surprise when he said he hadn't a penny left; he had already
borrowed a few pounds from his sisters in order to save a
family in the direst necessity. 'What can a Bishop do,'
he exclaimed, 'when a poor man asks for help, on his
knees?'"

A Canon of Treviso was once having a meal as the guest of
Cardinal Sarto. The Cardinal interrupted the meal to
comment: "I can scarcely swallow a bite!" and added after
a pause, "Just think, a working-class family would have gone
hungry to-day had I not sent them the bare essentials for a
meal. I wonder how many others are in the same necessity?"
With visible emotion he then spoke of the hundreds of letters
he received requesting help in one form or another.

For himself he never sought anything nor did he think of putting anything away for his old age. His only complaint was that the money he received for his own upkeep could never keep pace with his charitable designs. When he had no longer any money to give, he did not hesitate to part with some of his clothing or things which were dear to him. " I am very sorry," he once said to a man who was very poor and needed help urgently, " just now I have no money, but take this crucifix; it belonged to the saintly Pope Pius IX; it is of great value and you will be able to get a good price for it."

Facts like these help us to understand why the people could call him " the poorest of the poor in Venice," and why he could say continually to his nephew, Giovanni Battista Parolin, parish priest of Possagno, " Giovanni, when I die you will find nothing."

All the poor were his friends: those from the slums, and those who had known better days, those born in poverty and those still dressed in silk and velvet, the last painful memories of former days of prosperity. No one left his Palace empty-handed. One of his close co-operators tried to limit the number of those admitted to him to ask for help, but he had given the order that no one should be stopped. More than once he reproached Mgr. Bressan, his secretary, for trying to prevent the poor entering. He would say: " Remember the poor have precedence over all others in my house."

But it was not enough for him simply to leave the doors of his Palace open to the poor, he himself went out to visit the miserable and forsaken in their hovels and attics. God alone knows the full extent of the sacrifices and denials he underwent in his effort to dry the tears of the sorrowful, alleviate sufferings, and encourage with his blessing and help those in dread of a dark and hopeless future. His life was a living out of the words printed around the apse in the chapel of St. Clement in St. Mark's, as an admonition to the Doges of former days: " Love justice, and give everyone his rights. Remember the poor, the orphan, the widow; all look to you with confidence as their protector. Be merciful to all; neither fear, nor hatred, nor avarice should have power over your soul."

MODESTY AND SIMPLICITY

The modesty and simplicity of the Cardinal, signs of real greatness, were not less admirable than his love for his neighbour. The reception of the Red Hat had not altered the tenor of his life. The magnificent halls and carpeted stairways of his palace served their purpose for the solemn reception of important visitors, but for himself there were two very simple rooms, nothing better than those of any country parish priest. He had but one servant and one gondolier, and depended on his sisters for the upkeep of the house. They also were very modest and went about their daily round of duties, shopping and the like, dressed like the housewives of the city. Audiences were given in the same informal manner as at Mantua: the Cardinal opened the door himself and dispelled the timidity of his visitor with a smile or a jest. His meals were frugal and modest and he was always content with what was put before him.

He was an enemy of all kinds of ostentation and pomposity. He walked through the streets dressed in an ordinary black cassock like any priest. The doctor had ordered him to take a short morning walk, but invariably he made his way down to the Lagoon to chat familiarly with the fishermen, buying a few fish from time to time, so as to give them something without appearing to be giving alms. With joy and pride he spoke to them of the poverty of the family from which he came and delighted to be called the poor Cardinal of the country. When they addressed him as " Your Eminence," he would reply, " I have come from a poor family of Riese . . . there is nothing eminent in that! "

In 1889 the Sisters of the Child Mary in Crespano del Grappa invited him to preside at the closing feast of their scholastic year. It was quite obvious that the good nuns would prepare a magnificent reception for him at the station of Bassano where he would leave the train. He therefore wrote to one of his friends in that town to ask him to meet two priests from Venice at a certain time and to take them in his carriage to the Convent, as one of them, being used to the gondola, was a bad walker. The friend was punctual in meeting the train, but immediately recognized the Cardinal and, overcome

with joy, was about to exclaim: " Oh! Your Eminence."
But the Cardinal put his finger to his mouth to indicate
silence, got into the carriage and reached the Convent without
being seen by the nuns.

His sisters treated him with the same intimacy as they had
at Riese long ago. They still called him Bepi, and because
of his kindness and consideration it was a joy for them to
be near him.

PRINCE OF THE CHURCH

Although he was now Patriarch of Venice and Prince of
the Church, at heart he was still the son of the poor Cursore
of Riese. But there was nothing in his manner which could
in any way detract from the dignity conferred on him by the
Church. Those who did not know of his humble beginnings
would have taken him for the son of a noble family.

The French Minister of Education, Chaumie, once said
of him: " He is a man of magnetic personality and splendid
appearance, with an open face from which decision and
firmness shine forth, but on the other hand the mildness of
his eyes tempers all severity. Every manifestation of dignity
is contrary to his nature, but there is nothing servile in him;
his manners are perfect; they are the manners of one who is
completely master of himself."

René Bazin, a member of the French Academy, calls this
the criticism of a passer-by. It is evident that the Minister
was attracted only by his outward appearance and had not
understood wherein the mystery of this perfection lay. The
Venetians sensed it; they said of him: "He lived continuously in
a supernatural atmosphere," and they venerated him as a saint.

The Venetians knew that Cardinal Sarto only lived for
the spiritual well-being of his people. They called him
" Our Patriarch " with great pride. When they heard that
he was in this church or that, they flocked to hear his words
and receive his blessing, and nothing gave them greater joy
than to succeed in kissing his hand. Such signs of affection
pleased him very much—he would smile, give his blessing
and embrace them as his children.

Cardinal Sarto took no notice of the many peculiar happenings which threw a prophetic light on the future. A confidant of his tells the story: "I accompanied the Patriarch once as he went to give a sick child Confirmation. A peasant woman passed us carrying a child in her arms which must have been but a few years old. As usual the Cardinal was dressed in a plain black cassock, but as soon as the child saw him it exclaimed: "Mama, Mama! that is a Pope!" I whispered to the Cardinal: "Ex ore infantium—Out of the mouths of infants," but he looked at me severely and said: "Don't be so silly." Christian hagiographers tell us time and time again that children, illumined from above, have been the bearers of divine messages.

In Mantua, Mgr. Sarto had had a similar experience. "I accompanied the Servant of God," says a priest from Mantua, "into a Jesuit house. There we met a simple, kind lay-brother by the name of Tacchini. As soon as the latter saw the Bishop coming he exclaimed: 'Here comes Sarto (in English, "tailor") who will repair the Church; he will first be Cardinal, then Patriarch, then Pope.'

" 'There! you see,' said the Cardinal, ' you see how wrong you are, for if that were to happen at all, I should first be Patriarch and then Cardinal.'

" 'No!' insisted Tacchini, ' you will become Cardinal, then Patriarch and then . . . just wait and see . . . Pope!' "

ON THE SUMMIT OF THE GRAPPA

Cardinal Sarto was invited to bless a great statue of the Blessed Virgin on August 4th, 1901. The statue had been erected on the top of a hill to commemorate the beginning of the twentieth century. The people feared that the climb of 1,500 feet would be too much of a strain for him, but he simply replied that to honour the Mother of God nothing was too great a strain. On the evening of August 3rd he reached Campo S. Croce at the foot of the Grappa. Ten thousand voices singing the praises of Mary sounded through the night: voices of children tinkling like silver, the high-pitched voices of women and the powerful bass voices of men united in a single melody of praise for their Queen. Bonfires, flares and torches awakened the sleeping mountain to life.

By sunrise the Patriarch had reached the summit of the hill. He celebrated Holy Mass, blessed the statue and then spoke to the multitude gathered about him, as only he knew how to speak, on the love of Mary. At the end of his sermon the crowd shouted: " Viva il Patriarca "—Long live the Patriarch; but he answered " Viva Maria! " An eighty year old woman succeeded in pushing her way through the crowd to kiss the Cardinal's hand. She exclaimed: " And now I can die happy."

As the Patriarch began to descend the mountain the people decorated him with the white *stelle alpine* which they had gathered on the hill. That was a memorable day for the Church and for Italy, for not even Cardinal Sarto realized that one day the enemies of Italy would come as far as the Grappa and stop at the feet of the statue of Our Lady which he had blessed that day. The enemies were the Austro-German armies, which were to meet the heroic resistance of the Italian forces during the last part of the first World War (1914-1918).

CHAPTER VII

FROM LEO XIII TO PIUS X
(August 4th, 1903)

FROM VENICE TO ROME

LIKE a flame which flickers and dies for want of fuel, the
"Lumen in Cœlo" passed away on July 20th, 1903.

The Pope who had illumined the world by the light
of his sanctity and wisdom for a quarter of a century passed
to his eternal reward, like a warrior after battle. Leo XIII
was dead.

While in the Vatican prayers were offered for the Church
bereft of its pastor, the Roman people knelt around the body
of the late Pontiff. The Cardinals began their journey to
Rome from all parts of the world in order to give Christendom
a new father, the Church a new Vicar of Christ and humanity
a new teacher.

In Venice Cardinal Sarto, deeply grieved at the news of
the death of the aged Pontiff, began his preparations for the
journey. In the afternoon of July 26th he bade farewell to
his sisters and departed from the Palace, without foreseeing
in the least what God had in store for him. He stepped
into the gondola, travelled down the Rio di Canonica (a
small canal) and reached the Grand Canal, while the bells of
the city of St. Mark chimed in unison with thousands of
cheering voices from the banks—a grand, affectionate
farewell for their beloved Patriarch. At the station a great
crowd of people awaited him. With one voice they shouted
again and again: "Come back soon, Eminence!" but it
seemed as if in this call there was a note of fear that perhaps
he would not return to the City of the Lagoon.

"Dead or alive I shall return to you," the Cardinal answered,
trying his best to restrain his emotion as he blessed his
beloved flock.

As the train moved out of the station at 2.35 p.m. an enthusiastic and repeated cry arose: " Long live our Patriarch! Long live our Cardinal! "

From the bridge over the Lagoon he once again looked back on the city which was so dear to him. He saluted the dome of St. Mark's and watched it disappearing slowly into the shining blue waters of the sea. In his heart he experienced all the bitterness and yearning of a child leaving home for the first time. He plunged his tear-moistened face into the palms of his hands and wept bitterly.

WHO WILL BE THE SUCCESSOR OF LEO XIII?

Were his tears a presentiment of what was to come? During the past few years, when anyone thoughtlessly expressed the desire to see him Pope, he would answer severely: " If you want to wish me evil; think of something sensible."

Mgr. Primo Rossi, Abbot of Castelfranco Veneto, was once speaking to Cardinal Sarto about the advanced age of the reigning Pontiff, and asked whom the Patriarch considered to be the most likely successor. " You ask a most inopportune question," the Cardinal replied, " No one can conjecture who will succeed so eminent a Pope." And after a short pause he continued, " Since Leo XIII has illumined the world by his wisdom, you can take it for granted that only a most distinguished person can be his successor. His successor will have to be a very holy Pope." Unwittingly Cardinal Sarto had described himself as the Pope the world demanded and needed.

B. Contardo Ferrini, who was a witness at the Beatification Process of Pius X, wrote towards the end of the lifetime of Leo XIII: " Now we have a Pope renowned for learning and wisdom, who by his keen judgment and extraordinary ability has advanced the honour of the Church in the world far beyond expectation, in a manner which seems almost miraculous. But after the death of Leo XIII the Church will need a Head to lead her back to the evangelical virtues of apostolic times, kindness, mercy, poverty of spirit, that

she may exercise great influence on the masses of the people.
The election of Cardinal Sarto of Venice is very desirable, for
he has a reputation for such virtues in a high degree."

THE CONCLAVE

The Cardinal of Venice arrived in Rome on the morning
of July 27th and took up residence in the Lombardian College,
which at that time was situated in the Prati di Castello.
He had no doubts about his return to Venice and the thought
of election to the Papacy was so far from his mind that he never
took the wishes of his friends and acquaintances seriously.
Furthermore, the devotion the Venetians had shown him on
his departure strengthened his desire to fulfil his promise
of returning, " dead or alive."

In one of the meetings held in preparation for the Conclave,
Cardinal Sarto was seated next to the French Cardinal
Lécot, Archbishop of Bordeaux. The French Cardinal did
not know the Patriarch and said to him in French: " De quel
diocèse est-ce que Votre Eminence est archevêque? "

" I'm afraid I do not speak French," the Cardinal replied
in Latin.

" Where do you come from? " returned the French Cardinal.

" From Venice."

" Then you are the Patriarch of Venice? "

" That's right."

" But if Your Eminence does not speak French you have no
chance of being elected, because the Pope must speak
French," commented the Archbishop of Bordeaux.

" I have no desire and no prospect of being elected Pope,
Deo Gratias! " replied Cardinal Sarto, much gratified that
at least one person thought the same as he did.

But God had different plans for the poor Cardinal from
the country who did not speak French. He possessed the
sanctity and knowledge to direct the fate of the Church and
show men the way to truth and salvation.

.   .   .   .   .

On the evening of July 31st, sixty-two Cardinals walked in

solemn procession to the Sistine Chapel to call down the Light of the Holy Spirit to guide them in their choice of a new Pope. The Dean of the Sacred College was Oreglia di Santo Stefano, created Cardinal by Pius IX. The Secretary of the Conclave was a young prelate, only thirty-eight years old, Mgr. Merry del Val, Archbishop of Nicaea, and President of the Accademia dei Nobili Ecclesiastici, who had already been charged with very important missions in the Pontificate of Leo XIII and who was greatly esteemed by all the Cardinals for his eminent piety and vast learning.

Clouds of anguish covered the countenance of Cardinal Sarto as he pondered the importance of the duty he was about to perform, though he hadn't the slightest fear of being elected himself; such a thought to him was a mere absurdity.

At the first ballot of the election, *per scrutinium,* five votes fell to him, and at the second in the afternoon ten. With his usual sense of humour he whispered to the Cardinal sitting next to him: " The Cardinals are amusing themselves at my expense." This he could say quite truly for Cardinal Rampolla had received twenty-nine votes, and it was evident that the number would increase.

The next day brought a decisive change. Cardinal Puzyna, Bishop of Cracow, for political reasons put in a veto in the name of His Apostolic Majesty, the Emperor of Austria, against the election of the Secretary of State of Leo XIII. He did not realize for a moment that that Aulic " Exclusiva " was to give events the course prepared by Divine Providence. The Dean of the Sacred College, Cardinal Oreglia, immediately negatived the attempt of a worldly power to bind the hands of the Sacred College in the election of a Pope and declared that the Cardinals should completely ignore the veto in subsequent ballots. Cardinal Rampolla no less firmly protested against the interference of a worldly power in the freedom of the Church and the dignity of the Sacred College, saying: " I protest against it with all my power, but as far as my own insignificant person is concerned I don't think anything more propitious could have happened."

After this interlude the voting continued on August 2nd. Cardinal Rampolla received the same twenty-nine votes at the first ballot as he had received the evening before. In the afternoon thirty Cardinals gave their votes to Cardinal Rampolla. The Cardinal of Venice who had received ten votes on the evening of August 1st, received twenty-one in the morning ballot of August 2nd, and twenty-four in the evening.

.   .   .   .   .

"I AM UNWORTHY . . . FORGET ME!"

Cardinal Sarto began to experience a sinking of heart as he realized that his votes were increasing. In order to rid himself of the danger of being burdened with the tremendous responsibility of the Papacy, he began to beg the Cardinals not to vote for him. He openly declared with absolute firmness that never, and on no conditions, would he accept the Pontificate.

Like a child about to receive a beating, he burst into tears, murmuring and sobbing (rather than saying): " My conscience tells me that it is my duty to inform you how absolutely unworthy and incapable I am of the Papacy. I have not the necessary qualities. It is your duty to forget me and give your votes to someone else. I am unworthy . . . I am incapable. . . For the love of God, forget me! " To persuade them more effectively he then proceeded to enumerate his many faults and weaknesses, his ignorance of languages, diplomatic affairs, and so on.

" But the arguments he adduced," testifies Cardinal Gibbons, Archbishop of Baltimore, " completely defeated their own purpose, because they were so full of humility and wisdom that far from diminishing the esteem the Sacred College had for him, they rather tended to increase it a hundredfold. We learned the true value of the man from the profound sincerity of the words he used to express his own lack of the qualities necessary for a Sovereign Pontiff. Every time he spoke there was a tremor in his voice and tears fell from his eyes."

On August 3rd at the first ballot Cardinal Sarto's votes

rose to twenty-seven, while those of Cardinal Rampolla fell to twenty-four. There could be no doubt now that the Patriarch of the City of the Lagoon was the Cardinals' choice. The Sacred College expected that Cardinal Sarto would now resign himself to accepting the Papacy, but he would have nothing to do with it. With repeated entreaties he once again insisted: " Let me go back to my Venetians; they are waiting for me. To elect me Pope is absurd."

" HAVE COURAGE, YOUR EMINENCE! "

The Cardinal Deacon was becoming a little anxious because the Conclave was going on too long and there was no sign of Cardinal Sarto's yielding to the wishes of the Sacred College. He therefore asked Mgr. Merry del Val to approach the Patriarch privately to ask him to accept the Papacy. Mgr. Merry del Val, years later, described that private meeting with the Patriarch as follows:

" After searching for some time, I was told that I would find His Eminence in the Pauline Chapel. I entered that dark, silent retreat and there I saw the sanctuary lamp flickering on the altar, two candles lighted in front of the picture of Our Lady of Good Counsel and the Cardinal kneeling on the marble floor, his head in his hands, absorbed in prayer. I knelt down beside him and after a few moments whispered the wish of the Cardinal Deacon. He raised his head and looked at me sternly through his tear-filled eyes. I cannot describe the tension of the few following moments as I awaited an answer from the unhappy Patriarch. Clasping my hands, he murmured: ' Ah! Monsignor, do ask the Cardinal Deacon to have mercy on me and forget me.'

" At this moment it seemed to me as if he were going through the agony of Gethsemani and urging like his Divine Master: ' Transeat a me calix iste—Let this chalice pass from me.' ' Take courage, Your Eminence, the Lord will supply the strength you need,' unwittingly sprang to my lips. He looked at me pensively and whispered, ' Thank you, my son.' I then left the chapel. Time will not efface from my memory the impression the Cardinal of Venice left on me. It was the first time I had spoken to the Patriarch, but from that moment I considered him a saint."

Hours of dramatic tension were to follow. The Cardinals crowded around the Patriarch of Venice using all the power of their eloquence to shake his firm intention of not accepting the Papacy. They were aware of his devotion to duty, of his love for the Church, of his submission to the Will of God, and they did not fail to use these virtues of his to bolster up their persuasive arguments.

" Go back to Venice if you wish," contended Cardinal Ferrari, " but until your dying day you will be plagued with qualms of conscience."

" The responsibility of the Papacy is too terrifying," returned the Patriarch with fear and trembling.

" The responsibility of refusing it will be far more dreadful," came the reply.

" I am too old, I shall die soon." The Cardinal of Venice was quibbling rather than answering the objection.

" Apply the words of Caiphas to yourself: ' It is expedient that one man should die for the people ' " (*John* xi. 49) returned the quick-witted disputant.

Cardinal Satolli now lent support to the arguments of Cardinal Ferrari: "Accept it! Accept it! God wills it; the Supreme Council demands it and the well-being of Christendom depends on it."

Like Daniel in the lions' den, the poor Patriarch saw that he was surrounded on all sides, but made one last heroic effort. " I have promised to return to my Venetian children, dead or alive."

Cardinal Satolli came immediately to the attack: " Your Eminence has done well to say dead or alive, for if you try to resist the Will of God, as Jonas did, could it not happen that God would punish you by making you the victim of a railway accident? What a responsibility would be yours if you had to face your Judge with numerous others, victims of your disobedience! " (The memory of the major railway catastrophe at Castel Giubileo, on the Rome-Florence line, was still fresh in the minds of all).

"For God's sake don't say things like that; they freeze the blood in my veins," answered Cardinal Sarto. But it was precisely to freeze the blood in his veins that Cardinal Satolli had used the argument.

"I say this to you, because you refuse to accept the dignity of the Papacy. By that you are flying in the face of God."

The Patriarch was defeated and he knew it. He did not answer a word; for a moment he reflected that it would demand a great sacrifice of him, but on the other hand he would be sure of the assistance of Christ. He then raised his eyes, wet with tears, and answered: "May God's Holy Will be done."

The ballot in the evening of the same day gave Cardinal Sarto thirty-five votes. "It was now certain that he would be elected the following day by a clear majority," says Mgr. Merry del Val.

"TU ES PETRUS"

When Cardinal Sarto took up his place in the Sistine Chapel on the very warm morning of August 4th he was unrecognizable. His face was disfigured by hours of weeping, and an indescribable expression of pain rested on his brow. That morning at the final ballot he received fifty votes—eight more than was necessary for the two-thirds majority required for valid election.

Pale and still weeping he sat there, his lips moving in prayer. The humble son of the Cursore of Riese bowed his head, silently accepting the Will of God, and murmuring to himself: "If it is not possible that this chalice pass away, but I must drink it, may the Will of God be done. . . I accept the Pontificate as a cross."

"What name do you wish to take?" the Cardinal Deacon demanded in accordance with the ritual.

For some moments there was no reply, but then the new Pope answered: "As the Popes who have suffered most for the Church during the last century were called Pius, I too shall take that name."

In this way the humble peasant from the obscure country village mounted the steps of the highest throne on earth. He was the successor of Peter, the head of the Universal Church, and the 259th Vicar of Christ, but for him the triple tiara was a mysterious crown of martyrdom. The hour of sacrifice had struck. The " ignis ardens " of the popular and symbolic prophecy had begun to blaze.

It was August 4th, 1903, and the big clock on St. Peter's showed exactly 11.45. The enormous dome of Michael Angelo looked like a gigantic tiara in the sunlight, and the statues of popes and saints which adorn Bernini's Colonnade seemed to spring to life, repeating, as it were, the words by which Christ promised perpetual assistance to His Church: " Tu es Petrus."

THE BLESSING " URBI ET ORBI "

A mighty crowd of people had collected in the Piazza of St. Peter's, waiting in suspense to know who had been elected. Cardinal Macchi, from the central loggia of the Basilica, announced in clear, solemn tones: " We have a Pope, His Eminence Cardinal Giuseppe Sarto, who has taken the name of Pius X." Then the people thronged into the spacious halls of the Basilica consecrated to the Prince of the Apostles. It was not long before the new Vicar of Christ, dressed in white cassock, appeared on the inner loggia, surrounded by the Sacred College of Cardinals and the noble guard. The enthusiastic cries of " Long live Pius X " resounded throughout the immense Basilica.

With one glance at that vast cheering crowd the new Pope perceived the affection of his children; with one fatherly smile and gentle salutation he manifested his appreciation of that affection. As the cheering gradually died down a solemn silence fell upon the people as His Holiness lifted his eyes to Heaven, stretched out his arms in the symbolic embrace of the whole world and in a steady voice pronounced for the first time the Apostolic Blessing to those collected around him, to those absent near and far, to the whole of Christendom. Once again shouts of jubilation hailed the humble Pope who showed deep emotion in this hour of glory.

As soon as the ceremony had finished, he withdrew to one of the rooms he had occupied during the days of the Conclave and kneeling before the crucifix poured out his soul in prayer. It was only here at the feet of his suffering Redeemer that the new Pontiff found his peace again. Consoled and strengthened he rose to his feet to begin a pontificate, which, though short in duration, was to be one of the richest and most glorious in the history of the Church because of the greatness of the works to be accomplished. The Cardinal of Venice had taken the name Pius, because of the sufferings of his predecessors, Pius VI, Pius VII and Pius IX, but his pontificate was a replica not only of their sufferings, but also of the burning piety of Gregory the Great, the strength and power of Hildebrand and the wisdom of Innocent III.

The following day he opened up his soul to his dear friend the Bishop of Pavia, Mgr. Giuseppe Callegari, to tell him of the great suffering it was to be elevated to a dignity which he had never sought or wanted. He writes:

" Your Excellency,

" I have scarcely recovered as yet from the great shock which I felt when this heavy cross was laid upon my shoulders. I hasten, nevertheless, to convey to you, my dear friend, my most affectionate greeting. What a great consolation it would be for me were you present, so that I could pour out my soul to you! But I haven't the courage to say: ' Come to Rome.' This first letter which I write from the Calvary whither the hand of God has led me, I bathe with my tears and press a loving kiss against its pages, and with it I send to you and all the members of your flock the Apostolic Blessing.

Most sincerely and affectionately yours in Jesus Christ,

PIUS PP X."

Vatican, August 5th, 1903.

FIRST MEETING WITH THE DIPLOMATIC CORPS

On August 6th Pius X had his first meeting with the diplomatic corps. "Each one of these diplomats was curious to know," Mgr. Merry del Val tells us, "how the new Pope would receive them. Would he be bashful and reserved? Would he be awkward, not being used to the splendour of court ceremonial? They had known him as a 'priest from the country,' untrained in the ways of aristocratic formalities and diplomatic finesse, so eminent in his predecessor. They felt they must prepare themselves for the worst."

But the impression they received at their first meeting was so completely different from what they had anticipated that it left them amazed. The Pope received the Ambassadors and Ministers with great courtesy and kindness and answered a speech made by the Ambassador of Portugal with fluency of word and profundity of thought.

The forty years of his priestly ministry had brought him into contact with many people and had taught him too much about life and human affairs to leave him a victim to the subtleties of the great ones of this world. He felt as much at home in the presence of the cosmopolitan diplomatic corps as with the poor in the Episcopal Palace of Venice.

The trained eye of the diplomat very soon saw that here was a superior intellect to be admired and respected. Immediately after the audience the diplomatic corps proceeded to the Sala Borgia where they met the Pro-Secretary of State, Mgr. Merry del Val. The latter was not slow to perceive an atmosphere of mystification and disillusionment; he tells us: "Their conversation was laboured and disjointed. To my enquiry as to how the Holy Father had received them, the reply was but a few platitudes: 'Very well!' 'Most cordially!' interspersed with periods of silence which made me feel quite uncomfortable. Had anything happened? Had there, perhaps, been some unpleasantness? What else could cause this reticence, I kept asking myself. Then quite suddenly the Prussian Minister put me the question: 'Tell us, Monsignor, what is it that this Pope has which charms one so irresistibly at the very first meeting with him?' Remarks from the other Ministers showed that all were extremely interested in the answer to this question. The question first of all seemed to confirm my suspicion that something unusual had taken place, so instead of answering I tried to ascertain exactly what had taken place at the meeting. They assured me that nothing unusual had happened; that the Pope had answered a speech made by the Doyen, the Ambassador of Portugal, and had then spoken to each of the diplomats individually. They were all charmed by his personality. I could only reply that I had known His Holiness but a few days and had come under the same spell. No one said, but all felt as I did, that the Pope was really a man of God, a saint."

The French statesman, Emilio Olivier, wrote of Pius X: " The new Pope has not the majestic appearance of Leo XIII, but instead an irresistible kindness and pleasantness of manner. His super-eminent gifts of mind, the keenness of his intellect, the clearness and precision of his thought, left a deep impression on me. He is an excellent listener and can pick out at once all the important points in a speech. His answers are short; in a few decisive words he can make a situation live. He possesses all the qualities of a great statesman; he has a remarkable foresight of what is possible and what is not. In his calm, courageous manner he is slow to condemn, but once he has made up his mind he is inflexible. I think he will be seen at his best when difficulties arise—then he will prove himself a hero and a saint."

THE FIRST PUBLIC AUDIENCE

The ceremonies of the solemn Coronation and the reception of the diplomats being completed, the people, who saw in him the father of all, began to gather to pay their respects to the Vicar of Christ. First of all came the parish priests of the Eternal City and then the Roman populace, which was very dear to him. Every Sunday the Court of St. Damasus was crowded with people, who gazed up at that balcony adorned by the paintings of Raphael, until the Sovereign Pontiff appeared. Then shouts of triumph greeted him as he smiled and raised his hand in blessing over his faithful flock. Silence was restored during the blessing and then the Pope proceeded to explain to them the Gospel of the day. It was clear from his words that his one wish in life, his one purpose on earth was to make God known and loved. The explanation of the Gospel text differed only from that given in the parish churches of Venice in the greater force lent to his words by the dignity of his position and the Apostolic Blessing.

" This great pastor of Rome and of the whole world," so wrote René Bazin, a member of the French Academy, " like St. Peter, spoke of Jesus Christ with certainty and love. All who heard him, especially the poor, felt that the Pope loved each one of them."

When the address was ended the people sang in unison the hymn, " Noi vogliam Dio," while the Pope who had loved the peasants of Riese and the gondoliers of Venice, stood over them with a gentle smile overshadowed by an air of sadness.

People came from Riese, Tombolo, Salzano, Treviso, Mantua and Venice to be received in the simple, homely audiences and to hear him speak of the love of God, the importance of prayer and the need for Christian sacrifice. He loved to remind them of the happy days he had spent ministering to their needs, as priest, Bishop and Patriarch. But sometimes while he looked down on that throng of people he imagined that he saw in the midst of them his mother, and then would come into his mind the thought of the Mother of Sorrows, standing at the foot of the Cross.

THE CARDINAL SECRETARY OF STATE

On the very evening of the memorable day on which the Cardinal Patriarch of Venice had been elected Pope, Mgr. Merry del Val, the Secretary of the Conclave, came to him and said: " Holy Father, my task as Secretary of the Conclave is now finished; I beg Your Apostolic Blessing before returning to the Accademia dei Nobili Ecclesiastici."

Pius X looked at him, smiled, and said somewhat reproachfully: " Why do you want to leave me, Monsignor? " and after a short pause, continued, " No! stay with me. Up

PIUS X CROWNED POPE
(9th August, 1903)

to now I have done nothing; I have decided on nothing; I have not found one to whom I can speak freely and on whom I can rely for prudent advice. Do me this favour; remain with me for the present and then we shall see."

Mgr. Merry del Val, deeply moved, replied: "It is not my wish to abandon Your Holiness, but my task is done. The Secretary of State whom Your Holiness appoints will take my place and continue looking after Church affairs."

"Take these papers," the Pope said, "and I beg you to exercise the office of Pro-Secretary of State until I have made the appointment. . . Do me this favour."

How could anyone resist so ardent a wish of the Vicar of Christ not to be left alone at the moment when he needed the assistance of an experienced Prelate for the performance of work so new to him? Mgr. Merry del Val complied with the wish of the Holy Father whom he already regarded as a saint. A few days later Pius X sent him his first photograph as Pope, dedicated to " Our Pro-Secretary of State."

Not many days were needed for the new Pope with his discerning eye to penetrate the soul of Mgr. Merry del Val and to see in him one possessed of all that was required for an excellent Secretary of State. Three months later, on October 18th, he nominated him to that office and created him Cardinal on November 9th with the title of S. Prassede. (At the same Consistory he gave the Cardinal's Hat to Mgr. Giuseppe Callegari, Bishop of Padua, whom he had served as chancellor in the years 1880-1882).

René Bazin writes: " It called for very great courage to elevate so young a prelate to so high a position. But Pius X had this courage because, as he himself said at the first Consistory, Mgr. Merry del Val possessed an extraordinary character, a great ability in dealing with Church affairs and a soul deeply imbued with the priestly spirit—considerations which must silence all worldly objections to his appointment."

The nomination of a Prelate of only thirty-eight years of age to so high a position as Secretary of State was the cause of no little surprise to the Prelates and Cardinals at the Consistory, but Pius X explained: " I have nominated Mgr. Merry del Val as Secretary of State because it is fitting

that the successor of so noble a prelate as Cardinal Rampolla
should be a person outstanding for piety and priestly virtues."

The Cardinals understood this unusual step of the new
Pontiff still more clearly when a few days later His Holiness
wrote to Cardinal Cenci: " I have chosen him because he is
a polyglot. Born in England, educated in Belgium, of Spanish
nationality, partly of Irish descent, living in Italy, son of a
diplomat and a diplomat himself, he is conversant with the
problems of every country. He is modest, humble and
saintly. He comes to me each morning and informs me of
the latest news on all political questions; I need never pass
a remark, for thoroughness is the hall-mark of all he does."

Mgr. Merry del Val was no less appalled at the news of
his appointment to the office of Papal Secretary of State
than the Pope himself had been at the news of his own election.
But Pius X consoled him, saying: " Let us work and suffer
together for the love of God and for the well-being of the
Church."

To work and suffer! Not a very attractive programme to
put before a young prelate, but how great a grace it was for
him to be called to share in the inevitable fatigues and sorrows
of the Vicar of Christ! From this hour Cardinal Merry del Val
did not part from the side of the Pope to whom the
tremendous task was allotted, " To restore all things in
Christ."

CHAPTER VIII

"INSTAURARE OMNIA IN CHRISTO"
(August 4th, 1903—August 20th, 1914)

FUTILE QUESTIONS

THE exaltation of the Patriarch of Venice to the Papal throne filled all minds with great curiosity. What can be expected from the new Pontiff? . . . Will he take the same lines as his predecessor? . . . Will he prove himself conservative or progressive; conciliatory or intransigent? . . . For or against democracy? . . . Can he be easily influenced? . . . Is he conversant with the religious and political state of the world?

Futile questions! A change of Pope does not mean that the Church changes. Difference in policy is due only to the changing conditions of time and circumstances, but time and circumstances can never in the slightest alter the fundamentals of the Faith. These questions were asked chiefly by those who, finding the teachings of the Church difficult to reconcile with their own ideas of progress, secretly hoped that the new Pope could be won over to their way of thinking, as Liberalism had once tried to win Pius IX. The greatest danger now was that the enemy was inside the Church, and hence the necessity for absolute clearness in teaching, lest the faithful be led astray by the wiles of these false teachers, who sought to alienate the Church from her proper purpose. Pius X made the aim of his Pontificate quite clear in the first encyclical Letter, *E Supremi Apostolatus Cathedra*, which aim could be summed up in the words "Instaurare omnia in Christo" (To renew all things in Christ). This had been his aim as Bishop and Patriarch, and there was now no reason why he should choose another motto.

The object of the Papacy has always been the spreading of the Kingdom of Christ on earth. Pius X had ascended the throne of Peter at a time when the rights of Christ were passionately denied, when this denial was, as he said, "the great illness of the age" and when man put himself up in the place of God and worshipped the golden calf of his own intellect.

The new Pope introduced himself to the world in this first encyclical letter, writing: "Supported by the power of God, We pronounce that We know for Our Pontificate no other programme than that of renewing all things in Christ that Christ may be all in all. There will be some who will try to interpret Our intentions and actions in accordance with their own earthly aims and private interests. From the outset We wish to disillusion them by making it quite clear that We have no other ambition than to be the Servant of God and the Bearer of His Authority. The interests of God are Our interests and We will use all Our power to defend them. The motto which will govern all Our acts will be 'Instaurare omnia in Christo.'"

It was his duty to lead humanity back to God, to direct and govern the modern man who lives as if there were no God to be served and no law to be obeyed. But how can man serve a God Whom he does not know, or keep a law which he has never heard? Ignorance is the root of many of the evils which afflict modern society and hence the Pontiff's insistence on the importance of the regular, systematic teaching of Christian Doctrine to young and old alike. He continues: "More hate Christ, despise the Church and ignore the Gospel because of ignorance than because of malice. These unfortunate people blaspheme a God Whom they have never been taught to love. This is a condition which prevails not only amongst the uneducated, but also, and even more so, among those whom the world calls learned. It is not the progress of learning which destroys the Faith, but the prevalence of ignorance. Where ignorance reigns, incredulity finds its kingdom."

The Pope went on to show that there was no possibility of a revival unless there was a general reform of the way in which the Catechism and Christian Doctrine were taught to the people. "We will take the greatest care to safeguard Our clergy from being caught up in the snares of modern scientific thought—a science which does not breathe the truths of Christ, but by its cunning and subtle arguments defiles the mind of the people with the errors of Rationalism or semi-Rationalism. And not only priests but each and every one of the faithful must keep in view, now more than ever, the interests of God and their own souls, and that by following the teaching of their Bishops, to whom alone it belongs to lead, teach and govern."

These severe admonitions of the Pope were not superfluous. He had taken over the government of the Church at a very critical moment in her history; at a moment when free rein was being given to the errors of false theologians and thousands of Catholics were being kept from a proper understanding of Catholic Action.

CHURCH AND POLITICS

Ought the Pope to concern himself with worldly politics? Would this Pope concern himself with affairs apparently extraneous to the work of the Papacy? In the speech given at the First Consistory on November 9th, 1903, Pius X gave a clear and decisive answer to these questions. He explained that politics is nothing more than the application of the Moral Law to the social life of the people, and as the Pope is the supreme teacher of the Moral Law it is his right and duty to play an integral part in the politics of the world. The proper purpose of politics is not party interests or national egotism, but rather the acknowledgement of God's Law and the keeping of His Commandments.

"It is astonishing," he said in his speech, "to see so many so solicitous as to the line of politics the Pope will follow. Is it not perfectly clear that We shall not depart from the policy of Our predecessor? It is Our programme to renew all in Christ; Christ is truth, and We shall make it Our first duty to preach and explain the truth in simple language that it may penetrate the souls of all and imprint itself upon their lives and conduct. Did not Christ make it clear that the keeping of His Law is the sign that We are in the ways of truth when He said: ' If you continue in My Word, you shall be My disciples indeed. And you shall know the truth; and the truth shall make you free ' (*John* viii. 31-32).

" We are convinced that many will resent Our intention of taking an active part in world politics, but any impartial observer will realize that the Pope, to whom the supreme office of teacher has been entrusted by God, cannot remain indifferent to political affairs or separate them from the concerns of Faith and Morals. And as he is the head and leader of the Church, a society of human beings, the Pope must naturally come into contact with the earthly governors of those human beings, heads of states and members of governments, if the peaceful security of Catholics is to be preserved in all countries.

" One of the primary duties of the Apostolic Office is to disprove and condemn erroneous doctrines and to oppose civil laws which are in conflict with the Law of God, and so to preserve humanity from bringing about its own destruction."

If we consider the spiritual and political conditions of the time in which these words were spoken, a time which had as its aim to oppose the Church in every possible way, we shall understand what great courage was required on the part of the new Pontiff to lay the axe to the root by formulating such fundamental principles. Pius X did not stop before any obstacle or difficulty; he feared no opposition or criticism he did not care about being despised and paid no attention to the threats which came from heads of states or governments His one thought was to defend the Church of Christ against all who dared to encroach upon its divine mission.

His speech left no room for doubt as to the aims and plan he would adopt during the perilous years which lay before him. His way lay towards Calvary; his light was the light which came from the Cross.

THE FIGHT AGAINST MODERNISM

The defence of the full and integral truth of the Church which was denied by the Modernist, was the first major action of the new Pontiff. Without truth there does no exist order, either in the religious, moral, or political sphere, and so he must deliver the death-blow to Modernism, which struck at the fundamental teaching of the Church and strove to undermine the spirit of the Catholic world by its insidious and subtle reasoning.

Many Catholics were of the opinion, either because of ignorance or fear of being considered reactionary, that the Church must bring her doctrines into line with modern development. A wave of insurrection against the teachings of the Church flowed throughout the world, and the saddest thing was that the leaders were recruited from the ranks of the clergy, from men holding responsible positions in schools and universities, from those working in the curiæ of Bishops, from priests teaching in seminaries and even from the Hierarchy. Not many were aware of the damage and the confusion of thought wrought by these modern theories, which were widely propagated in books, newspapers and periodicals.

At this critical moment Providence had called to the throne of Peter a man without fear of the defiance and protests of those who in the name of progress and Christian culture, sought to give a new orientation to the Christian way of life, a new character to the Church and a new social call to the clergy. But Pius X followed strictly the lines of his predecessors Pius IX and Leo XIII and declared war on this new tendency and exposed its manifold errors.

THE ENCYCLICAL "PASCENDI DOMINICI GREGIS"

Many Popes had already condemned the attempts of those who, under the guise of working for the development of dogma and making a return to a " pure Gospel," denied revealed truth, opposed the authority of the Church and the decisions of Councils and took it upon themselves to make an exegesis of the Bible suited to their own way of thinking. Efforts to bring them back to the doctrines of the Church met with the answer that the Pope was an enemy of progress and that after nineteen centuries the Church had lost her ability to adapt herself to the spirit of the times.

What is Modernism? C. Périn, in the *Revue Trimestrelle*

of Paris (October 15th, 1851) called it "an attempt to
exclude God from social life," but this definition only views
one aspect of the many-sided phenomenon. Modernism was
basically a system of errors which denied to human reason
any possibility of understanding things not perceived by the
senses.   Pius X calls it: "The synthesis and poison of all
heresies which tend to undermine the fundamentals of the
Faith and to annihilate Christianity."   The Modernist, of
course, regarded this definition as exaggerated and false, but
the encyclical *Pascendi* was to demonstrate its precision,
and at the same time to proclaim the wisdom of the Pope
who pronounced it, of the Pope whom the Modernists
imagined to be an ignorant priest from the country. Instead
of weakness they were confronted with irresistible strength;
instead of finding an ignorant, timid country curate they had
to bow down before the profound wisdom of a saint.

In the encyclical the Pope writes: "Modernists place the
foundation of religious philosophy in that doctrine which is
commonly called agnosticism.   According to this teaching
human reason is confined entirely within the field of
phenomena, that is to say, to things that appear, and in the
manner in which they appear; it has neither the right nor the
power to overstep these limits.   Hence it is incapable of
lifting itself up to God, and of recognizing His existence,
even by means of visible things."

The Holy Father then exposes the erroneous reasoning of
the Modernist philosopher who jumps from the principle
that man cannot know God to the conclusion that God does
not exist: "It may be asked in what way do the Modernists
contrive to make the transition from agnosticism, which is
a state of pure nescience, to scientific and historic atheism,
which is a doctrine of positive denial. . . Let him answer
who can.   Yet it is a fixed and established principle among
them that both science and history must be atheistic; and
within their boundaries there is room for nothing but
phenomena; God and all that is divine are utterly excluded."

But the Modernist had to find some explanation for the
fact of religion, which did exist.   Natural theology and
revelation had been rejected, so that, no explanation for the

fact of religion being possible outside man, they sought to
find an explanation in man.   They explained that in special
circumstances man experiences a need for the divine in the
subconscious; this subconscious need was ascribed to a
principle known as vital immanence."   The Modernist then
tries to show that this need for the divine is termed Religion.
Since they hang all religion on the slender thread of
agnosticism and vital immanence, it is easy for them to deal
with Faith and Revelation in the same way.   The encyclical
continues: "But we have not yet reached the end of their
philosophizing, or, to speak more accurately, of their folly.
Modernists find in this sense, not only faith, but in and with
faith, as they understand it, they affirm that there is also to
be found revelation.   For indeed what more is needed to
constitute a revelation?   Is not that religious sense which is
perceptible in the conscience revelation, or at least the
beginning of revelation?"

This is, in brief, the philosophical background of
Modernism.   Agnosticism represents its negative aspect,
while its positive aspect is the principle of vital immanence.
By means of these false and groundless principles Dogma, the
Sacraments, the Holy Scriptures, the Church and ecclesiastical
authority can be dispensed with readily.

Dogma is the result of reflection upon faith; hence the
saying of the Modernist: "Man must think his faith."   These
elaborations of the intellect, if they finally receive the
approval of the supreme magisterium of the Church,
constitute Dogma.

Divine worship, or cult, springs from the need of giving
religion a sensible form.   This need is also an explanation
for the Sacraments which, like dogmas, are for the Modernist
merely symbols.   Divine inspiration and the Sacred Books
receive the same treatment.

"The Sacred Books," the encyclical says, "according to
the principle of the Modernists, may be described as a
summary of experiences, not indeed of the kind that may now
and again come to anybody, but those extraordinary and
striking experiences which are the possession of every religion.
And this is precisely what they teach about our books of the

Old and New Testament. . . Inspiration is in nowise distinguished from that impulse which stimulates the believer to reveal the faith that is in him, by words or writing, except perhaps by its vehemence."

This need can also be used to explain the origin and spread of the Church. To explain this the encyclical *Pascendi* says: " They begin with the supposition that the Church has its birth in a double need; first, the need of the individual believer to communicate his faith to others, especially if he has had some original and special experience; and secondly, when the faith has becomecommonto many, the need of the collectivity to form itself into a society and to guard, promote and propagate the common good. What then is the Church? It is the product of the collective conscience, that is to say, of the association of individual consciences which, by virtue of the principle of vital permanence, depend all on one first believer, who for Catholics is Christ." [1]

It was once believed that the Church had her authority from God, but the Modernist denies this, saying: " Every society needs a directing authority to guide its members towards the common end, to foster prudently the elements of cohesion, which in a religious society are doctrine and worship. Hence the triple authority in the Catholic Church, disciplinary, dogmatic, liturgical. The nature of this authority is to be gathered from its origin, and its rights and duties from its nature. . . Authority, like the Church, has its origin in the religious conscience, and that being so, is subject to it. Should it disown this dependence it becomes a tyranny."

The Church bears the same relation to other societies as Faith does to knowledge. Hence Church and state have nothing in common. In temporal matters the Church must submit to the state, the Catholic to the citizen. " Every Catholic, from the fact that he is also a citizen, has the right and the duty to work for the common good in the way he thinks best, without troubling himself about the authority of the Church, without paying any heed to its wishes, its counsels, its orders—nay, even in spite of its rebukes."

---

[1] Extracts from *Pascendi* are taken from the C.T.S. translation.

As in philosophy and history, so also in politics all religion must be ignored and hence there remains nothing but a hopeless subjectivism, complete incredulity and radical denial of the existence of God. This is the logical and inevitable outcome of the doctrine of vital immanence and agnosticism on which the Modernist system is built.

THE ECHO OF THE ENCYCLICAL

September 8th, 1907, is a memorable day for Christendom, and equal in importance to September 9th, 325, the day on which the Council of Nicæa dealt the death blow to Arianism. All who lived in the conviction that chaos is the inevitable result of trying to live without Christ and His truth, understood at once the importance of the encyclical.

Had Modernism been propagated in the Church, it would have been on account of its parading under the guise of a Catholic truth and thus hiding its own vague and contradictory ideas. There was thus a need of making a thorough and implacable examination of these false doctrines, and causing inevitable offence to their supporters.

It is difficult to conceive the efforts made by the Modernists to elude the consequences of the defeat inflicted on their theories by the encyclical *Pascendi*. Pius X must have had a most bitter struggle, but the victory was his; his encyclical triumphed and is held among the most famous doctrinal documents of the century; it is a glorious demonstration of the power and strength of the Church against which Modernism in its folly and unmeasured pride had dared to cry: " Change or die." By the encyclical of September 8th, 1907, they and not the Church met with the death sentence, and history can write an epitaph on their tomb: " Mentita est iniquitas sibi ' (*Ps.* xxvi. 12). " Iniquity hath lied to itself."

THE POPE OF REFORM

The task of a Pope is a double one: to preserve the truth intact by careful vigilance against every error, and with that truth to further the well-being of men. To the Pope could be applied the words of God to the prophet Jeremias:

" Lo, I have set thee this day over the nations, and over
kingdoms, to root up and to pull down, and to waste and to
destroy and to build and to plant " (*Jer*. i. 10).

At the time Giuseppe Sarto stepped upon the throne of Peter
many thorns and brambles had sprung up in the mystical
vineyard of the Lord, and these he must root out at once or
else the good seed would be choked. He must root out the
Modernist ambition to revolutionize the Church, the atheistic
tendency of modern scholarship and the idolatry of modern
science.   But how could the people know the word of God
when it was preached to them in a language they did not
understand, in a language full of high-sounding words and
flights of fancy which rang in the ear but never penetrated
the heart ? The Patriarch of Venice had eradicated oratorical
abuses from his diocese, and the Pope was no less determined
and active in eradicating them from the whole Church.

What had become of Catholic Action? Every year
Congresses were held faithfully, speeches and exhortations
were delivered in beautiful words and carefully prepared
academic arguments were propounded, but nothing ever
happened; how could these picturesque but artificial trees
be expected to bear fruit? The result of this was violent
anti-clericalism in Italy and bitter persecution of the Church
in France and other countries.

Before the new Pope lay a great task which called for a man
of more than common wisdom, experience in government
and apostolic courage. Pius X had started at the lowest
grade of the clerical state and passed through every step of
the hierarchy. He possessed the required characteristics
and this he proved by the organic and all-embracing
programme of renovation and reform which he laid down as
soon as he received the Pontifical Tiara.

BISHOP OF ROME

As Bishop of Rome, it was most fitting that Pius X should
begin his reform in the Eternal City, the centre of the
Catholic Church and a city most dear to his heart. In the
apostolic letter of February 11th, 1904, he announced a

Pastoral visitation of the city and commissioned his Cardinal Vicar, assisted by prelates and priests renowned for doctrine, prudence and probity of life, to carry this out. The very astonishment with which this news was received made it clear to him how necessary it was.

At that time in Rome there were many priests from other dioceses who had come there in quest of an easier and more remunerative career and for whom, in actual fact, no fixed duties had been prescribed. In the work of God they had proved themselves more of a hindrance than a help and were very often a bad example to the people whose spiritual needs they feigned to serve. Pius X, who had such great experience in the care of souls, knew the damage such priests, living far from the vigilance of their superiors, were capable of causing. He did not hesitate to make a firm and resolute decision, ordering all extradiocesan priests, residing in Rome without valid reasons, to return at once to their own dioceses. As usual there were not wanting those who decried this measure as over-strict and censured the Pope for taking it, but the order and regularity which resulted from it very soon showed how prudent and necessary it had been.

Statistics taken at the visitation made it clear that the population of Rome was rapidly growing, that many new parishes ought to be established and many of the old ones divided. But to undertake such a programme the Pope must spend large sums of money, make many enemies for himself by offending existing interests, and overcome the resistance of cherished and long-standing customs. The Holy Father could not reflect without emotion on the crowds of Roman people who were without the consolation of religion for want of priests. He could allow no difficulties or obstacles to stand in his way. The indomitable Pius X came to the attack with a determination not to be thwarted.

What was the result? The boundaries of the parishes clustered together in the heart of the city were revised; new parishes were established and new churches built wherever housing schemes were in progress; the newly erected parishes were staffed with zealous, efficient priests, and the income of curates was carefully determined so that they could give

their whole time and attention to the interests of souls.
It was not long before the fruit of these measures became
evident by the increased reception of the Sacraments and the
flourishing religious life of the city.

THE POPE OF THE CATECHISM

Nothing was more painful to Pius X than that he could not
leave the Vatican to move amongst his children, teaching
them the Catechism and giving instructions in Christian
Doctrine as he had done at Mantua and Venice. But if he
was prevented from bringing to them the comfort of his
blessing and his words, they could come to him. Hence a
spectacle never seen before was beheld in the Vatican.
Every Sunday the gates were thrown open to an ever increasing
multitude eager to see their beloved Pontiff and to hear him
comment on the Gospel of the day and explain the Catechism,
as he had done in the parishes of Tombolo and Salzano.

The encyclical, *Acerbo nimis*, which the Pope sent out on
April 15th, 1905, to the Bishops and priests of the world,
admonished them to give the greatest attention to the
teaching of the Catechism and to adapt their methods and
their language to the needs of the people. As Bishop of
Bishops it was his duty to look not only to the spiritual
needs of the Roman people but to see that the faithful
throughout the world were thoroughly instructed in the
fundamentals of their faith. The onslaught of false doctrines
could only be checked effectively if the rampart of true
doctrine were built firm and strong. The weeds of error
flourish only in the soil of ignorance. It is of little use to
hoe at the weeds while the soil remains unfertile. From
the lips of Pius X fell the lament of the prophet Osee: " There
is no knowledge of God in the land. Cursing and lying and
killing and theft and adultery have overflowed: and blood
hath touched blood. Therefore shall the land mourn and
every one that dwelleth in it shall languish " (iv. 1-3).

There was only one remedy for so great an evil—the
Catechism. In the encyclical, *Acerbo nimis*, the Pope
attributes the religious crisis and the havoc caused in the

Church by Modernism to ignorance of Christian Doctrine, and points out how necessary it is for the faithful to attend regularly the weekly instructions and for the clergy to teach with zeal, constancy and perseverance, because Christian Doctrine is the foundation of the sacerdotal ministry. Preaching against error in defence of the truth is truly praiseworthy and always to be commended, but it is useless unless preceded by a thorough grounding in the elements of the Faith. The seeds of religion, fallen upon the barren soil of ignorance, must needs perish. The Catechism is the plough which opens up the soul and prepares it for seeds of grace. Preaching to an ill-prepared congregation is so much waste of time.

In the encyclical strict regulations were laid down for the teaching of the Catechism, and many congresses have since been held to discuss the most practical means of applying these regulations to the needs of various nations and mentalities. Although this encyclical appeared two years before *Pascendi Dominici Gregis*, they really belong together. Both have the same aim—to lead the world back to a true recognition of God and to buttress the faith of the people against the storms of error and immorality.

As Bishop of Mantua, Mgr. Sarto had sent a proposal to the President of the First Catechetical Congress, held at Piacenza in 1889, that a standard Catechism should be drawn up, suited to the needs of all. It was now possible for him to put this plan into operation. He appointed a commission of theologians who, under his leadership, would formulate the questions and answers of a new Catechism according to the ideas which he had found most useful and practical in his own teaching at Mantua and Venice. The Catechism thus produced was used first of all in the diocese of Rome and later spread throughout Italy. It has been translated into many European languages. There are two books in it; the first is intended for younger children and treats the essentials rather summarily, and the second goes into more detail, but does not repeat the wording of the first.

Fifty years have passed since the publication of *Acerbo nimis*, but it is still important to-day, for the Church must be

on her guard now as then against the destructive influences
of the false teacher. At the International Catechetical
Congress held in October, 1950, Pius XII said: " The value
of any law or decree intended for the improvement of public
morality depends on religious instruction." The necessity
has not changed, and the passage of time has but made the
dilemma more pressing and urgent: " The Catechism or
destruction! "

" SINITE PARVULOS . . ."

The life of Pius X brings into relief the attraction he felt
for little children. His own purity of soul and innocence
of life were mirrored in their sinlessness and simplicity.
We have seen how, as a priest, he was able to come down to
their level and take part in their games and amusements
while, at the same time, opening up their minds to the truth
and their hearts to the infusion of divine grace, and we
know how he considered the Eucharist the best means for
procuring for these children the treasure of those graces
most necessary for them.

When he started his priestly ministry, children were
debarred from the altar rails by the severe views then
prevalent as to the age at which children ought to make their
First Holy Communion. Don Sarto as parish priest of Salzano
did not escape harsh criticism when he ignored those views
and permitted the children of his parish to approach the
Table of the Lord long before they had reached the usual age.
He was able to justify himself by quoting the " Summa " of
St. Thomas, who taught: " As soon as a child is capable of
distinguishing between the Sacred Species and ordinary
bread, he can be admitted to the reception of the Holy
Eucharist " (Summa Theol., 3rd Part: Quest. lxxx). This
teaching of the Angelic Doctor is based upon the practice
of the Church until the thirteenth century, and it has never
been frowned upon by Popes or Councils. If a child can
distinguish between good and evil and is thus capable of making
use of the Sacrament of Penance, why should he be denied
the benefits of the Holy Eucharist, which nourishes virtue
in his soul and turns his will away from sin?

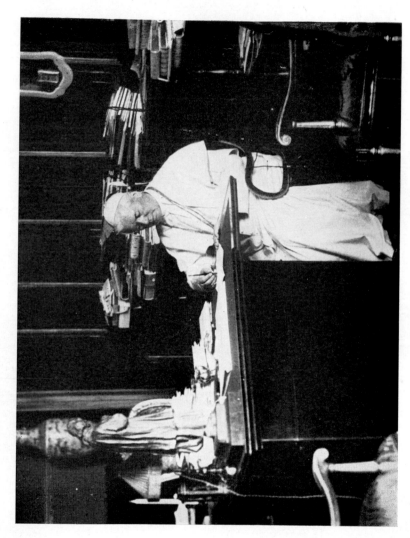

PIUS X IN HIS STUDY

Such severe views were the result of Jansenism, which taught people to regard the Holy Eucharist as a reward for virtue rather than as "an antidote and a medicine for human frailty." But Divine Providence had chosen as Pope one who would bring back to the minds of the people the fundamental truths about the Eucharist which had been forgotten, and with a strong hand wipe out an attitude towards it which was never intended by the Saviour at its institution on Holy Thursday.

December 20th, 1905, is a memorable day for all who love the Blessed Sacrament. The decree *Sacra Tridentina Synodus* once and for all put an end to heated discussion between those who thought of the Eucharist as a reward and those who thought of it as Christ Himself did, and threw open the tabernacle to all who desired to partake frequently and even daily of this Heavenly Bread. This was, indeed, the wish of the Saviour in instituting the Eucharist: that the faithful should nourish the life of their souls daily by partaking of the Food He gave, just as they nourish their bodies daily by eating ordinary food. Had there been any doubt about this, the Council of Trent would not have exhorted Catholics to receive Holy Communion every time they were present at Mass. If the right dispositions of faith, devotion and love are present in the soul, there is no reason why the faithful should refrain from the reception of Holy Communion and "especially," as the Pope said, "in times when the Catholic religion is everywhere attacked and charity has grown cold in the hearts of men."

Still greater was the happy decree of August 8th, 1910, *Quam singulari Christus amore*, which fixed the age for the reception of First Communion. It is difficult to see why there should have been such doubt and hesitation about permitting children to receive Holy Communion at an early age, when the Church had so long before determined the matter and the decrees of the Sacred Congregations in recent years had but repeated and confirmed ancient decrees. Not only did the Church permit it but she positively frowned upon those who had held the opposite view, as had been shown in her attitude to the Provincial Ecclesiastical Council of

Rouen, which had fixed the age for First Communion at a minimum of twelve years.

There is thus no real practical justification for the criticism which was widespread especially in France, of the decree of Pius X which stated: " Children should be led to the Table of the Lord at seven years of age and in some cases even earlier." The Pope had anticipated this criticism and now ignored it, leaving it to die the natural death which was soon to be its lot. Its death was signalized by the pilgrimage of a multitude of French children who came to Rome especially to thank the Holy Pope for allowing them to receive their Lord in Holy Communion at an early age.

REFORM OF THE CLERGY

Having established the foundations of the two major items on his programme of " Restoring all things in Christ," Pius X now turned his attention to the clergy. The principles of Modernism had caused a slackening of discipline and had diminished in many priests the true estimation of their dignity and vocation. While but a few priests followed the teachings of Modernism theoretically, many were influenced by its tendency to criticise the Church as " out of date " and in need of reform, and so the spirit of obedience and submission was greatly undermined.

Pius X knew that the world was in need of saintly priests, and that his plans for reform could only be realized if he started his reform in the sanctuary. He had already mentioned this in his first encyclical, when he recommended that " we priests must grow in sanctity of life and purity of doctrine if the people are to be formed in Christ," in exactly the same way as he had exhorted the clergy of Venice on September 5th, 1894, in his first pastoral letter as Patriarch: " Each one," he wrote, " must do his best to reform himself, because society is a mirror which reflects the spirit of the individual, of the family, of the city; and if each of us does his best to let Christ reign in his heart, then the whole society will be conquered for Christ."

The priesthood is a supernatural state created by God for a supernatural mission, in which knowledge plays an important but by no means the most important part. The ministry of the priest depends on his virtue and sanctity and therefore the Pope stressed time and time again that Seminaries should be on their guard against preparing young men for a worldly career, instead of training them to be true servants of God. The Cardinal Patriarch of Lisbon on May 5th, 1905, wrote that Seminaries should be what the Council of Trent wished them to be: " Homes of study and furnaces of piety." The Pope was determined that the greatest prudence and attention should be exercised in the choice of candidates for the priesthood, before admitting them to the Seminary, and that before they received Minor Orders the genuineness of their vocation should be tested by a strict scrutiny, lest any unworthy person should find his way into the Sanctuary. Those in authority should not be misled by eminent gifts of intellect or outstanding natural talent, but should judge the candidate by his foundation of true piety, the first sign of which is obedience to authority and absolute submission to the Church. The document which most clearly shows the priestly spirit of the Pope was the *Exhortation to the Catholic Clergy*, written on August 4th, 1908.

On September 18th, 1908, Pius X celebrated the golden jubilee of his own Ordination to the priesthood. It was the earnest wish of the Pope that the commemoration of such a date should not consist of a useless and empty outward display. For himself he wished to spend the day in silence and recollection, and he thought it fitting that the whole Church should join with him in thanking Our Lord for the fifty years of priesthood that He had granted to His Vicar on earth. It was at the same time a very suitable opportunity for putting before the minds of his priests the dignity and sanctity of their vocation. Without offending against modesty Pius X, a priest according to the Heart of God, could repeat the words of the Divine Saviour Whom he represented on earth: " I have given you an example that as I have done, so you do also " (*John* xiii. 15). The diversity of offices which he had held during the course of fifty years of priestly life

made it possible for him to stand as an example for all. His
life was the norm for all priestly activity: his every act and
word was a lesson to be studied and imitated by those who
wished their ministry to yield the greatest fruit.

The *Exhortation to the Clergy* was little more than a
description of his own virtues, though he would have
been the last person in the world to claim this. He
pointed out that the priest should be ever mindful of the
dignity of his vocation to offer the Holy Sacrifice of the Mass,
to preach the Gospel, and to act as physician of souls; that
a vocation so sublime, having a divine and not a human origin,
carried with it a strict obligation of striving for holiness and
ought to foster in his heart a deep sense of his own nothingness
rather than cause the recipient of so great a grace to become
puffed up with self-complacency. If a priest's life is not
modelled on that of his divine Master, it is empty and
meaningless.

While learning is of great importance to the priest in the
exercise of his mission, the abuse of knowledge could be a
great evil. But those, on the other hand, who are well
grounded in the science of the saints are certain to bring
a blessing on the souls under their care, even though the
world may regard them as ignorant and untalented. The
company of saints who adorn the pages of history is a proof
of this, for they did not work wonders because of the richness
of their intellect but because they were crucified to the
world.

The Pope then asks what means a priest must use in order
to become a tower of strength, and work amongst men as
an " alter Christus." The means are prayer, meditation,
regular examination of conscience, spiritual reading and the
practice of obedience, humility, mortification and penance.
He stresses these virtues because the priest, before all others,
is called to lead a life of self-denial in imitation of his divine
Master. These are the virtues stigmatized by the Modernists
as " passive virtues " in contrast to the " active virtues," but
Pius X warned his priests against this " heresy of action "
in the following words: " There are those who maintain that
the success of a priest lies in the care he takes of others, and

attach no importance whatever to the practice of interior virtues. They call these virtues 'passive' and demand that a priest should give all his strength to the development of the active life. Beware of this fallacy; it is fraught with error and breeds destruction.

"Christ does not change with the course of time, but is the same 'yesterday and to-day: and the same forever' (*Heb*. xiii. 8). His admonition, 'Learn of me, because I am meek and humble of heart,' was not meant for a particular phase of history, nor was the example He gave when 'He humbled Himself, becoming obedient unto death' only intended for the men of one age. In every age and in every phase of history the words of the apostle are valid: 'They that are Christ's have crucified their flesh, with the vices and concupiscences' (*Gal*. v. 24). The virtues of penance, mortification and self-denial are to be practised by all men but especially by priests who should apply to themselves the words of our predecessor, 'Oh, may the number of those priests increase who, like the saints of by-gone days, exercise the virtues of humility, mortification and obedience; they were mighty in action and their preaching was of the greatest value not only to the cause of religion but to the well-being of the state.'

"If a priest is governed by the odious vice of lust for worldly goods, self-gratification, or a constant effort to satisfy the desires of flesh and blood; if he seeks the praise and adulation of the world or if human wisdom alone inspires his direction of souls, it is because he has refused the invitation of the Master: 'If any man will come after Me, let him deny himself and take up his cross and follow Me' (*Matt*. xvi. 24)." The Pope closed his admonition with the prayer: "Holy Father, sanctify my priests."

Cardinal Bourne, Archbishop of Westminster, thus commented on this document which so eminently synthesizes the striving for priestly perfection: "This springs from the heart of a true priest and rings true to the heart of the divine Master . . . may the zealous words of this holy Pope, who was Christ's Vicar on earth for eleven years, imbue the hearts of all priests with their fundamental lesson."

" THE GOOD COUNTRY CURATE "

Had the documents and decrees published by Pius X as Bishop of Mantua and Patriarch of Venice been better known, and had modesty not concealed his outstanding ability, he would never have been called " the good curate from the country." Long experience had taught him that his programme, " to renew all things in Christ," was quite impossible unless he had a well educated and efficient clergy. The progress of learning, the new findings of science and the activity of his enemies convinced him still more that his reform must start in the Seminaries. Unless these divine workshops produced a continuous stream of young priests thoroughly instructed in the Christian Sciences and distinguished for holiness of life, he could not hope to grapple with the ever increasing forces of evil.

Lack of means and of professors deprived many dioceses of Seminaries of their own, and the same privations hindered others from running their Seminaries with all the efficiency desirable. The Pope's plan was to amalgamate the smaller Seminaries and so provide each group of dioceses with a large one which should aim at the high ideals he proposed.

The plan met with great difficulties and much resistance as soon as he had mentioned it in his letter of November 16th, 1913, to the Rector of the newly-founded Seminary of the Lateran. To many Bishops the thought of being separated from their own candidates for the priesthood was distasteful. Pius X understood such antipathy and to some extent regarded it as justifiable, but he would not alter his firm decision, for higher interests were at stake. Only those dioceses were excepted whose Bishops could guarantee for their seminarians a thorough education, a strict discipline and a firm grounding in the spiritual life, and for their Seminaries a stable economic footing.

The decline of the spiritual life so noticeable in many Seminaries was due largely to the substitution of modern ideas and up-to-date systems of study for traditional methods. Pius X wrote to the French Bishops: " It is very sad to observe in the younger members of the clergy many new ideas which are often erroneous as to the very fundamentals of Catholic

Faith. What is the cause of this? It is undoubtedly contempt for the methods of scholastic philosophy and disregard for a discipline to which the Church has always given the greatest praise."

Leo XIII had been aware of the attempt to abolish Scholastic Thomistic philosophy. His encyclical, *Aeterne Patris,* of August 4th, 1879, showed how this great Pontiff had foreseen the injurious effects which must be the outcome of so perilous an attitude. He had done his best to check the tide of new ideas which swept the Church in his day, but his commands had not been heeded. The high esteem which the Modernist had for the so-called " active virtues " and positive sciences had roused a storm of resistance against the studies which were the key to all wisdom. Pius X showed clearly why so many promising young intellectuals had wandered from the path of truth: because their intellectual activities were not founded in the basic principles of sound philosophy. Modernism did not want to destroy the Church, but to reform it and adapt it to its own way of thinking; many of its supporters went so far as to prophesy the end of the Church and tried to quote Aquinas in defence of their fallacious teaching.

Pius X saw in the teaching and philosophy of St. Thomas, which had shone so splendidly down the course of the centuries, an incomparable means for the defence of truth. He ordered that all philosophical training should be carried out according to the principles of the Angelic Doctor. St. Thomas should have the place of honour in the Seminaries and Universities because only on the foundation of his all-embracing and thoroughly Christian philosophy could a successful course of studies be built. Similar commands given by Leo XIII had been largely ignored.

The condemnation of Modernism would have lost its purpose if it could at the same time be shown that the Church, far from fearing the advance of science, was well equipped for dealing with anyone who dared to raise his voice against her teachings. For this reason Pius X wanted to found a Biblical Institute in which the Sacred Scriptures should be studied with all the modern methods of linguistics and archæology. As Bishop and Cardinal, Pius X had shown great interest in the progress of Scriptural studies; soon after his elevation to the throne of Peter he published the apostolic letter, *Scripturæ Sanctæ*, in which it can be seen what great importance he attached to the study of the Bible. He wrote: " It is the duty of Our apostolic office . . . to see to the advance of the study of Holy Scripture among the clergy as much as possible, especially in our time when the human intellect tries to overstep the boundaries of its own limitations and attack the fountain of divine revelation."

The encyclical, *Providentissimus Deus*, of Leo XIII showed that the founding of a Biblical Institute in Rome had been in the mind of the predecessor of Pius X. But the project had gone no further than the planning stage. In 1902 a Biblical Commission had been appointed to encourage the study of the Sacred Scriptures and to direct the exegesis of the inspired text. Pius X went still further. He gave the Biblical Commission a certain foundation and ordered them to watch carefully over all books published on the Scriptures. The Biblical Institute was to make use of the most modern means of research and was to show the world that the Church with her inflexible dogma was not a thing of the past but a leader in modern scholarship, in the proper sense of the term. Though Pius X had this plan in mind right from the beginning of his pontificate, lack of funds made it impossible to see its realization until 1909.

.   .   .   .   .

Another glorious work of Pius X, which we cannot pass over, is his collecting into one book the laws which govern the discipline of the Church, a book now known as the *Code of Canon Law*. An eminent Italian lawyer said that this work of Pius X deserved the same praise as the work of Justinian in the codifying of Roman Law. Not many days after his election to the Papacy, he made known his intention of undertaking this work which was of such great importance to the Church. As Pastor of Souls in Venice and Mantua he had realized the extraordinary difficulty of referring to decrees and important documents on Church discipline which had never been compiled into one book but were dispersed through many. Furthermore, it was difficult to know exactly what decrees were to be followed, for many of them had been annulled by more recent ones.

A clear, well-ordered collection was urgently demanded. On March 19th, 1904, Pius X ordered, by his Motu Proprio, *Arduum sane munus*, that the Law of the Church should be codified as quickly as possible. He added: "We hasten this measure, for advanced age makes us fear that We will not see its completion."

But strange are the ways of Providence. After eleven years of untiring work during which he followed the progress of the task step by step, the completion was left to his successor. When Benedict XV in a solemn speech announced to the College of Cardinals on September 4th, 1916, that the Laws of the Church had finally been codified, he referred to the necessity there had been for it and the great benefit it would bestow upon the Church, concluding: "Divine Providence has arranged that the honour of bestowing this termendous service on the Church goes to Our predecessor, Pius X, of happy memory. You all know with what great fervour he undertook this gigantic task from the very beginning of his Pontificate and the zeal and perseverance he exercised in striving for its speedy completion. While it was not granted to him to see its completion, the honour of the work is his alone. Therefore his name will be celebrated in the pages of history alongside such eminent names as Innocent III, Honorius III and Gregory IX, who did so much for the development of Canon Law. It is with the greatest satisfaction that We publish what he created."

"I LOOK AT THE CRUCIFIX"

The greatest sorrow which lay upon the heart of Leo XIII when the Lord called him to his reward was that he had not effected religious peace in France, and that he had failed to bring to a halt the development which had as its aim a complete break with the Church. The series of laws hostile to the Church, which had been initiated in 1880, had not in the least been changed by the famous Pastoral, *Au Milieu*, of February 16th, 1892. It was evident that the purpose of the French Government was to ignore the terms of the Concordat and to bring about a complete break with Rome. The milder members of the Government were opportunists for the most part and easily yielded to the more radical elements.

The last attempt to come to an understanding with the President of the French Republic was the letter which Leo XIII addressed to M. Loubet on March 23rd, 1900, in which he wrote: " It would be bitter indeed for Us, nearing the close of life, to see the failure of Our efforts, which were influenced only by good-will towards the French nation and its Government. We have repeatedly given you proofs not only of careful attention but also of Our special affection." The exile of Religious Communities from France in 1901 was proof that the good-will of Leo had been disregarded and that his efforts had failed.

The struggle with Pius X started almost immediately after his coronation when the revenues allotted to the Archbishop of Marseilles by the Concordat were stopped for no apparent reason. It was clear that the plan of the French Government was to provoke protest on the part of the Church, in order to establish an excuse for breaking off diplomatic relations with the Holy See. But the Pope was well aware of this and he was determined that if diplomatic relations were broken off the world should know who was responsible.

The long desired excuse was found on April 24th, 1904, when the Prime Minister of France, M. Combes, paid an official visit to the Italian king. Because of the unusual relations which existed at the time between the Italian State and the Holy See, the French Government felt sure that such a visit would provoke a protest. This plan of the Freemasons would have failed had it not been for the indiscretion of the Prince of Monaco, who informed the public of the protest which Cardinal Merry del Val had directed to the states in diplomatic relations with the Holy See. The French Prime Minister used this protest as an excuse for the withdrawal of his ambassador. This was May 28th, 1904. While the withdrawal of the ambassador did not immediately signify the breaking off of diplomatic relations, it was a preparation for it. The immediate cause was the action of Pius X in deposing two French Bishops, the Bishops of Dijon and Laval, who had shown themselves wholly unworthy of their office. The reasons which prompted the deposition of these Bishops were purely ecclesiastical and in no way the concern of political powers.

The French Prime Minister immediately declared publicly that there was no hope of coming to an understanding with the Vatican, and that he had therefore decided to break off diplomatic relations. The mission of the Apostolic Nuncio in Paris was regarded as finished, and he was immediately invited to leave France.

The speech which Pius X made three months later on November 14th, 1904, to the Consistory, left no doubt as to the paradoxical nature of the objection brought against the Church and showed who was responsible for the breach of diplomatic relations with France. He showed how the French had manifested complete disregard for the agreements they had made: the obstacles they had put in the way of the free exercise of religion; how disrespectfully they had treated bishops and priests; the interference of the secular power in the Seminaries; the determination to abolish Religious Instruction from the schools and utter contempt for the authority of the Vicar of Christ. He added: "Unfortunately we cannot hope that this opposition to the Church will soon come to an end, but on the contrary we must be prepared for incidents of a more serious nature; but they will find us fearless, armed with the strength of the Words of Christ: 'The servant is not greater than his master. If they have persecuted me they will also persecute you. . . In the world you shall have distress. But have confidence. I have overcome the world '" (*John* xv. 20; xvi. 33).

This address exposed to the world the insidious aims of the French Government and left a deep impression on all the faithful. Attempts were made in Paris to damp that impression by telling the people that the breach with the

Church was the "inevitable consequence of circumstances and had in no way the character of a reprisal."

In the meantime in the French Parliament long and heated discussions were held with a view to formulating the new law against the Church. On December 9th, 1905, the law was finally passed and two days later published. The injustice of the law was self-evident; its aim was not so much the suppression of the Church as its subjection to the State.

The Pope watched the development of the situation with keen attention, and on February 11th, 1906, in the encyclical *Vehementer* he made known to the world what he thought about it. He opened his letter by expressing his deep sorrow that the century-old bond which united France to the Church had been ruthlessly severed. He examined the clauses of the "Law of Separation" and condemned in the strongest terms those who attempted to justify it. The spirit of the law was that Church and State were two absolutely distinct societies and that between spiritual and temporal affairs there could be no connection. He said: "This opinion is completely false and an insult to God. It is the primary duty of the State to assist its subjects in every way possible to reach their eternal salvation. In any Christian State separation from the Church is reprehensible, but in France it is far more so, because she has for so many centuries been preferred before all other nations by the Church, and her glory and her greatness rise largely from her connection with the Holy See. The breaking of the traditional union must necessarily despoil her of much of her moral power and prestige."

If principles of gratitude made no appeal to France, principles of honour should have made her blush before the nations of the world to disregard her part in a bilateral agreement such as the Concordat of 1801. Even if the separation of Church and State could have been tolerated, there still remained a duty on the part of the Government to respect the freedom and independence of the Church; but these too had been abolished by the clauses of the law, which sought to subject the Church to the State and despised her Divine Institution.

There was a certain group of Catholics in France who, while confessing allegiance to the Pope, represented to the French Hierarchy that the Church ought to give the new law a fair trial. A meeting of the French clergy which took place from May 30th until June 1st, 1906, gave these opportunists the answer they deserved. They pointed out that most of the clauses of the new law were not in harmony with the divine constitution of the Church. While the squabble as to the possibility of a compromise for the sake of saving the property of the French clergy went on in France, discussions were held by the Cardinals in Rome under the presidency of Pius X.

The Cardinals of the Roman curia were divided in their opinion. Some held the view that the future of the French clergy depended on the reaching of a satisfactory compromise. They knew that unless a compromise were reached the clergy would be expelled from France and their property and possessions confiscated, and they were of the opinion that no greater evil could take place. Pius X listened to the opinions of all; pondered them, prayed about them. For him it was not a question of deciding between loss of property or adaptation of the Church to the new French law, but simply a question of right and wrong. Speaking to a Frenchman he said: " We are not a diplomat; Our task is to defend the Law of God. The Church is divinely instituted by Jesus Christ, and no earthly power can force her to yield her rights or her freedom. We know that many are concerned about the goods of the Church but Our concern is her good. We would prefer to suffer the loss of churches of stone than risk the destruction of the Church herself."

One day during the course of the discussions he looked at the crucifix with an expression both inspired and inspiring, and exclaimed: " I look upon the crucifix! " Cardinal Ferrata, who had defended the " compromise " most strongly in order to save the property of the Church in France, was so touched by these words and gestures of the Pope that he approached him and said: " Holy Father, we have stated our view, but if Your Holiness sees fit to decide differently we are most willing to submit."

The outcome of the discussions in Rome was the encyclical *Gravissimo Officii munere*, which made it quite clear that the Church had no intention of bowing down to the civil power and that the Holy Father regarded all ideas of compromise as odious. At the beginning of the letter the Pope repeated that the Church could not possibly accept the new law of the French Government as this was contrary to her God-given constitution. Then he declared: " Our conscience would not permit Us to tolerate any form of experiment on this question in order to save the French Catholics from the dangers which threaten them. . ."

Superficial observers began immediately to criticize the Sovereign Pontiff for this decision, regarding it as a thoughtless step and an unnecessary surrender of the property of the French clergy. In reality it was the decision which saved France. The immediate result of it was the loss to the Church of tremendous possessions and the extreme poverty of French priests. How right was Senator Vittorio Emanuele Orlando when he wrote: " No greater stand has ever been witnessed than that which Pius X took in utterly rejecting all compromise. This rejection meant for French Catholics the loss of all their possessions."

He was asked how he expected the Archbishop of Paris to exercise his office without church, income or house. But the Pope replied: " We can give the office to a Franciscan who is bound by his Rule to live on alms and to exercise absolute poverty." The decision of Pius X is magnificent in its apostolic spirit. It is true that victory cost the Church millions of francs, but the object achieved far exceeded any sacrifice that could be made.

Pius X had won a moral victory but the French Government wreaked vengeance by the confiscation of the property and possessions of 30,000 parishes and 100,000 priests—a measure which had been threatened by the law. Mgr. Montagnini, who had remained in Paris after the expulsion of the Apostolic Nuncio, was quickly conveyed to the frontier. The archives of the Nuncio's residence were broken open and searched in the hope of finding some document which could be used in evidence against the Church. M. Briand declared in

Parliament: " The law has been so framed that the Church cannot glory in the honour of persecution."

In the letter *Une fois encore*, of January 6th, 1907, which the Pope addressed to the Church in France, he once again outlined the indefensible behaviour of the Government. In a touching way the Pope described how much he suffered in union with the faithful and clergy of France and what a great consolation their loyalty and obedience had been to him. He then briefly repeated the history of the breach with the Church, showing how it was to be ascribed to the malice of the Government and protesting strongly against the specious arguments by which they sought to justify the pillage of ecclesiastical lands and property. He continued: " The Church has not yielded up her right to these possessions; they belong to the worship of God and have been ruthlessly confiscated. The Church was faced with the choice between material ruin and the surrender of the rights given her by God. She courageously refused the latter though this meant the loss of all the world holds valuable. She still refuses and will continue to refuse the provisions of that perfidious law which is absolutely incompatible with her mission. What a lame and impotent conclusion the Government has drawn in saying that the Church has relinquished her right to property by her refusal to accept an unjust law, and that their own robbery of her property is merely distribution of goods which have no owner! "

At the end of the encyclical the Pope once again solemnly declared: " No other course of action was left open to Us without greatly offending Our conscience. Fearlessly, therefore, we look to the judgment of history, for it was never Our intention to humble a civil power or oppose any particular form of Government, but merely to defend the rights of the Church founded by Christ Jesus Our Lord."

This letter of the Holy Father caused great surprise in France. No one had expected that he would take such a firm stand. Clémenceau said: " Diplomats had foreseen much of what happened, but no one conceived what resistance the Pope would show to the new law." The enemies of the Church had rested in the hope that they would succeed in creating a split between the French hierarchy and Rome, but what they actually achieved was a strengthening of the bonds which united them and ultimately brought victory to the cause of God.

As soon as the State ceased to care for the support of priests the faithful began to contribute to it abundantly, as Pius X had foreseen that they would, when he said: " The life of the French clergy does not depend on the Government." French Catholics were fully aware of the reasons for the Pope's decision, and they were fully prepared to stand by him in support of that decision. The generosity of the faithful, rich and poor, was an unparalleled spectacle of unity and discipline. The Pope wrote on November 18th, 1908: " We shall never cease thanking God for the spirit which inspired Our children in France. Our counsel to follow Us in suffering was obeyed gloriously. Our only sorrow is that We cannot participate in all the bitterness of the battle which you experience. Now France has really shown herself worthy of the title, ' Eldest daughter of the Church.' Whilst We have recited with tears the psalm ' Miserere ' on account of the tribulations and sorrows which have broken over the Church in France, We have chanted the ' Te Deum ' with joy and gratitude for the consolation of witnessing the spirit of sacrifice and loyalty of the faithful to the Church."

In future years when the Pope spoke of the incidents that took place in France, it was with an expression of joy on account of the love the people had shown to the Church rather than of sorrow for the injustice the Government had shown to the people. Nor did France forget the heroism of the Pope. On the morning of August 20th, 1914, when the news of his death was announced, an atmosphere of deep sorrow settled upon the Catholics in France, and the spectacle seen at Notre Dame as 30,000 people clustered around the catafalque covered with the banner of Joan of Arc was a manifestation of the sentiments which carried that Catholic nation to victory.

The Pope had prophesied that the future would know that his decision in that hour of darkness was justified. The future has indeed shown the wisdom and inspiration of that great

PIUS X AT MASS

Pope who declared to the French clergy: "We lose our churches, but the Church remains secure; it is better to sacrifice property than freedom."

CHURCH MUSIC

Even a brief treatment of the reign of Pope Pius X would be incomplete without some mention of the work he did for the reform of Church music. We have already seen the active part he played in this respect as Bishop and Patriarch in the dioceses he governed; that same activity was extended to the Universal Church when she was committed by Divine Providence to his guidance.

In his Motu Proprio on Church music he explains that one of the chief functions of the Vicar of Christ is to maintain and promote the decorum of the house of God wherein the divine mysteries are celebrated. The object of such decorum is first of all the worship of God and secondly the uniting of the faithful in common prayer. The abuse most prevalent in his time was that which affected the sacred chants. This, the Pope explains, is due chiefly to the fact that music like all arts changes with the spirit of the age. In modern times, Church music has been affected by the theatre and by prejudices which, even among pious and responsible persons, have caused a reaction to the injunctions of the Sacred Canons and the decrees of many Popes.

In recent years, he goes on to explain, much has been done for the restoration of the spirit of the Church in this respect, especially in the Eternal City where groups of illustrious men have united into societies to restore Church music to its proper place of honour. This, unfortunately, is not general. The Pope considers it his duty to condemn all that is out of harmony with the rules and spirit of Church music.

The Christian spirit demands the sanctity and dignity of the temple. It is useless to hope for the blessings of God while putting into the hands of the Redeemer the scourges with which of old he drove unworthy profaners from the temple.

Music suitable for the house of God must be governed by the three rules of sanctity, beauty of form, and universality. Its sanctity must defend it from the profanity of modern theatrical melodies, its beauty of form must give it an artistic nature and its universality must make it suitable for all nations.

The two forms of music most in keeping with these rules are the Gregorian chant and the classic polyphony. The closer a piece of music is to the Gregorian chant the more sacred and liturgical it becomes. The works of Pierluigi da Palestrina, though differing vastly in form, can be placed beside the melodies of the Gregorian chant because of their rigid adherence to the three rules above mentioned.

Modern music is not to be condemned because it is modern, but in its composition and use great care must be taken to avoid a theatrical style. Though laymen sing these melodies they should resemble a liturgical choir as much as possible, and hence, whenever solo singers are permitted, they should not be allowed to predominate. It would be better to select for the soprano and contralto parts young boys rather than women.

While the use of the organ is permitted for the purpose of accompanying the singers, preludes and interludes must be governed by our three rules and should not be allowed to interrupt the flow of the chant. Frivolous instruments such as drums, cymbals and bells must never be used in the church, but bands may be allowed in processions outside.

The Pope closed his Motu Proprio with an exhortation to Bishops and Pastors to promote with zeal these reforms, which for a long time had been demanded by the faithful of the whole world, so that contempt should not be shown for the authority of the Church which had so repeatedly inculcated them.

Chapter IX

CHARACTERISTIC VIRTUES

THE POPE OF THE SUPERNATURAL

NOTHING could have been more true or exact than the title which the Piedmontese Bishops ascribed to Pius X: "The Pope of the supernatural." Those who were fortunate enough to have known him carried away a life-long impression of his gentle smile, the sympathetic tones of his voice and his kindness and consideration for the needs and opinions of all. All who spoke with him have commented upon the glowing expression of his countenance; and, referring to this, one Cardinal concluded: "Pius X is a Pope not of this world but of Heaven." We are told that it is quite impossible for anyone who has not seen him to comprehend the charm which emanated from his kindly soul and which filled those about him with a fervour and love previously unknown.

Mgr. Baudrillart, a member of the French Academy, who became Cardinal in 1935, paid a special visit to Rome every year from 1907 to 1914 to see Pius X. He writes: "His appearance, his words and his personality manifested his generosity, firmness and faith: generosity revealed the man, firmness the leader, and faith the priest, the Pope, the man of God. A more spiritual man it would be hard to imagine. 'Deus providebit,' which was ever on his lips, characterized the faith burning in his soul. When he had made a decision he did not worry about the consequences any more, in the knowledge that God would change insignificant and passing evil into useful and permanent good. He seemed to have a special intuition for always doing the right thing. Calm and unperturbed, he pointed out evil wherever he came across it, and he never allowed fear of men to make him deviate from the path of duty. Never was there a Pope

who fulfilled more perfectly the rôle of reformer. Ever
faithful to his principle ' Instaurare omnia in Christo ' he
set about and accomplished his task with incomparable energy.
While Governments feared him, the people loved him and
were inspired with confidence by his fatherly spirit."

Cardinal Henri Luçon, Archbishop of Rheims, wrote in
a letter of August 15th, 1923: " In the many audiences I had
with His Holiness Pius X, I always felt deeply impressed and
edified by his spirit of faith, his completely Christian outlook
and by the sanctity of his words."

The Argentinian Ambassador to the Holy See, Señor Daniele
Garcia-Mansilla, testifies: " The first impression the Servant
of God made on me was that here was a man from whom
piety emanated. I could not restrain my tears—a sensation
I had never before experienced. I must add that of all the
Popes whose acquaintance I had the honour to make, none
made a deeper impression on me than Pius X."

The Servant of God, Don Luigi Orione, who is so dear
to the Italian people on account of his love for his neighbour,
says: " On more than one occasion the countenance of
Pius X seemed to me as though illumined with a supernatural
light."

Another member of the French Academy testifies: " It
was not possible to come into contact with Pius X without
being deeply moved by his affability and magnanimity.
Pilgrims from every part of the world commented on his
kindness. At public audiences he appeared with all the
majesty of the Vicar of Christ, while his eyes seemed to look
into eternity."

EVANGELICAL SIMPLICITY

No other Pope in history is known to have passed through
all the grades of the Hierarchy before ascending the Chair
of Peter. But while the rustic boy of Riese received honour
after honour until he became the saintly Bishop of Rome, his
character never seemed to change. The only visible change
was his clothing The deep humility which inspired him as
he begged from door to door in a remote country village in

order to collect sufficient money to defray the necessary expenses of seminary life, was only deepened and solidified as he was carried into St. Peter's on the Sedia Gestatoria and suffered nothing at his being proclaimed throughout the world Vicar of Christ and head of the Church.

Until his dying day, Pius X never succeeded in overcoming his natural dislike for all forms of ostentation and splendour, and the only moment he welcomed on solemn occasions was that in which he could take off his magnificent vestments and return to his humble way of life. He permitted himself only that pomp which was demanded to preserve the traditional solemnity of the ceremonial. Personal attention was wholly repugnant to his sensitive nature, and he was often heard to say: " It is so distasteful to see people suffer inconveniences for my sake," or " With me everyone should feel at home."

As soon as he was elected he broke the century-old custom that the Pope should dine alone. He took his meals as simply as any parish priest and dispensed with attendants at table. The Aiutanti di Camera or the Noble Guard accompanied him only when they were essential and never in the Vatican Gardens. The number of servants in his Anticamera was reduced to a minimum. He forbade applause when he entered the Basilica of St. Peter's, and at private audiences he would not allow the kiss of the foot. Visitors were greeted with a few homely gestures: he bade them sit down and sometimes even fetched a chair for them. With great simplicity he conversed with his gardeners and Aiutanti di Camera, showing great interest in their welfare, their families and the work they were doing. He often pressed a few coins into their hands. When the complaint was made that he was lowering his dignity, he always replied: " Who is higher and who is lower in the eyes of God? Don't forget that God sees things on a different plane."

Governors of States, kings, princes and ambassadors, simple peasants and world famous personalities, fervent Catholics and orthodox Jews could all feel at ease in his presence, sure of being received with incomparable kindness and a simplicity that won all hearts to him. Like the divine Master in the

midst of the multitude in Palestine, Pius X stood among his
people as one of them, but at the same time a grace and
affection went out from him that was not of this earth.
When the people of Tombolo or Salzano came to visit their
Don Giuseppe they approached him as easily as long ago they
had approached their curate or parish priest. Their visits
carried his mind back to the days of his youth, to the time he
loved so much and to which he would gladly return if such
were the will of God.

The spectacle which took place at his public audiences
left a lasting impression on all who attended them; a
friendliness and spirit of brotherly love seldom seen in large
crowds of people seemed to prevail. Many with tears in
their eyes went away feeling inwardly changed. These
audiences have been aptly described as " A mission for the
people."

A young Hungarian of Rumanian descent was admitted to
one of the private audiences. When the Pope entered the
room he was covered with confusion because he was a member
of the Orthodox Church. Pius X approached and immediately
embraced him, saying: " Catholics and Orthodox, all are
my children." The Hungarian was so deeply moved that
after the audience he inquired from one of the prelates in
the Anticamera how he ought to set about being instructed
in the Catholic religion, as he did not want to leave Rome a
non-Catholic.

POPE OF THE CHILDREN

The poorer and simpler the visitor, the happier Pius X
seemed to be. In the company of children his love knew
no bounds, for in their eyes he saw reflected the purity of
the children of God, and in his heart rang the words of the
divine Saviour: " Suffer the little children to come unto me
and forbid them not, for of such is the kingdom of heaven "
(*Mark* x. 14).

He had shown a deep love for children as curate of Tombolo
and parish priest of Salzano; why should it not be so now
when he was pastor and father of all souls? A replica of

the scene which took place on the hills of Galilee, as Jesus stood in the midst of the children, could often be seen in the Cortile della Pigna as the holy Pope standing on a platform looked down on a multitude of young people. They listened carefully to his every word as though it came directly from heaven, and the thousands of little hearts beat in unison with the great, pure, generous heart of the father of Christendom. When he had finished speaking to them about Jesus and explaining the Catechism, he walked among them speaking kindly to those near him and often picking the smaller ones up in his arms. Here there was no room for formalities or restrictions; all was freedom, love and kindness.

The kind old man moving among the children, talking to them about the little Jesus of Nazareth, answering their simple questions in a still simpler way and telling them about their dear Mother, Mary, is no other than the author of *Pascendi*, the man of iron who smashed the resistance of the Freemasons in Venice, made the lofty theories of the Modernists appear like old women's tales, and stood out, almost single-handed, against one of the most powerful nations in Europe. It was the same power he used to counter the wiles of the French Government as to kindle the love of Jesus in the hearts of his children.

The mothers of Palestine delighted to carry their little ones to Jesus to get His blessing on their innocent souls. Pius X was determined that the innocent souls of children should receive the Blessing of Jesus in Holy Communion before the evils of the world had a chance to influence the course of their lives. Again and again he repeated: " It is better for children to be sanctified by the reception of Jesus in Holy Communion, while their hearts are still pure, than to wait until the devil has got his grip on them."

The genuine holiness of the Pope was alone responsible for the decree of August 8th, 1910, which permitted and encouraged children to make their First Communion at as early an age as possible. While this decree was welcomed with joy throughout the Christian world, there were not wanting those who immediately began to criticize it as rash and unnecessary.

To some of the Cardinals Pius X described as the happiest moment of his life that in which a remarkable incident took place as the result of this decree; 400 French children who had just received their First Holy Communion at an early age, made a pilgrimage to Rome to thank the Holy Father who had made it possible for them to receive their Lord so young. They presented him with an album containing the signatures of 135,000 French children who also wished to convey their gratitude and love for the Pope who had made such a difference to their lives.

The Superior General of the Assumptionists accompanied the children to Rome. Solemn Mass was celebrated by Cardinal Vincenzo Vannutelli in the Basilica of Santa Maria Maggiore. After the Mass the Superior General said: " Emperors and kings have come to Rome in order to kneel at the feet of the Vicar of Christ; knights and crusaders have come to beg his blessing; representatives of all nations and classes to pay theirrespects to the Head of the Church, but never till this day has a crusade of children come to the Holy City to thank His Holiness for a benefit which he has bestowed upon them."

Two days later the children were received by the Pope in the Sistine Chapel in solemn audience. They were full of excitement and enthusiasm; they pushed each other, stood on their toes, jumped on to benches in order to catch a glimpse of the Head of the Church of whom they had heard their mothers speaking so much. They saw the stately old man, dressed in white cassock, enter the chapel. On his face was a look of kindness and an affectionate smile. They listened to his words and each received from his hands a little silver medal in token of his appreciation of the gratitude and love of the little pilgrims. Those who were near handed him letters, others spoke to him without any signs of shyness or timidity, asking him for all sorts of favours and blessings. . . " Restore health to my sister, Holy Father," " Convert my mother, dear Holy Father," " Bless my parents," etc. As the children left the Sistine Chapel they turned and with one voice thanked the Holy Father, and finished with the words, " We shall come again, dear Holy Father."

HIS MEEKNESS

Did Pius X lacerate his body with the discipline? Did he fast on bread and water, or attempt living on the top of a pillar? Was he raised from the ground in ecstasy? No! There is not the slightest shred of evidence for anything of that sort in his life, but the Process of Beatification assures us that he constantly practised interior mortification and denial of his own will. Many witnesses observe that his life was a constant struggle in order to gain complete self-mastery, and no physical mortification could be greater than this. He was not born with a big generous heart: this was the result of prayer and self-denial. By nature he had a fiery temperament, but his wonderful strength of will converted him into one of the meekest of men. One of his private secretaries asked him how was he able to control himself in the face of such grave dangers and difficulties. " Only with the self-mastery which is gained by years of practice," came the simple reply, which gave evidence to the internal struggle he continually waged.

Whether on account of small, irritating daily inconveniences or major difficulties which left the honour of the Church and his own good name at stake, no one ever saw him angry. " I can safely assert," wrote his Secretary of State, Cardinal Merry del Val, " that I have never noticed in him an ungoverned movement, not even in things which caused him the greatest internal pain. Even when he was obliged to reprove, he always remained completely master of himself and expressed his grief and displeasure with tranquillity, mildness and fatherly care. He manifested a just anger only when the rights of the Church were in danger or God was blasphemed."

From the fact that he succeeded in preserving during the eleven trying years of his Pontificate, his happiness, mildness and untiring zeal, it is quite evident that he did not depend on himself or work for himself. He worked for God and so could not be frustrated; his ambition was God's glory and so he learned the triumph of failure.

As he relied wholly on Christ, it made no difference to him that his purpose of renewing all things in Christ was

criticized, opposed and mistaken for self-glorification. In
spite of all the disappointments and calamities of his reign,
he was never known to utter a word of bitterness or complaint.
Sometimes in moments of great sorrow and loneliness
he would breathe the words of Isaias: " De gentibus non est
vir mecum—And of the gentiles there is not a man with
me " (lxiii. 3).

HUMBLE OF HEART

The humility which had characterized the son of the
Cursore of Riese, as bare-footed he ran messages for his
mother or assisted his father in his modest employment,
shone in all its splendour and aroused universal admiration
when he had ascended the throne of St. Peter as Head of the
Universal Church.   His Secretary of State, Cardinal Merry
del Val, wrote: " His humility was truly heroic and admirable.
It showed itself particularly when difficulties arose.   I have
never seen anything quite like it, for it seemed second nature
to him."   This evidence is corroborated by a host of witnesses
and incidents.

Pius X always considered himself insignificant; he showed
dislike for any kind of fuss about his person and carefully
avoided any manifestation of a domineering attitude.   Cardinal
Merry del Val writes: " He never let his authority be felt
except in extreme cases as a last resort.   He preferred to
govern his priests by force of gentle persuasion rather than
by his authority as Pope.   Nothing could be more disagreeable
for him than imposing new burdens on others or asking
others to make sacrifices."

He seldom spoke about himself, but when he did he
discussed things which others would have carefully avoided—
his humble origin, the great poverty of his childhood days, the
fact that he had no academic degrees.   These topics were
often introduced into the conversation at audiences, but
they never had the effect of lowering him in anyone's
estimation.

On April 14th, 1904, when the Archbishop of Palermo,
Cardinal Celesia, died, a deputation of nobles came to Rome

to beg the Pope to preserve their tradition of having as Archbishop an aristocrat and a Doctor of Theology. The request immediately brought to the mind of Pius X the thought of the little cottage of Riese. He replied sternly but with a touch of humour: "I know a curate who was neither a noble nor a Doctor of Theology who was appointed parish priest; that parish priest was made a Canon and then a Bishop; that Bishop who was neither a Doctor of Theology nor an aristocrat was created Cardinal and then elected Pope, and it is the Pope who is now speaking with you."

Pius X was proud. He was proud of his little home in a remote village, of his humble, saintly mother, of the hardships of his childhood, his long journeys to Castelfranco Veneto, the simple meals of coarse food taken in the dim light of an oil lamp which burnt in the kitchen. With the greatest pleasure he recalled the little white church, the shrine of the Madonna of Cendrole and the happy hours he had spent there with the other children of the village.

The thought of the great dignity that had been bestowed upon him kept constantly before his mind the thought of his own unworthiness. When he was told that his politics were criticized both within and without the Vatican and that he had been named the " good country curate," he smiled and said, "I know I haven't the subtle mind of a politician; I am only a poor peasant and have only one point of view— the Crucifix."

Never did he attribute success to his own initiative, ability or experience though he had many gifts of spirit and intellect, by which, as the Minister Orlando says, " he ranks among the greatest Popes of the Church." When he astonished statesmen by his detailed knowledge of all branches of learning and by his wisdom in dealing with human and national problems he would call them " old reminiscences of school life," or say that he had heard them from other people. Cardinal Merry del Val wrote: " The Prince of Bülow had immense admiration for Pius X. The Pope surprised the statesman by the lucidity with which he comprehended every situation and by his foresight and clear judgment about men and things. Speaking of his audiences, the statesman

told me: ' I have made the acquaintance of many rulers and
princes, but I have rarely found in any of them such a clear
and all-embracing knowledge of human nature as in His
Holiness.' " Count Golochowski, Count Sturza, Sir Wilfrid
Laurier, Mr. John Redmond and many other eminent
statesmen have spoken in a similar strain about the capabilities
and characteristics of the Pope.

All who had the privilege of attending his audiences
have commented on the inexplicable attraction which they
experienced for the white-clad figure who spoke to them,
smiled at them and made them feel that they were in the
presence of a saint.   When people mentioned this fact to
him he would interrupt their eulogies with: " This is the power
that has been bestowed on me; I have nothing to do with
it; it is your faith and not my virtue."   To those who asked
him to work miracles he would reply jokingly: " Don't you
know, I don't work them any more? "   If the people hailed
him as " Papa Santo " (the holy Pope) he was ready with the
witty remark: " You err in one consonant.   I am Papa
Sarto."

Pius X was always ready to listen to advice and if he realized
that he had made a mistake, he was prompt to admit it and
follow the counsel of his consultors.   A prelate once took
the liberty of criticizing the Pope on an important matter.
Pius X listened to him patiently and concluded: " Monsignor,
you are perfectly correct; I am grateful for your advice and
shall act upon it."   The prelate was astounded at his humility,
for he had expected quite a different reply.   Whenever he
presented the draft of his letters to his secretaries, he gave
them full liberty to correct them as they thought fit.   Just
as he had read his sermons to Don Constantini as curate
of Tombolo and submitted to the criticism of his pastor, so
as Pope he read his speeches to his secretaries, for he always
respected their opinion.   When his Secretary of State made
a suggestion to him he would sometimes reply: " Why not,
if you think so? "   Documents which he had drafted with
much care and labour were pen-marked, pruned and
sometimes even torn up at the mere suggestion of Cardinal
Merry del Val, whose opinion he esteemed so highly.   He

was not the kind of person to adhere tenaciously to his own ideas as though incapable of error. In a letter of December 15th, 1886, he wrote to a friend in Treviso: " Those are to be pitied who, obstinately clinging to their own ideas, find opposition at every step, because they lack the tact which humility teaches."

To Cardinals and Bishops who came frequently for audiences, he was full of consideration and kindness. Should one of them be kept waiting because he was engaged with someone else, he never failed to apologize for the delay, and if they knelt to him he would beckon them to rise, saying: " Don't kneel to me, Monsignor, I am the least of the priests of God." He never closed a conversation without recommending himself to the prayers of others, asking them to pray that the Lord would forgive him his sins and grant him the grace to work for His greater glory. To Bishop Macerata he wrote: " If the favourites of the Lord do not pray that I shall be able to carry the cross which has been placed upon my shoulders, how can I ever hope to climb Mount Calvary? "

When he wanted to ask his Cardinal Secretary for counsel he would send him a letter in order to save him the trouble of coming. He spared no pains to lessen the work of his secretaries. A Monsignor testifies: " I noticed one morning at an early hour that His Holiness had already written fifteen letters, and I took the liberty to advise him not to overtax his strength. He replied: ' Oh! that doesn't matter to me, but I like to save my secretaries as much work as possible.' "

His humility, self-forgetfulness and consideration for others made meeting him a pleasure. He tried as far as possible to reduce the work of his domestics to a minimum by performing himself many of the little tasks which should ordinarily have fallen to them. During the visit of his nephew, Mgr. Battista Parolin, to the Vatican, the Pope very often served his Mass. One heavy summer afternoon he was talking with his nephew in his private library. During the course of the conversation the Pope exclaimed: " Oh! I do feel thirsty." The nephew rose to call the servant, but

Pius X stopped him, saying: "Let's not trouble the servants on account of a little thirst."

One of his Maestri di Camera said: "To be served and to give others trouble was for him a sacrifice. His commands were always introduced with such phrases as 'Do you mind,' or 'I should be grateful if . . .' and when asked if he required any service, he would reply: 'I am here to serve; I am the servant of the servants of the Lord; I don't need anything . . . I was born poor . . . I have spent my life in poverty and I shall die poor.'"

The words "Thank you" were continually on his lips for even the smallest services rendered to him; he asked pardon for any trouble he gave to others and sometimes showed his gratitude by giving little presents.

In 1908 he celebrated the golden jubilee of his priesthood and in 1909 his silver jubilee as Bishop. On these occasions he would not permit any ovations or testimonies of gratitude for the work he had done. He did not want plaques, monuments or anything to immortalize his name. All he asked was the prayers of the people, their Communions, their acts of piety and charity.

"The Pope would be very sad," he wrote on December 23rd, 1908, "if the Venetians persisted in their plan of putting a memorial stone in the Cathedral. He is certain of their devotion and does not need to have it shown this way."

To the parish priest of Riese he wrote on April 25th, 1909: "Remember this; I expressly forbid that a memorial stone be fixed in the Baptistry where I was baptized and the same applies to the shrine of Cendrole."

On January 14th, 1910, he wrote to the Canons of Treviso: "If the Reverend Canons of the Cathedral of Treviso are desirous of pleasing the Holy Father they will remember him in their Masses and prayers and abandon the thought of 'Stoning him.'"

HIS GENEROSITY

We have already seen much of the goodness of Pius X which was born in him and purified by the continuous

practice of virtue. In the Vatican he was referred to as the
"kind-hearted Pope." In the great questions concerning the
administration of the Church he showed extraordinary
resolution and firmness, but to the individual all was kindness
and gentleness. Whenever it was his duty to reprove anyone,
he suffered more than the culprit. His Cardinal Secretary
of State tells us: "Then he passed mournful days and sleepless
nights. . . One could perceive the sorrow of his soul in
his eyes, which seemed to say, 'I suffer . . . but this is a
sacred, imperative and unavoidable duty.'"

Trustworthy witnesses assure us that his severity was always
tempered with the tenderness of his fatherly love, and as
Cardinal Mercier said, "In him was a wonderful blend of
gentleness and firmness which gave his soul an unshakable
equilibrium and a joy which by its charm attracted men of
all races."

Cardinal Merry del Val once found the servant of God
depressed and weeping. He had not slept the previous night
because he was tortured by the thought that on the following
day he must admonish an unfortunate individual for neglect
of duty. He asked the Secretary of State to say a little prayer
that the Lord would inspire his words and that the poor man
would listen and so do away with the necessity for further
steps. A few hours later the Holy Father returned full of
joy and said: "The poor man has seen his mistake. He
submitted even though I did not spare him any of the
chastisement he deserved. We must now do all we can to
help him."

Pius X was full of consideration for human weakness and
always tried to construe a fault which had been reported to
him in the best possible way. If he were told that he had been
criticized, he would reply: "It is not for us to judge, but the
Lord." If a conversation turned to criticizing anyone he
made use of his sense of humour and quick wit to turn it
to some other subject. Insults, calumnies and injuries were
immediately forgiven, for he always looked upon himself
as an instrument of the Lord, and as such his every action was
influenced by the love of God. He was once presented with
a bundle of letters filled with severe reproach and stern

criticism. He refused to read them but made the Sign of the Cross over them and exclaimed "Parce Sepultis."

At the beginning of his Pontificate he was informed that among the group of pilgrims to whom he was about to give audience there was a certain Commendatore, Secretary of the Charity Organization of Venice. Pius X knew this person only too well, for when he was Patriarch of Venice the Commendatore had taken care that every case recommended by him for charity should be left unattended. He was a strong supporter of anticlericalism. When the Pope heard that this man was among the pilgrims he seemed very happy. He asked a prelate to bring him the golden rosaries which lay in the secret safe. With his usual broad smile and kind words he greeted each one of the pilgrims, until he stood face to face with his former adversary. Then he said: "Ah! how nice it is to see you. How is your mother? How are things in Venice?" With incomparable kindness he concluded: "Take this golden rosary for your mother; tell her that I send her my blessing." Tears burst from the man's eyes, wetting the hand of the Pope. When he left the Vatican he told everyone he met: "Pope Sarto is a saint; I didn't think it possible that he would forgive and forget so easily the injuries and inconveniences I caused him at Venice."

No one caused the Pope so much sorrow as the Modernists. But even these erring sons of the Church, who in their blindness thought themselves her new blood, were pitied and welcomed. Before he took such measures against them as were necessary for preserving the integrity of the faith and discipline, he made sure he understood their ideas clearly. He wished that all possible means should be used to point out to them the error of their doctrines, and only when every other means had failed did he impose on them canonical censures. This he did with deep sorrow, exclaiming: "Maerore animi maximo."

One day a prelate gave expression to his astonishment that a certain well-known Modernist, Murri, had not been more severely punished for the continual opposition he had shown to the Church. The Pope answered calmly, "It is

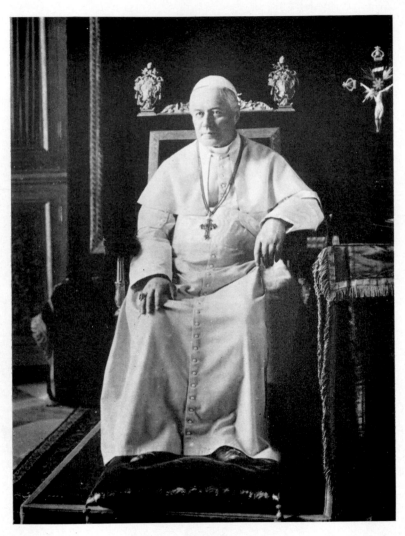

PIUS X
TOWARDS THE END OF HIS LIFE

not for the Pope to make martyrs. Leave the Modernists alone and they will bury themselves." In order to better the financial position of this Modernist he allowed him a fixed monthly pension, and he did not withdraw it when the man left the Church. In this way he put into action the words he had spoken in the Consistory on November 9th, 1903, in his first speech: " Since we are forced to fight for the truth let us embrace with love the enemies of the truth and commend them to divine mercy."

The same spirit of charity inspired his first encyclical, in which he exhorted all the Bishops and priests of the world to the practice of love for their neighbour. They should show charity even to those who were their enemies and persecuted them, for it often happens that we consider them worse than they are in reality. It is only the flame of Christian love which can banish darkness from their souls and bring them to the light and peace of God.

In 1908 he wrote to the new Bishop of Châlon, the diocese to which belonged Abbé Loisy, who had fallen under excommunication on account of his continual support for Modernist ideas. " You are also the Bishop of Abbé Loisy; treat him with kindness, and if he takes one step towards you, advance two towards him."

As Patriarch of Venice he had come to know a priest whose ideas about the temporal possessions of the Papacy were not altogether in keeping with the ideas of the Church, and who had signed the " Letter of Petition " drawn up by Pater Passaglia. Pater Carlo Passaglia, S.J., was famous for a theological work on the Immaculate Conception. He later adopted the view that temporal possessions were of no importance to the Papacy and that the Papacy should not be possessed of worldly power. He drew up a petition, had it signed by a great number of Italian priests, and presented it to Pius IX. The Pope ignored the petition. Pater Passaglia later had to leave the Society of Jesus, but in 1882 he submitted unconditionally and finished his life on March 18th, 1887, in an edifying way.

Our priest, Don Angelo Volpe, was one of those who had signed this petition, but he had not been willing to submit

when Pater Passaglia had submitted. He had been Chancellor
of the diocese of Belluno. His Bishop, Mgr. Giovanni Renier,
esteemed him highly and had tried to persuade him to change
his views. Don Volpe soon tired of these admonitions and
reproofs and left the diocese for Turin. In 1862 he became
Professor of the Royal Lyzeum in Faenza and was regarded
as the leader of the Liberal National Party. He wrote and
published a pamphlet, " La Questione Romana e il Clero
Veneto," which proposed the view that Italy had a right to
Rome. The Italian Government rewarded him for that
work by appointing him Rector of the National School of
St. Catherine in Venice, now known as " Marco Foscarini."
There the Patriarch had demanded a retraction of what he
had written, but sooner than submit he renounced his priestly
vocation. Cardinal Sarto was deeply grieved to learn that
there was a priest in his Patriarchate in this evil condition
and did all in his power to persuade him to come back to
the path of truth.

When he was elected Pope it troubled him to think of
the evil effect an unfrocked priest might have on the Venetian
clergy, so he invited Volpe to come and see him. Volpe
was greeted with the usual grace and affability of the Pope,
who said: " Don Angelo, let's bring this matter to a head,
and if possible conclude it once and for all."

" For forty years I have longed for this," replied
Volpe.

" Then make a very simple retraction," Pius X encouraged
the unhappy priest with a gracious smile. But these words
only caused the blood to rush to his face, and he exclaimed
resolutely: " I am sorry, I cannot retract anything. I said
it forty years ago and I still feel certain that Providence
' wanted ' the renunciation of all worldly power by the
Papacy." The Pope looked at him solemnly and replied:
" Let us say Providence has ' allowed ' it." The substitution
of ' allowed ' for ' wanted ' brought about an immediate
change in Don Volpe's countenance. Without hesitation
he made known his intention of making a total retraction
of the work which had caused so much scandal. A few days
later with downcast eyes and heart filled with contrition,

he stood before his Bishop and was once again admitted to the service of the altar.

INFLEXIBLE FIRMNESS

His kindness and consideration for the opinion of others did not in the least diminish the decisiveness of the Pope's actions. When it was necessary to protect the revealed Word of God against the misinterpretation either of the enemies of the Church or of her sons, he was inflexible. On such occasions he showed a resolution which no earthly power dared resist. While he respected the opinion of others the yard-stick of his actions was the Will of God. At the beginning of his Pontificate he was questioned as to what his policy would be; he raised his eyes, looked at the little crucifix over his table and replied: " This alone is my policy." It was this policy which was to stabilize the Church at the beginning of the stormy twentieth century.

One of the old Venetian fishermen exclaimed, when he heard that the Patriarch had been elected Pope: " The new Pope is a man of iron." " An iron made of charity and of faith," added a Mantuan later; but it was an iron so firm that if Bonaparte had to deal with it, he would not have reached his aim so easily.

Before Pius X took a decision, he weighed all the facts very carefully, pondered them for a long time, prayed about them and sought the advice and counsel of his Cardinals, whose opinions helped but never ruled him, for he knew the responsibility rested on his own shoulders. But once made, the decision was inexorable. Cardinal Merry del Val tells us: " There was no shade of weakness in him. As soon as there was any question of defending the rights and freedom of the Church, or the integrity of her doctrine or discipline, Pius X showed the full strength and power of his character. He had the inflexible firmness of a ruler fully conscious of the responsibilities which his high office imposed on him, and determined to fulfil them, cost what it might. All attempts to shake his firmness, to intimidate him by threats, or to persuade him by merely human reasoning, were futile."

After days of careful study of a particular problem and sometimes sleepless nights of anxious thinking, he made known his final decision in a few well-selected words. In pronouncing those words the usual expression of gentleness left his face, and in its stead came a look of severe determination. Then it was clear that there was no more to be said on the problem, and that the final word, however distasteful, had been spoken.

The contrast between meekness towards their fellow-men and lack of consideration for all human feeling when the rights of God were at stake, was the characteristic of all the saints; but in none of them was the contrast more pronounced than in Pius X.

Cardinal La Fontaine, Patriarch of Venice, tells us: " When Pius X wanted to appoint me in 1905 Bishop of Cassano, I presented every possible reason to save myself from the burden of the Episcopacy. The Servant of God looked at me sternly and said: ' Monsignor, I am the Pope, and it is for you to do the will of the Pope.' "

For the diocese of Bovino Pius X had a certain Monsignor consecrated Bishop, who after the consecration refused to accept the government of the diocese. The Pope pleaded with the new Bishop and begged him to undertake the work to which he had been appointed by God. It was of no avail. The Pope then told him that if he did not obey at once every vestige of Episcopal dignity would be taken from him. The Bishop knew that the Pope meant business and showed no further signs of hesitation.

Negotiations had been going on for a long time between the Papacy and the Italian Government about a very difficult problem. The Italian Prime Minister then had the unfortunate idea of telling Pius X that he would bring the affair to a speedy and equitable conclusion if the parish priest of his home town were appointed Bishop. The Pope simply replied: " Tell the honourable Prime Minister that the Pope doesn't sell Sees."

Pius X was not a man to be intimidated. The patient acceptance from the hand of God of trials, privations, poverty and sacrifice throughout his life, had hardened his spirit and taught him that in this world only one thing really mattered.

NOTHING FOR HIMSELF

Throughout the whole course of his life Pius X preserved the spirit of Christian poverty in which he had been brought up, so that at the end of his days he could say with truth: " I was born poor, I have lived in poverty, and shall end my days a poor man." Ambition for wealth and perishable possessions lay far from him, and the closer he got to them the more he despised them. At the beginning of his Pontificate he admonished the two private secretaries whom he had brought from Venice, that if they used their position in the Vatican to better their position in society he would have them dismissed at once. Nothing roused his indignation more than attachment to money in those engaged in the Service of Christ, who " had not where to lay His head." He condemned in the strongest terms those priests who, sprung from poor families, were able to leave a considerable inheritance to their relatives as a result of their priestly ministry. While thousands of pounds passed through his hands every year, he was scrupulous to see that the last penny was spent for the honour of God and the needs of the Church.

The splendour of the Papal court was for the Vicar of Christ, but for the son of the poor Cursore of Riese only the bare essentials were necessary, because he loved poverty no less than did St. Francis. His meals often consisted of but a little cheese and a few nuts, and if any kind of spirits were put before him at table he would refuse it saying: " That is only for gentlemen." His private rooms were very simply furnished. The only luxury in his bedroom was a blue fox skin which had been presented to Leo XIII. Except for his cassock his clothing was of the same kind as he had always worn at Mantua and Venice. His handkerchiefs were of an inferior cotton, and he still used the same watch as he had at Tombolo.

On the day of his election to the Pontificate a jeweller presented him with a golden pectoral cross, to which was attached a chain of specially fine workmanship. He accepted it thinking it belonged to the Papal insignia, but when, a few days later, he was informed that it had to be paid for he exclaimed: " No, certainly not! You must not pay so much for a cross which I am to wear; there are so many crosses used by my predecessors, and besides I still have the one I used at Venice." Without further reasoning he took off the cross and had it sent back to the jeweller.

He took the greatest care of all his possessions in order to prolong their life. He strictly forbade the spending of any money on his own comfort, and those in charge had to argue with him to make him avail himself of even the most essential things. The only argument which seemed to have any effect on him was that these things would be useful to his successor. He regarded himself as the administrator of money and not as the possessor. He kept a thick ledger in which all receipts and expenditure were carefully marked down, and no amount of persuasion could prevail on him to use money for a purpose for which it was not intended.

After the dreadful earthquake which devastated Sicily and Calabria he was asked to donate a small portion of the money collected for the victims to some other pious undertaking. His answer was: " No! not a penny. Money given for one purpose shall not be used for another, be it ever so good and meritorious." On another occasion he was asked to subsidize a certain newspaper in the hope of preventing the spread of anticlerical propaganda. He was adamant in his refusal and in his determination not to use the Church's money for such purposes.

HIS RELATIONS

Pius X was the opponent of all forms of nepotism. His relatives lived poor and unknown, after he had ascended the throne of Peter, as they had done before. While he preserved the same friendly relations with them he was anxious to see that they remained in the modest conditions in which they were born. The humble cottage of Riese was left unaltered; the rough furniture which he had used as a child was never changed. To-day it stands a symbol of glorified poverty.

On the day of his election to the Papacy he was asked what title he would give to his three unmarried sisters, those pious, humble women who had remained near him through all the stages of his life. " What title? " he repeated; " call them the sisters of the Pope; could there be a more honourable title than that? " When he met his sisters for the first time in the Vatican he admonished them to take great care to persevere in the modest, unostentatious way of life they had lived until then. The sisters of the saintly Pope were not ladies of magnificent villas, or proprietors of country residences, but tenants of a humble flat on the third floor of a house in the Piazza Rusticucci. As sisters of the guardian of Truth it became them to be true to their state of life; as sisters of the humble Pope it was fitting that they should despise the snobbishness of the world. Towards the close of his life, Pius X commended his sisters to the care of his successor requesting that they be given a pension of a few pounds to keep them in their old age after a life of fidelity to the Church in his person.

The only brother of the Pope, Angelo, was still living as an employee of the Postal Service. He lived in a little town near Mantua close to the Grotto of the Madonna delle Grazie. His brother-in-law, Giovanni Battista Parolin was an innkeeper in Riese. Shortly after Pius X had become Pope his brother and brother-in-law made a visit to Rome to find out what kind of life they were expected to lead now that one of the Sarto family had been raised to the highest dignity on earth. Pius X solved their difficulty in two sentences: " When you have become gentlemen you can cease working and vegetate in ease and luxury, but until then you must work if you want to eat. Do you expect to become gentlemen simply because I have been given a cross to carry? "

The Marchese di Bagno, a Member of Parliament, had come to know the Pope well while he was Bishop of Mantua. He took the liberty during an audience to suggest that as a Member of Parliament he could arrange that the Pope's brother be promoted from Delle Grazie to a more honourable and more remunerative position in the Post Office in Rome.

He begged the Pope to agree to this. But Pius X frowned
and in a decisive tone replied: " My brother ought to stay
where he is; I cannot understand why my election to the
Papacy should interfere with his work." " But would you
have him receive no promotion at all? " asked the astonished
Marchese. " None whatever; he must live now as he has
always done," answered the Pope. Angelo Sarto remained
in Delle Grazie until his death on January 9th, 1916.

His nephew, Don Battista Parolin, of whom the Pope was
very fond, received the same treatment. Cardinals, prelates,
and consultors continually expressed the wish that this
exceptionally worthy priest should be near his uncle, and
begged the Pope to let him come to Rome. The answer
was always in the negative. The Roman people, too, expected
that the Pope's nephew would become a Cardinal, but such
a thought never entered his uncle's head. He left his nephew
in Possagno as parish priest, and whenever he paid a visit
to Rome, Pius X tried to hasten his departure so as not to
keep him from his duty. Years later, under pressure of much
persuasion, he finally gave him the title of Domestic Prelate,
but in handing him the document, said: " Take this, Battista;
the people have repeatedly requested that you become a
Monsignor."

When it came to the Pope's ears that his niece, Ermenegilda
Parolin, had received an offer of marriage from a member
of the noble guard, he exclaimed: " What does she need a
count for? She is of humble origin; it would be better if
she married one of her own class."

A car had been presented to the sisters of the Pope by a
rich American. When Pius X heard of this he exclaimed to
his niece, Ermenegilda Parolin: " What a distressing sight it
will be to see the sisters of the Pope driving through the
streets of Rome in an automobile! Nothing could grieve
me more." A few days later the car was sold by his order.

His brother Angelo had two nephews who had lost their
mother. The boys were attending a high-class boarding
school at Cremona, and at the end of the year, being unable
to pay the school fees, Angelo asked the Pope for help.
The Pope replied: " Very well, for this year I shall pay the

fees for them to save you from shame, but see to it that the boys are removed from this school at once, for it is only intended for the sons of gentlemen, and we are too poor to afford such luxuries."

All his relations, near and far, remained poor to their dying day. If they received presents of money from the Pope the sums were no greater than those granted to other poor people. Any complaints against such treatment met with the answer: " The money does not belong to me, but to the Church; you must work now as you always have done, and do not count on inheriting anything at my death." This was the answer the Canon of Treviso had given to his sisters when they lived with their mother in the cottage of Riese.

It sometimes happened that benefactors granted large sums of money to the Pope to be used according to his wishes. Who could have blamed him for giving such money to his relatives? But no! He would not give in to his natural inclinations, arguing that such presents were given to him because he was Pope and not because his name was " Sarto."

A far more precious gift than gold or silver did Pius X grant to his relations and to the Chirch—the example of his sanctity and the holiness of his life.

" PAUPER ET DIVES "

Pius X was poor in the goods of this earth, but abundantly rich in that love which won all hearts to him. His doctor, Professor Marchiafava, tells us that one morning the Servant of God asked him to accompany him on his morning walk in the Vatican Gardens. Leaving the room the doctor made as if to lock the door, but the Pope stopped him, saying: " You may as well leave it open; there is nothing there; this morning I gave away the last penny." Just as in Salzano, Mantua and Venice, so in Rome he gave all he had and grieved only that he could not give more.

On December 28th, 1908, a major earthquake devastated the two flourishing towns of Reggio in Calabria and Messina in Sicily; 100,000 lives were lost and untold damage was done to property. The Pope lost no time in making an urgent

appeal to the Catholics of the whole world to send funds to
relieve the distress of the homeless, the suffering and the
bereaved.   A delegation of volunteers was sent to render
first aid to the suffering.   The gates of the Vatican were
opened to welcome the wounded and terror-stricken; 575
children who had lost their parents were taken within its
walls—snatched from the hands of anti-Catholic philanthropic
societies.

The efficiency and speed with which every kind of assistance
was organized was so great that even the Freemason press
could not avoid giving expression to its astonishment
and admiration.   Houses, seminaries, churches, schools,
orphanages and hospitals sprang up under the guidance and
direction of the Pope; large sums of money, clothing and
other necessaries were sent to bring life where before was
destruction and death.   " Calabriæ ac Siciliæ orphanis Adjutor
et Pater " (Helper and Father of the orphans of Calabria and
Sicily) was the title Pius X merited in those sorrowful days.

Il Giornale della Sicilia, a newspaper by no means over-
friendly to the Church, wrote concerning the prompt action
of the Pope in bringing help to the victims of the earthquake:
" Never, perhaps, has such great assistance been administered
so speedily and so efficiently.   While committees and
commissions set up by the Government quarrelled and
disputed as to the means of helping these unfortunates, the
doors of the Vatican were quietly opened and closed,
accepting the wounded and discharging the cured.   With
our own eyes we saw houses and homes for the sick, the
orphan and the service of God, being rapidly constructed
and put to use, without fuss, without ostentation and without
counting the cost.   To this spirit of duty and true Christian
charity could be attributed the efficiency, speed and
thoroughness of the wonderful work accomplished."   About
eight million people could turn to Pius X in gratitude for
the work he had organized to make life once again possible
for them.

In Mantua he had given an alms to a certain Pietro Lazzè
who lived in the greatest poverty.   In June, 1893, when
the Bishop of Mantua became Cardinal, Pietro Lazzè had

congratulated him, saying amongst other things: " You see, Your Eminence, humanity is divided into two classes, the prosperous and the unfortunate. I belong to the second class and Your Eminence to the first. Now you are a Cardinal and they will soon make you Pope."

" Bravo! " answered the Cardinal and added jokingly: " When I am Pope I shall make you Commandant of the Noble Guard, and then you too will be one of the prosperous ones."

Lazzè did not forget this promise made in jest, and whenever he wrote to the Patriarch to ask an alms—not seldom and never in vain—he signed himself Pietro Lazzè, Commandant of the Noble Guard, in spe (in hope).

When Pius X was elected Pope, Pietro Lazzè wrote the Holy Father a letter in which he expressed his joy, and closed with the words: " I dispense Your Holiness from the promise, and sign myself, Your most obedient Pietro Lazzè, Commandant of the Noble Guard, in otio (in retirement)." A few days later the good Lazzè received a hand-written letter from the Pope, accompanied by a generous present. This letter went from hand to hand in Mantua, because the people there had not forgotten the generosity of their one-time Bishop.

In 1865 an Austrian soldier, Giovanni Baier, suddenly took ill while passing through Tombolo. The curate of Tombolo, Don Giuseppe Sarto, hurried to give him assistance and showed him great kindness. About forty years later, when Pope, he received a letter from Austria, recalling the incident and expressing the sincere gratitude of the poor soldier. Pius X was deeply moved by this letter and answered it in his own handwriting, enclosing a generous alms.

His boundless confidence in Divine Providence inspired him with courage to undertake works for the honour of God and the salvation of souls, which humanly speaking seemed impossible. He wrestled with God in prayer and always experienced, as he himself says, " the visible help of Divine Providence." The foundations of seminaries and churches were very frequently laid when the means for completing the buildings seemed unobtainable, but the Pope looked to God for help and his confidence was always justified.

From all quarters money poured in, in such abundance that even the Pope himself could not explain it. He once said to a Roman lady: "So much money comes in and out of that drawer that I myself cannot understand it." It was with full truth that he could say: "The more I give in alms the more I seem to receive," and at another time: "The left hand receives, the right hand gives, but through the left more seems to pass than through the right." This latter statement he made against the criticism that his charities would drag the Holy See into financial ruin.

In 1911 the Masonic Government of Portugal passed laws against the Church. Bishops and priests were persecuted and deprived of all rights as citizens. The Bishop of Porto came to Rome as a delegate of the Portuguese Episcopate to beg help from the Pope. At the news of the situation the Pope was deeply grieved and asked at once how much would be needed for the moment. The Bishop answered "About £50,000." "That much I haven't got," was the reply, "but come back to-morrow and the Lord will help us." The following day the money was there when the Bishop arrived. The Pope then called a Prelate and asked him to count the money. While the counting was in progress the chamberlain announced that a certain gentleman who spoke with a foreign accent had urgently requested an audience with His Holiness. The Pope made a gesture to the Bishop to take the money and leave the room through a small door, while the chamberlain ushered the stranger in through the main entrance. The gentleman did not stay long with the Holy Father, but left the room as soon as he had concluded his business. When the chamberlain returned, the Pope said to him with a broad smile on his face: "There it is you see, it goes out through one door and comes in through the other," while he showed him the cheque for £50,000 he had received from the foreign visitor.

THE PRESENCE OF GOD

The inexhaustible fount of virtue and the secret of the abundant fruitfulness of his ministry was his intimate union with God; he could well apply the words of St. Paul to himself: " And I live, now not I: but Christ liveth in me." (*Gal*. ii. 20).   Midst the confusion of human affairs, the continual daily preoccupation with men and things, the weight of work and cares which overloaded the Holy Pope, he had learned to live constantly in the presence of God. Frequently during conversations with people of varying rank, he would stop for a moment and say: " Let us reflect that God is watching our every thought and word."

One of his Maestri di Camera tells us: " He seemed to be constantly absorbed in God; every time he looked at us or spoke to us we could not but feel that we were in close contact with the Divinity; in his words and actions there seemed to be something inspiring and supernatural."

His Cardinal Secretary of State tells us much the same thing: " In all his actions the Servant of God was led by super-natural reasoning which showed that he was always in the presence of God.   In the more important matters he would look at the crucifix and exclaim: ' He will tell us the answer.' "

Pius X was a man of prayer.   When engaged in friendly conversation at the audiences he would from time to time lift his eyes heavenwards as though drawn and directed by a celestial power.   Mgr. Tait testifies: " He prayed with such deep recollection that sometimes it seemed that he left the earth in order to collect his thoughts in God."

The change from prayer to work and from work to prayer was natural and spontaneous with him, for his whole life was one long communion with God; his work was but another form of prayer.   Many of his more intimate friends tell us that they would frequently find him in his private chapel absorbed in prayer.   His prayer was most intense when he was faced with major decisions which concerned the welfare of the Church.   Before he took the decision to condemn the Freemason Government in France for their policy of separating Church and State, he spent a night of prayer in the Basilica of St. Peter's, prostrate before the tomb of the first Vicar of Christ, begging light and strength to take a decision which would have irrevocable consequences for the Church.   Of these hours of fervent prayer, he himself tells us: " No one can imagine how much I have suffered and prayed, but the Lord has strengthened and enlightened me."

How ardent was his love for God! One of his close companions assures us: " He took meticulous care to avoid every venial sin and imperfection; in every action he showed himself a mirror and example of great virtue." A shadow of inexpressible anguish came over his brow whenever he heard of scandal or grave offences committed against God. His burning love for God was the power which guided and stimulated him in the reforms he brought about among the clergy, first of Rome and then throughout the world. He did not spare himself in uprooting all forms of abuse and diminishing as far as possible all occasions of sin.

In times of distress expressions would sometimes escape him such as: " Paradise, Paradise! how sweet it will be in heaven." His love of God was the root of his submission to and confidence in Divine Providence and caused him to exclaim: " Let the Will of the Lord be done . . . the Lord wills it, so let it be." His love of God was responsible for the angelic recollection with which he celebrated the Holy Sacrifice of the Mass, for his desire to receive Holy Communion daily when he was confined to bed in 1913, and for his Eucharistic Decree—the act of his Pontificate most rich in blessings and the act which won for him the title " Pope of the Eucharist."

Endless testimonies have been written on the love of the Servant of God for his Creator, e.g., " Love of God inspired all his thoughts and words," " Love of God shone in his eyes," " His whole countenance spoke of the love of God in his soul."

LOVE FOR MARY

From his early childhood a tender and solid love for the Immaculate Mother of God burned in his heart. On his mother's knee he had learned to love Mary, and we have already seen with what joy of heart Giuseppe Sarto led his playmates to the shrine of the Madonna of Cendrole. As pastor of Salzano his sermons on Our Lady attracted crowds of people, not only from his own parish but from neighbouring parishes. The day he was consecrated Bishop, Mantua was celebrating the feast of his Queen; in this the new Bishop perceived a pledge that Mary would take his episcopate under her very special protection.

While he was Bishop of Mantua scarcely a day passed that he did not speak to the seminarians about the love of Our Lady. Nothing gave him greater joy than to lead these young men to the Shrine of the Madonna delle Grazie to sing hymns and recite the Rosary in honour of the Mother of God and to listen to his simple but profound words as he expressed his own love for Mary and his desire to see all priests loving her.

It was well known in Venice what a great veneration the Patriarch showed for the statue of Our Lady of Grace in the Cathedral of St. Mark. The statue was known as the Virgin Nicopeja. When he was elevated to the highest dignity on earth, his love for Mary never diminished. He consecrated his Pontificate to her and laid all his troubles, cares and anxieties at her feet. At mid-day and in the evening when the bell tolled for the Angelus he would interrupt any business, however important, to salute his Queen and to renew his intention of living for her, and on his daily walks in the Vatican gardens he never omitted his visit to the grotto of Our Lady of Lourdes. On the 50th Anniversary of the Definition of the Dogma of the Immaculate Conception, he extended the solemnization of the Feast of Our Lady of Lourdes to the whole Church and sent a letter to the Catholics of the world exhorting them to love her who was conceived without stain.

In spite of the burden of excessive work and anxious cares which weighed on his shoulders, he never omitted his daily Rosary. In reciting it he appeared to have forgotten all about the earth; he said the *Aves* with such recollection that it seemed as if he stood in the visible presence of the Mother of God. He had chosen her Queen of his Pontificate; for her, his Queen, he lived, suffered and worked until the day God called him from the battle of life to celebrate with her the eternal victory.

Chapter X

LOVED ALIKE BY GOD AND MEN

THE GIFT OF MIRACLES

BOTH within the walls of the Vatican and outside, it was well known that the Blessing of the Pope effected miracles. When this came to his ears he treated it as a joke and said: " Now they are saying and printing in papers that I have started working miracles, as if I haven't enough to do already. . . . What will they want next? " But the people were not wrong.

At the very beginning of his Pontificate the holy Pope had astonished everyone in the Vatican when Cardinal Herrero y Espinosa, Archbishop of Valencia, who was over eighty years of age, had suddenly fallen ill during the conclave. In spite of the great burden which had just been laid upon his shoulders, and the agitation of his mind, the new Pope hastened to the room of the sick Cardinal accompanied by Cardinals Sanminiatelli and Satolli and Mgr. Merry del Val, in order to console the dying Cardinal in his last agony. When Cardinal Herrero y Espinosa heard that the newly-elected Pope was present, he opened his eyes and in a weak voice begged the Apostolic Blessing before departing from this world. The Holy Father prayed for a moment, placed his hand on the forehead of the sick Cardinal and gave him his blessing. At that very moment the Cardinal began to feel considerably better and those around the bedside noticed a change. Three days later the Cardinal was completely restored to health and returned to Spain attributing his cure to the blessing of the Holy Father.

The very appearance of Pius X in the audience halls brought huge masses of people spontaneously to their knees. Everyone seemed enraptured at the very sight of him, and as he passed through the crowds timid voices uttered humble petitions, begging for consolation and strength in the trials of life. The sight of the Pope, clad in white, lifting his eyes to heaven and blessing an anxious but silent crowd of people was like an apparition from another world. It seemed as if all sufferers felt themselves irresistibly drawn to him to ask his help, feeling certain that the touch of his hands and his Apostolic Blessing would bring them consolation in their every sorrow, light in their doubts and help in their necessities. Miracles were so numerous that in his presence one could not help feeling oneself back in the days when the Divine Master walked through Palestine, " doing good and healing all " (*Acts* x. 38), but Pius X attributed everything to the power of the keys and never to his own holiness.

It is quite impossible even to mention all the miraculous happenings that took place during his reign, so we will mention but a few of them, asking for nothing more than human faith in the testimonies of reliable witnesses.

A PARALYZED ARM

Walking among the people at a general audience, Pius X noticed a man with a paralyzed arm who had abandoned all hope of being cured by natural means after consulting many doctors. He had but one hope left—the power of the Blessing of the Pope—but in this his confidence was unshaken. As the Pope moved slowly through the crowd, stopping every now and then to speak to various people, the poor man waited anxiously. The long-awaited moment at last arrived when the eyes of the Pope fell on the misshapen arm of the unfortunate man, who cried out: " Holy Father, Holy Father, heal me that I may earn bread for my poor family." The Pope looked at him for a moment without saying a word and then took the paralyzed arm in his hand and exclaimed: " Have confidence in the Lord . . . only have faith and the Lord will heal you." At that very moment life returned to the man's arm, as the Pope turned to walk away. The man was filled with amazement and joy, and he tried to force his way through the crowd to tell the Pope that the miracle had been worked. He shouted at the top of his voice, " Holy

Father! Holy Father!" Pius X turned around and put his
finger to his lips to indicate to the happy man that he was to
hold his peace.

"MAMMA I AM HEALED!"

A young Irish girl had her head covered completely with
sores. "If you bring me to Rome to the Holy Father,"
she often said to her mother, "I shall be healed, because if
Jesus gave His apostles power to work miracles, why should
He not have given it to His Vicar on earth." The importunity
of the child finally prevailed upon her mother who, against the
advice of the doctor, decided to undertake the journey to
Rome.

The brave woman, standing in the midst of an Italian crowd
and holding the hand of her little daughter, whose head was
almost entirely covered with bandages, presented a pitiable
sight to the saintly Pope as he moved slowly through the
general audience. When he saw the little girl he put his
hand on her head, blessed her, and smiled gently at her
mother. Suddenly the child called out "Mamma, I am
healed!" It is difficult to imagine the astonishment and joy
of that Irish mother as she rolled off the bandages from the
head of her daughter to find not even the slightest trace of
a sore.

CONSUMPTION CURED

A Sister of the Congregation of the Holy Wounds in
Florence was in an advanced stage of consumption. In 1912
she wrote to her Mother Superior General for permission to
go to Rome to visit the Pope, expressing her great confidence
in him. When the Pope saw her kneeling before him,
he said smiling: "What are you worried about, Sister; you
look much better than I do." He blessed her and she was
completely cured.

.   .   .   .   .

"One of our novices, Sister Maria Frontuto," wrote the
Mother Superior of the Sisters of the Holy Family, "became

very ill with consumption. Within a few weeks the disease
had made rapid strides, and great alarm was caused when
she began to spit blood and exhibit other symptoms which
showed that the end was near. The doctors held out no hope.
I then resolved to comply with the wish of the novice to be
taken to Rome to the Holy Father. The audience took
place on July 13th, 1913. In reply to her earnest supplication,
' Holy Father, I beg to be healed,' the Pope exclaimed,
' But why? Don't you feel well? Your health is very
important . . . do you understand? ' Filled with emotion
the novice plunged her head into her hands and wept. A
moment later she felt as if a great burden had fallen from her
shoulders. She stood up and returned to her convent to
resume the ordinary duties of the novitiate."

" HEALING ALL MANNER OF SICKNESS " (*Matt.* iv. 23)

One of the chamberlains who regularly attended the Holy
Father testifies: " A German, about fifty years old, came on
one occasion to visit the Pope. He had been blind from birth
but came full of confidence that he would receive the gift
of sight if the Pope blessed him. The Holy Father touched
his eyes, admonishing him to have great confidence in God.
At the touch the man saw for the first time in his life."

All the unfortunate, weighed down with sufferings and
sorrows, had a claim on their common father, but to suffering
children he was most kind and sympathetic. In one of the
audiences he met a woman carrying in her arms her little
child who had been born blind. The compassionate glance
of the Holy Father met the sorrowful, pleading eyes of the
mother as she indicated the malady of her child. " Pray to
the Lord, and have confidence," said the Pope. Immediately
the child opened its little eyes, looked into the face of the
Pope and was privileged to behold, as its first sight on earth,
the face of the saintly Vicar of Christ.

At another audience he heard loud sobbing as he walked
through the crowds. A woman from Lyons was making
desperate efforts to get near him to present her little son

who had been born deaf. Though some distance from her, Pius X turned and called to the woman: " Have confidence, Signora, have confidence." It was as though the Divine Master had repeated: " Be thou opened," for the child heard from that moment.

In 1911 a young Bavarian girl was very anxious to enter the Carmelite Convent of St. Remo, but as a consequence of a severe cold she experienced acute pain and a constant rumbling noise in her left ear. The specialist diagnosed perforation of the ear-drum accompanied by otitis of the middle ear. He prescribed various remedies, but the pain continued to increase. In such a condition, there was no possibility of entering the order. With great personal sacrifice the girl undertook the journey to Rome, full of confidence in the Pope, of whose miraculous powers she had heard. Standing before him the girl bravely made known her wish to become a Religious, and begged him to make this possible for her by curing her ailment. He listened patiently as the girl described what was wrong with her. " And do you think I can cure you? " he asked when she had finished. " Yes, Holy Father, you can do it; heal me, I beg of you! " The sorrow of the poor girl filled the Pope with compassion. He touched her ear, and whispered: " If you believe." The girl was received into the Convent very shortly after her miraculous cure.

As he passed through the crowd at an audience one day, the Pope's eyes fell upon a pitiful sight. A lame child accompanied by father and mother, who had come all the way from Germany in the hope of benefiting by the sanctity of the Pope, stood full of woe pleading for a cure. The child was lying on the ground. Pius X bent down in fatherly tenderness, picked up the child in both arms and said: " Come, come, now, you must try to walk." He put the child down on both feet and it ran to its father and mother.

In 1913 a poor mother begged the Pope to heal her daughter, who had been lame for many years. " I cannot do that," he replied, " only God can work miracles." " You can," repeated the Mother, not losing hope, " if only you ask God." Seeing how strong was the faith of the poor woman, he whispered, "Have confidence, the Lord will heal your daughter." At that moment the girl rose to her feet and walked, to the amazement of all present.

The number of miracles worked by Pius X is astonishing; but still more astonishing was the ease and naturalness with which he worked them. Defying the course of nature, belying the prognoses of world-famous physicians, and bestowing a life of happiness on one who would otherwise have been condemned to live maimed or disabled, the great Pope stood with a gentle smile on his face and loving words on his lips, treating the suppliant as a father treats his child. He performed astounding miracles as if it were the easiest thing in the world, and joked about them as if they were insignificant.

A Roman schoolgirl had contracted a serious periostitis of one foot and had been a cripple since she was one year old. A friend of hers had managed to procure one of the Pope's socks in the hope that wearing it she would be healed. The hope of the pious person was justified, for as soon as the girl put it on all pain ceased and she was able to run about like any child of her age. News of the miracle very quickly reached the ears of the Pope, who roared with laughter and commented: "What a joke! I wear my own socks every day and still I suffer from constant pains in my feet, but when others put them on, all pain vanishes . . . peculiar, peculiar." It is known that Pius X did actually suffer great pain in his feet on account of a serious attack of uricaemia but this never prevented him from giving audiences and continuing his ordinary round of duties.

The Mother Superior General of the Franciscan nuns in the Via Castro Pretorio, Rome, had a serious throat complaint which endangered her life. Human science could only suggest a tracheotomy, the results of which would be at best doubtful. The sister had great confidence in the power of Pius X, of which she often spoke familiarly to her nurse. One night, when her suffering had reached its climax and she was scarcely able to breathe, Pius X appeared to her in a dream and assured her that she would be cured. Next morning she took up her place in the chapel for meditation

with the other sisters, much to their astonishment. At
breakfast she related the miraculous dream with which she
had been privileged, but in the twentieth century credence
is not easily given to such " likely tales." A few days later
she went to see the Pope to thank him personally for the
favour that had been granted her. He did not give her a
chance to speak, but addressed her by name and said: " You
are the sister that I have healed."

Miraculous cures were of such frequent occurrence that
letters poured in from all over the world asking for the
Apostolic Blessing, and relating a vast variety of benefits
which had already been derived from it. The Secretariate of
State had to work overtime to cope with the enormous
correspondence.

We will quote but a few instances here of how Our Lord
manifested His power through His faithful servant, healing
not only those who came to visit the Pope, but those who
lived at great distances from Rome.

" The six-year-old son of my cousin Giuseppe and Anna
Corradi," so writes a Roman gentleman, " had a fall which
damaged the kidney and punctured the bladder. The doctor
only gave the child a few hours to live. That day I was going
to see the Holy Father, and I decided to ask a blessing for
that family. He listened to the story, and with a look of
pity on his face said, ' Poor mother, yes, I shall gladly send
her my special blessing.' Immediately after the audience
I went to the house of the sorrowful family to bring the good
news that the Holy Father had sent his blessing. As soon as
the mother heard it she began rushing about the house,
exclaiming: ' Thanks be to God, my Giorgio will be healed.'
And so it happened. Within a few days the little boy was
on his feet again, not having received any surgical attention
whatever. Some months later I visited the Holy Father
again and reminded him of the blessing he had sent to the
family. ' Did the boy die?' enquired His Holiness. I
replied that the boy had been almost instantaneously restored
to perfect health by the blessing which he had so kindly
sent. He answered: ' The Pope blesses all; it was the faith
of the mother that merited the healing.' Giorgio Corradi

to-day enjoys excellent health after spending some years in the artillery in the first World War."

A Canon of the Cathedral of Trent reports: "At the beginning of November, 1908, I was summoned to Rome, but feared to undertake the journey because my mother had been in bed for two months seriously ill and likely to die at any moment. She was about seventy-six years old and could not take any nourishment. Sitting by her bedside one evening, I told her that I had resolved to postpone my visit to the Eternal City. She remonstrated with me for some time and assured me that if I fulfilled my duty and asked the Holy Father to bless her that she would be healed. I set out the next day and having arrived in Rome arranged with the Maestro di Camera, Mgr. Bisleti, for an audience. As soon as the Servant of God saw me he enquired as to the state of my mother's health. I told him that she could not live long and that she requested his special blessing. He lifted his eyes to heaven, prayed for a moment and then clapped me on the shoulder saying, 'I have prayed that she will be spared for many years to come.' After the audience I sent a post-card to my mother to tell her that the Pope had blessed her and prayed for her recovery. It was not long before I received a letter from my sister reporting that my mother had got out of bed, had taken some nourishment and had been restored to normal health. The healing took place at precisely the same moment that the Pope had prayed for it."

The mother of a Brazilian Bishop had contracted leprosy. The fame of Pius X's sanctity had been spread far and wide by the year 1914 when the infection was discovered. The Bishop set out for Rome at once and pleaded with the Holy Father with much insistence to heal his mother. Pius X told him to have recourse to Our Lady and the saints and to put his trust in God. Nothing daunted, the Bishop begged that at least the Pope would utter the words of the Divine Saviour: "I will, be thou made clean" (*Luke* v. 13). Pius X whispered the words and the woman was completely cleansed of leprosy.

In April, 1911, Marquis Galeani of Turin was confined to bed because one of his legs had become gangrenous. It was too late for an amputation. The sister of the sick man requested the Holy Father to offer Mass for the cure of her brother. Shortly after, Dr. Galle, who had attended the patient, expressed his astonishment that the man had been completely cured. Professor Murri of Bologna was asked for his opinion on the case, and he said that either the doctor had erred in his diagnosis—which was most unlikely—or an event had taken place which was humanly inexplicable. It was discovered that the healing took place at the time the Holy Father was offering the Mass for that intention.

The Belgian Consul in Rome, M. Charles Dubois, had for a long time suffered with carbuncles all over his body. Being a man of some means, he had consulted the most famous doctors in the country and had tried every remedy which human wisdom could suggest; but all to no avail. His condition became gradually worse. On the morning of September 8th, Madame Dubois resolved to turn to Pius X and put her trust in the sanctity of the Pontiff. The Pope looked at her, joined his hands and turned his eyes to heaven for a moment; then he said: " Confidence, Signora, your prayers will be heard." Full of confidence she returned home to meet her husband who had been completely cured of the affliction which had refused to yield to any natural remedy.

A reliable eye-witness of Treviso relates: " Having become involved in a dispute, I had to have recourse to a lawyer for legal advice. I went to Signore Paleari of Milan, but perceived, as I related the details of my legal complications, that the poor man was sore depressed and found it difficult to concentrate on what I was saying. He told me that his little boy, whom he dearly loved, was on the point of death. I needed the lawyer's assistance and so, without telling him, I at once sent a telegram to the Vatican to request a special blessing for the little boy. After an hour or so the answer was wired to me, informing me that the Holy Father had sent his special blessing. I took the telegram to the lawyer's house and showed it to the sick child. He stretched out his arm from under the bed-clothes, took hold of the telegram and immediately rose, completely cured."

The Mother Superior of the Orphanage of the Sisters of Canossa in Belgaum, India, had worn away to a skeleton from a chronic, incurable ailment of the stomach. She had consulted the most eminent doctors of both Bangalore and Bombay, had carefully followed the prescriptions of her physicians and had undergone major operations, but all without success. On January 18th, 1914, the little orphan girls who had just made their first Holy Communion resolved to write a letter to the Holy Father to implore him to heal their Mother, whom they all loved. They wrote the following letter:

Belgaum, Convent of St. Joseph,
January 18th, 1914.

Dear Holy Father,
We have been privileged to make our First Communion while we are still very young. We are very grateful to Your Holiness for this great blessing and we wish to thank you. Our Mother Superior has been ill for fifteen years and for the past twelve years has lived only on milk. We would like so much to see her well again and humbly beg for this great blessing. We often pray for Your Holiness and with great joy we sing the hymn ' God Bless Our Pope." Bless, O holy Father, our Sisters, pupils and orphans.

Sisters, pupils and orphans of Belgaum.

But the poor Mother Superior became worse and worse. She could no longer take any nourishment, and on February 7th as it was feared that she would die the Sacrament of Extreme Unction was administered. The next day the Sisters received the following telegram from Rome : " The Holy Father graciously grants the Apostolic Blessing requested "—Cardinal Merry del Val—Rome, February 7th, 1914.

The telegram arrived just before supper. Alone in her room the Mother Superior opened it and was filled with unspeakable joy and confidence in the Pope's blessing. She rose from her bed, dressed and sat in a chair. There was great excitement in the Convent that night. Some thought that she should take nourishment, others that she should return to bed and all that she should wait for a few days before

attempting the normal routine of the community. But the
Superior rejected all suggestions and demanded that soup,
bread and meat be brought to her, which she enjoyed
thoroughly and resumed her place in the community the
following day.

The condition of the Senator Pasquale de Giudice,
Professor of the History of Law in the University of Pavia
and successor of the famous jurist, Contardo Ferrini, was
becoming progressively worse in July, 1914. He was suffering
from gall-stones, and all the doctors consulted were unanimous
in affirming that only an operation could cure him. Such
an operation was impossible because he was seventy-one
years of age and the condition of his organs would not allow
it. His wife had heard of the wonders worked by the
blessing of Pius X, and she lost no time in writing to
Mgr. Achille Ratti, Prefect of the Vatican Library, who
was a friend of the Senator's, to ask the Holy Father for his
blessing. On July 21st Mgr. Ratti answered that the Pope
had blessed the sick man. The Senator was very much
relieved by the news and expressed a wish to receive the
Blessed Sacrament. He made his confession to Mgr. Dolcini,
Vicar General of Pavia, and received Holy Communion.
Three hours later, without the slightest effort and without
pain, a large gall-stone left his body, and he lived in good
health for another ten years.

Among the charismata given by God to Pius X was his
power of reading the secret thoughts of men. One of his
private secretaries testifies: " It was well known that the
Servant of God could read the secrets of the heart intuitively.
It would frequently happen that when a person came to speak
to him about a certain affair he would bring up the topic
before the visitor had a chance to mention it. This was told
me first by people who had been closely connected with him
as Bishop of Mantua." Another secretary adds: " I have
spoken to many people, who told me that they had the
impression that the Pope knew what was in their mind as
soon as he looked at them. In his presence I would not
dream of telling a lie, for I felt certain that he would know the
true facts in any situation." The Maestro di Camera says:

" Sometimes I felt that the Servant of God was looking into my soul, and therefore when speaking to him I was careful to observe the greatest exactness in the facts I was relating."

One day the Superior of the Roman Trappist Monastery of Tre Fontane, faced with a decision of great moment, went to the Pope to ask advice. He had just fallen to his knees in front of the Holy Father when he was given detailed direction and counsel as to the course he should follow, though he had not spoken a word on the subject.

The secrets he discovered, however, were not always to the comfort of the visitor. Once a distinguished prelate introduced a priest of his diocese to the Pope, giving him the highest praise and declaring his anti-Modernist attitude. The unusual severity of Pius X astonished and embarrassed the prelate, who repeated the praises merely for the sake of conversation. It was not very long before it became evident to the prelate why His Holiness had disregarded the praises he had lavished on the undeserving cleric.

When the Servant of God, Don Luigi Orione, had to go for an audience with the Holy Father he made sure that both body and soul were prepared. He shaved, put on his best clothes, polished his shoes and wore his almost new Ferraiuolo and hat. Then full of joy he set out for the Basilica of St. Peter's to confess his sins. The time was not very suitable for confessions in the Basilica, and he found all the confessionals empty. He hurried off to the Chiesa della Traspontina and there made his confession to a Carmelite. Because of the delay he did not have a lot of time to spare, but the Carmelite prolonged his exhortations and advice while Don Luigi, as it were, knelt on fiery coals. Finally he interrupted the confessor, begging him to give absolution at once as he had an audience with the Pope within a few minutes. He left the church, ran all the way to the Vatican and reached the top of the stairs breathless, but had still a few moments to wait before the appointed time for the audience. When his turn came he entered the study of the Pope. As soon as the Holy Father saw him he smiled and said: " Don Luigi, you could have come to see me without going to Confession, but if you insist on going to

Confession in future before an audience, then leave yourself a little more time." No one knew that Don Orione had been to Confession.

Apart from the gift of miracles and reading the secrets of the heart, the holy Pontiff had the power of prophecy. This was declared at the diocesan and apostolic processes for the Beatification.

A distinguished Mantuan, who lived in Rome and had known Pius X when he was Bishop of Mantua, testifies: " On August 29th, 1901, my son died in the flower of his youth, at the age of eighteen. The sorrow of his mother was so great that it was feared she would lose her reason unless something were done immediately. The Patriarch of Venice, Cardinal Sarto, wrote her a letter of consolation and soon after came to Rome to encourage her with motives of Christian resignation. At the close of the conversation he said to her: ' Have courage; the Lord sometimes takes in order to give in more abundant measure. Have confidence, Gaetana, He will give you another son.' This prophecy made no impression on my wife because she had had an operation in 1884, after which experienced doctors had told her that it was impossible for her to bear any more children.

" But to the surprise of all, nineteen years later she became pregnant. In February, 1903, the Servant of God came to Rome once again. As soon as I met him he greeted me and commented: ' You don't mean to say your wife will be a mother again soon, do you? ' and with a smile continued: ' Are you still as incredulous as ever? ' To my enquiry as to how he knew this he simply replied: ' It is enough that I know it; now which would you prefer, a boy or a girl? ' I immediately said I would prefer a boy in the place of the one I had lost. The Patriarch then said confidently, ' Tell your wife that she will soon bring forth a son, but she must have great confidence in God.' On July 8th, 1903, my wife gave birth to a boy who received his First Communion from the hands of the Pope at the age of seven."

On another occasion the Pope was giving the Sacrament of Confirmation to a number of schoolgirls. He noticed that one of them was crying and asked her what was the matter. The girl explained that her mother and father had separated and that now there was no one to look after her. The Pope put his hand on her head and consoled her, saying, " Have courage, my child, when you go home you will find things all right." After the ceremony the child returned home to be greeted by her father and mother who had been reconciled.

The prophecy which was most painful to Pius X was that of the dreadful conflagration which broke over Europe in 1914. In the year 1906 Mgr. Luçon, Bishop of Belley in France, received orders to come to Rome at once as the Holy Father wished to speak to him. As soon as he entered the Pope's study, he was astonished by the words, " I appoint you Archbishop of Rheims." Mgr. Luçon put forward many reasons against this and pleaded with the Holy Father to permit him to remain in his own diocese. The Pope concluded the interview with the words, " I appoint you Archbishop of Rheims not for your own glory or as a recognition of your merit, but because a heavy cross awaits you there. Can a Bishop refuse the cross when he gazes on the crucifix? You are already a Bishop and have a cross to carry, but in Rheims you will find a far heavier, but also a far more meritorious one." The prelate thought the Holy Father was referring to the conflict which at that time raged between Church and State. But eight years later when the towers of the magnificent Gothic Cathedral were destroyed by German shells and a large part of the town lay in ruins, Mgr. Luçon, who was then Cardinal, recalled the prophecy of Pius X and realized why he had been so horrified in making it.

Pius X felt keenly the approach of the death and destruction which were soon to befall Europe and often referred to it with a tremor in his voice. " I see a great war coming," he often said to his sisters, who tried to console him, admonishing him not to think of such things. But he refused to be consoled and added gravely, " Yes, but it will be a very great war."

" Eminence, things are looking bad," he often said to his Cardinal Secretary of State, who was amazed at the insistence and certainty with which the Holy Father spoke. " I do not speak of this war," he said in 1911 at the time of the interven-

tion of Italy in Libya; and during the Balkan wars in 1912-13
he declared, " All this is as nothing in comparison with what
is to come."   Whenever Cardinal Merry del Val commented
that a war was not expected, or that if one did come it would
not be for many years, the Pope exclaimed prophetically,
" Eminence, before the end of the year 1914! "

In 1912 a nobleman from Venice suggested to the Holy
Father that he should acquire certain property and buildings
for a religious institute in Gradisca.   " Quite impossible,"
replied the Pope, " all these buildings will be destroyed."
Three years later the district experienced the havoc of war
and the property became valueless.

On May 30th. 1913, the Brazilian Ambassador presented
himself to the Holy Father for a farewell visit.   " How
fortunate you are, sir," the Pope said, " you can go to Brazil
and so be spared the pain of witnessing the horrors of the war
which is soon to break out."   " I thought His Holiness was
referring to the Balkan war," the minister wrote later, " but
the Holy Father added that the Balkan war was but the
beginning of a great conflagration which he could neither
prevent nor outlive."   Fourteen months later, on June 28th,
1914, the portentous crime took place in Bosnia which was
to summon the Apocalyptic horsemen to the gates of
Europe.

CHAPTER XI

A BROKEN HEART
(August 20th, 1914)

DAYS OF PAIN

THE last days of Pius X on earth were darkened by great
anxiety and dreadful pain. In the early months of
1914 it was reported to him that the Mexican Bishops
had been forced to flee their country and that the Archbishop
of Durango had been condemned to sweep the streets. A
deep sadness came over him and the expression of joy which
had shone on his face from early youth was banished forever.

An observer who saw him at that time in St. Peter's wrote:
" Slowly the Sedia Gestatoria moved through the crowd.
The Holy Father's face was sad, and it seemed that his soul,
altogether unconscious of the pomp and splendour which
surrounded him, contemplated only the things of heaven.
The expression of sadness on his face was so pronounced that
it seemed he would never smile again. A sudden movement
in the crowd caused the Pope to halt. It was as though he
were torn from his contemplation. He lifted his face to
heaven, and then, like a sunbeam flashing across a wintry
sky, an infinitely lovable smile coloured his countenance.
He looked at two Italians who stood next to me as they
exclaimed: ' Bless us, dear Holy Father, bless us! ' "

On May 20th, 1914, Pius X held his last Consistory.
Though it then appeared that peace would bless the world
for many years, the Pope addressed the College of Cardinals
in grave words. He began his discourse by pointing to the
Cross of Christ as the only fountain of salvation and peace
for suffering humanity, and continued: " To-day more than
ever we must search for that peace as we look on helplessly
at the hatred which the different nations and classes bear
one another, fearing that the growing discord will develop
into dreadful battles. There are men of skill and authority

who, foreseeing in their hearts the fate of their states and the destruction of human society, search for possible ways and means to prevent the cursed tumult and butchery of war. Their purpose is, indeed, a blessed one, but their success will be small unless desperate efforts are made to plant justice and love in the hearts of all men."

The truth of these words became evident to all only two months later, when justice and love of neighbour were trodden underfoot, and all saw clearly that Europe was making steady strides towards destruction and slaughter, because one thing was missing—God in the life of the people.

Pius X had always lived among the people. He saw the influence materialism exercised on their lives and realized that sooner or later it must bear its bitter fruit. In the first encyclical of his pontificate he had declared: "The will for peace without God is absurd, for justice flies from where God is absent, and it is hopeless to wish for peace without justice."

On June 28th, 1914, newspapers all over the world reported that the heir to the throne of the Austro-Hungarian monarchy, Archduke Franz Ferdinand and his wife had been assassinated for political reasons. This was the match that was to kindle the fire which would cause much destruction and heartbreak and consume much of the good seed scattered by the labours of the Holy Pontiff. Pius X was deeply depressed by the news, for he had often prophesied that apostasy from God would give rise to the senseless murdering of people which was now imminent. On hearing the news he hastened to the chapel and spent hours wrestling in prayer with the Almighty that He would forgive the people their sins and have mercy on the children of this world. Under his direction Pontifical diplomacy did all in its power to prevent the impending war. The Pope begged, implored and admonished with all the authority of his elevated office that governing powers should not stain themselves with blood and should seek to preserve the peace at any cost. The whole Christian world looked to their beloved Pontiff, for they realized that he was their only hope of peace, that he alone could save them from the threatening onslaught.

PIUS X ON HIS DEATH-BED

But in those days of passion who would listen to invocations for peace? The rulers and powerful ones of the earth were blinded by pride, eaten with cupidity and deaf to the authority of Christ.

As the Pope worked hard for peace, eight nations mobilized their armies for war. Day and night Pius X prayed fervently, constantly and feverishly. He lay prostrate for hours before the Blessed Sacrament, repeating over and over again the words of Jesus in the Garden of Gethsemani: " Father, all things are possible to thee: remove this chalice from me; but not what I will,.but what thou wilt " (*Mark* xiv. 36).

His fatherly heart suffered in anticipation all the pains and sorrows which were to overtake humanity. Vividly before his eyes he could see the battles, the cruel hatred, towns reduced to ruins, homes broken and deserted, the weeping widow, the orphan and the broken-hearted mother in place of the unity of hearts and the harmony of nature intended by the Creator. Repeatedly he tried to prevent the horrible misfortune of war or at least to stem its tide. He dared to hope against all human hope. The Austrian Ambassador asked the Holy Father to bless the armies of the Danube monarchy, but he replied: " I bless not armies, but only peace." It was all in vain. The war had started.

HIS LAST EXHORTATION

On August 2nd, the Pope sent a moving exhortation to the Catholics of the whole world, to the world which was busily engaged celebrating orgies of bitter hatred and preparing to destroy the lives of thousands of young men in its ambition for power and wealth. This exhortation reveals the heartfelt sorrow of the universal Pastor in the face of the butchery which was to come.

" While practically the whole of Europe is torn in a whirlwind of furious war, the destruction and consequences of which cannot be visualized without pain and terror, Our soul is filled with a deep anxiety for the salvation and life of so many Christian peoples who are dear to Our heart. We admonish the Catholics of the whole world to take refuge,

full of confidence, at the throne of divine mercy. The clergy
should lead the way by their example and should organize
in their parishes public devotions and prayers that God will
be moved to compassion and will extinguish as soon as
possible the torches of war and will instil into those who
are charged with the government of the people, thoughts of
love and peace instead of hatred and war.

PIUS X.
Vatican.   August, 1914."

This was his last exhortation.

When he appeared the following Sunday in the courtyard
of St. Damasus to bless the people, there was seen not the
strong, smiling, happy Pope, but a weak old man, weighed
down by anxiety and bitter worry, his face wrinkled and his
thoughts distracted—a man broken by the evil of the world.
The war had broken his heart. His kind, generous soul felt
untold compassion for his people—" My poor children, my
poor children . . ." he called out several times with tears
streaming from his eyes. This he constantly exclaimed as
news was brought to him of new armies mobilized, of new
battles fought, of young lives lost. Day and night he continued
to pray, beseeching the Almighty to have compassion on his
" poor children." " I wish to offer my life as a holocaust
to prevent the destruction of so many thousands of my poor
children." He was inconsolable at the thought that so many
priests and candidates for the priesthood were already in the
battlefield, forced to fight against each other—those members
of the army of Christ's love, fighting in the armies of man's
hatred.

Only those to whom his last confidences were entrusted
could have any intimation as to how much he suffered on
account of the sins of men, on account of the deafness to his
admonitions of governors and rulers and because, the peace
of Christ having been rejected, men took upon themselves
the grave responsibility of the tragedy which had befallen
humanity. In tremendous pain he whispered repeatedly:
" I suffer for all who die in the battlefield. . .   Oh, this

war! . . . I feel this war will be my death." But in spite of his deep sorrow he never lost his resignation to the Will of God.

THE SUPREME HOLOCAUST

The anguish of Pius X reached its zenith when he held a farewell audience for the theological students who were forced to leave the Eternal City and abandon their sacred studies in order to return to their various countries to fight one another. He blessed English, French, Slavs, Austrians, Germans and Belgians, realizing that these young men who now stood side by side united in their love for the Pope would, within a few months, meet again as enemies at the battle front. With tears in his eyes he admonished them solemnly: " Show yourselves worthy of the Faith you profess, and in war don't forget mercy and compassion." He paused for a moment and turned his eyes to heaven as though in a last desperate effort to plead with the Almighty for peace and harmony among men, but his prayer went unanswered. This sorrow was plainly too much for him; he recalled the words of the Divine Master: " I am the good shepherd. The good shepherd giveth his life for his sheep " (*John* x. 11), and offered his life a holocaust for the salvation of the world.

The robust constitution of the Pope which had weathered the storm of attacks on the Church in Mantua and Venice gradually broke under the painful impact of the war. " He was tired in soul, shaken and depressed," wrote his doctor, Professor Marchiafava. On the afternoon of August 15th, 1914, he felt extremely ill and had to retire to bed. The 16th and 17th he spent struggling from bed to study-table time and time again in the hope of spending his last ounce of energy in the cause of the Church. On the 18th his condition fluctuated, and while at moments the end seemed near, at other times he felt sufficiently well to conceive the hope of recovering and returning to his work. The morning of the 19th brought an unexpected relapse, and it became certain that the end was nigh. The Pope was now fully convinced that all hope of recovery must be abandoned, and he resigned himself, breathing, " Father, into Thy hands I commend my spirit." All anxiety and worry had left him and an air of peace and joy surrounded the dying Pope. " There was no sign of excitement and no word of complaint," said Cardinal Merry del Val. Fully conscious, he received towards midday the Viaticum and Extreme Unction with great joy and peace.

Towards evening the big bell of St. Peter's sounded solemnly to proclaim to the Romans that Christ's Vicar was dying. All the bells in the city took up the peal simultaneously, and a heavy cloud of sorrow covered that city whose children were about to lose their beloved father. Churches were filled with people praying fervently, many offering their lives that God might prolong the life of the Pope. Men, women and children lifted their hands to heaven and begged that God would not deprive them of their only hope in those days of dreadful anguish. But God had decided differently. While the whole world trembled with anxiety, Pius X lay in bed calm and recollected. He whispered fervent ejaculations, asking God to forgive him his sins and to spare His sinful people who were so mercilessly destroying one another.

He gave his last farewell greeting to his faithful friend and loyal co-worker, the Cardinal Secretary of State, who had stood at his side for the past eleven years and had shared his sorrows and joys. The dying Pope could no longer speak, but with a look of great joy and love used his last ounce of strength to embrace and kiss the hand of his friend. The silent gesture gave expression to his whole-hearted gratitude and love. Then he smiled at his sisters and the other Cardinals present around his bedside, inviting them to turn their eyes heavenwards as he breathed his *consummatum est*. He fell asleep and after a few moments moved once again to make the Sign of the Cross; then he folded his arms, and a mysterious look came over his face as though he beheld the presence of a heavenly visitant. At 1.15 on the morning of August 20th, he kissed his little crucifix and closed his eyes forever.

" His death could not have been more peaceful," testifies Professor Marchiafava, who was present. The Archbishop of

Pisa, Cardinal Maffi, gave expression to the general opinion when he said that Pius X was one of the first victims of the war. Sorrow for his children, delivered to fury and hatred, had broken his heart.

In the early hours of the morning a little altar was erected in the sick-room, and a few Cardinals, prelates and confidants of the Pope celebrated the Holy Sacrifice of the Mass. Others approached the bed and touched the body with their rosaries, medals and crucifixes to be preserved as precious memories and relics. The same pathetic scene was witnessed again the following day when the body, clad in Papal vestments, was exhibited in the Throne room, where crowds of people of all classes and nationalities came, blocking the courtyard of St. Damasus, the Vatican stairways and many rooms, not so much to pray for the dead Pope as to beg his intercession before the throne of God. The multitude was so great that the Vatican Guards had to come on the scene to maintain order. Two Monsignori stood by the body of the Pope and touched it with religious objects which the crowds presented for that purpose.

The whole world, even the enemies of the Church, bowed in reverence before the greatness and sanctity of this unique personality. The great Protestant newspaper of France, *Le Temps* of Paris, wrote on August 21st, 1914: " Pius X was never led by the motives which determine human decisions. He was above the things of earth and wholly orientated to things divine. His faith alone was the light which illumined his path. The reality, power and sovereignty of his spirit was evidenced by his determination to preserve the rights and freedom of the Church." On the same day *The Times* of London wrote: " All who appreciate the true meaning of sanctity must unite themselves with the Catholic Church which weeps to-day for the loss of a holy priest, a great bishop, and a famous Pope."

The Socialist paper *L'Humanité* of Paris wrote: " A great Pope has died. His politics were extremely simple; they consisted in restoring the values of faith with apostolic force. He could conduct this policy with authority because the simplicity of his soul and the sincerity of his virtue was never doubted. Judge him as you wish, you must admit he was a great Pope." A democratic newspaper of Rome did not hesitate to assert: " We have seen living in our midst the form of the poor man of Assisi—Pius X is a saint."

His death caused very great sorrow among the diplomats and ambassadors who had had dealings with him during his life. Cardinal Merry del Val reports: "I saw several diplomats moved to tears. One of them, a non-Catholic, spoke to me the morning after his death and told me that he had it in mind to request his Government to appoint him to a new field of action because, whoever the new Pope might be, without Pius X, Rome would not be for him the capital of the world. Another diplomat, speaking of the general chaos into which Europe had fallen, said that with the death of Pius X the last hope and light had been extinguished and now nothing remained but darkness all about."

THE LAST TESTAMENT OF PIUS X

Pius X wrote his last testament on December 30th, 1909. It resembles those of the Popes of the earliest Christian times. It reads: "I was born poor, I have lived in poverty and am sure that I shall die a poor man. I commend my sisters, who have always lived with me, to the generosity of the Holy See and beg that they be allowed a small sum of money each month to support them in their old age. . . I expressly command that my body shall not be touched or embalmed. According to the custom it should be exposed for a few hours and then buried in the crypt of St. Peter's."

Two days after his death the contents of the last testament were made public. The spirit of sacrifice and humility expressed in it made a deep impression on the people, who were amazed at his heroic sanctity. "Pius X will certainly be raised to the honour of the altar . . . he is a saint," was on the lips of all. A correspondent of Le Temps, Jean Carrère, telegraphed his paper in the following words: " This testament reveals the truly evangelical spirit of Pius X. It caused a magnificent manifestation of public feeling in the Basilica of St. Peter's, where the whole of Rome, kneeling before the body, called out together, ' St. Pius, pray for us.' I have seen impressive ceremonies in Rome, but never have I witnessed anything like this magnificent spectacle at which a gigantic crowd of people of all classes unanimously declared the Pope who had just died a saint . . . Vox populi, vox Dei."

IN THE PEACE OF THE VATICAN GROTTO

On the evening of August 23rd, 1914, the humble son of Riese was buried according to his wish in the crypt of St. Peter's. His grave was on the right of the little stone stairway which leads from the Basilica to the grotto under the statue of St. Andrew. The body was laid in a plain marble sarcophagus adorned only with the words " Pius Papa X." On the floor in front of the tomb there was a plate with an inscription which synthesizes the character, the virtue and the Pontificate of Pius X. It reads:

PIUS PAPA X

PAUPER ET DIVES

MITIS ET HUMILIS CORDE

REIQUE CATHOLICÆ VINDEX FORTIS

INSTAURARE OMNIA IN CHRISTO

SATAGENS

PIE OBIIT DIE XX AUG. A. D. MCMXIV

" Pius X; poor and rich; meek and humble of heart; strong defender of the rights of the Church; labouring to restore all things in Christ, died piously on August 20th, 1914."

The body remained here until 1943, when the excavations in the Vatican Grotto caused it to be removed to a chapel in the grotto. In 1944 it was brought into the Basilica and placed in a niche in the wall of the chapel of the Annunciation.

A Prelate said at the burial service, " Pius X is dead, but he still lives on in the memory of the people and in the history of the Church. I have no doubt but that this part of the Vatican grotto will become a place of pilgrimage." This prophecy was fulfilled; from near and far men of all nations came to pray at the grave of the holy Pope. The number became so great that it was impossible for the crypt to hold the crowds, and many knelt in the Basilica itself just over

the tomb. Cardinals, bishops, prelates and priests celebrated
Mass on the little altar near the tomb, and many of the faithful
showed their devotion to Pius X by receiving Holy Communion
at this altar. They brought candles, flowers and votive
plaques which were immediately removed, so that the
veneration of the people would not become a cult, and so
delay the Beatification process.

In order that the faithful might easily find the spot in the
Basilica directly over the tomb, Cardinal Merry del Val
had a metal plate with the inscription " Pius Papa X " set
into the floor. On the 20th of each month the pious Cardinal
celebrated Holy Mass on the little altar in the grotto near
the tomb, uutil February 20th, 1930, six days before his
own unexpected death.

All felt that they had in Pius X a new helper and intercessor
at the throne of God. The devotion and confidence of the
people grew continually in a way that was, " humanly speaking,
inexplicable," as a Cardinal said.

Finally, the Cardinals resident in Rome, with one accord
demanded that the processes for Beatification and Canonization
be started immediately. This was the ardent wish of millions
of the faithful, including bishops, prelates and princes. It
is unique in the history of the Church that the processes
should be started by the Cardinals. On February 14th, 1923,
they appointed Don Benedetto Pierami, Abbot of the Roman
Benedictine Abbey of St. Prassede, Postulator for the Cause.
At the same time the canonical diocesan processes were
started in all the places in which Pius X had lived. These
were concluded when the Congregation of Rites introduced
the Cause of Beatification on February 12th, 1943.

Immediately after this followed the Apostolic Process
to investigate the virtues of the Servant of God. On
September 3rd, 1950, after thorough and diligent investiga-
tion, the process concluded with the declaration of heroic
virtue and gave him the title " Venerable." Never once was
it necessary to seek petitions for the Beatification; they poured
in in thousands. The deep inner conviction of the sanctity
of Pius X caused the faithful of the whole world to fill the
archives of Postulation to overflowing with petitions for his
Beatification.

CHAPTER XII

APOTHEOSIS
(1923-1951)

THE MONUMENT IN ST. PETER'S

PERHAPS never before has a celebration in memory of a Pope found such a strong echo among the people as that which took place on June 28th, 1923, in the Basilica of St. Peter's, at the unveiling of the statue of Pius X. This monument was not only the traditional token of honour presented by the members of the Sacred College to the Pope who created them Cardinals, but also an expression of the love and admiration of the whole Catholic world.

No sooner was it intimated that a monument was to be erected to the memory of Pius X than from all five continents subscriptions and donations poured in. Rich and poor gave what they could, for all wanted to play an active part in honouring the memory of the beloved Pontiff. Most of the gifts were accompanied by letters of petition for the early Beatification of Pius X—a proof that he had long ago erected a monument to himself in the hearts of the people.

The statue is of white marble and is very true to life. It seems as if Pius X were trying to step out of the niche and walk towards the altar of the Chair to celebrate the Sacred Mysteries. His arms are outstretched in a gesture of urgent appeal to the whole world and at the same time of total sacrifice of himself. In no more characteristic way could the memory of the great Pontiff have been transmitted to the world. He seems to beg for peace and mercy and puts all into the hands of God Who directs the faith of the people.

On the occasion of the unveiling of the statue Pius XI said: " The dead Pope still speaks; he truly speaks; he speaks by the magnificent simplicity of the whole work; a simplicity which is so much in accord with the humble life of the glorified Pope. It seems to Us that his posture in the statue gives expression to his whole being as father, saint and Pope.

The outstretched arms of the father speak of love, beneficence and pardon. The saint seems to say ' Sursum Corda.' He seems to tell us that our path is heavenwards and to remind us that above the perishable things of this earth the eternal riches of heaven await us. He seems to encourage us to strive for heaven, and for closer union with God, ' Venite Adoremus.' He offers to divine Justice the immaculate gift and holy sacrifice of his heart. He offers himself for the salvation of the world. All this the monument seems to say; but it also awakens the memory of the beautiful and saintly life he lived amongst us. To all who look upon it it is an encouragement to pray, to sanctify themselves, to pardon injuries and to do good. This monument is an honour which even the humble child of Riese could not refuse in spite of his great humility."

A GLORIOUS CENTENARY

On June 2nd, 1935, a century had passed since the day on which " a great saint and a great Pope " was born in a poor little cottage in a remote village. The whole Catholic world felt the urge to celebrate this centenary with great splendour. They could not tire of paying honour to the Pope who was, in Pius XII's phrase, a " glowing flame of charity and shining splendour of sanctity."

The people felt that Pius X was near to them, and they longed for the day when they could acclaim him " Beatus." The fame of his sanctity spread more and more, not only through Italy, but throughout the whole world, and crowds still continued to stream into the Vatican grotto to visit his tomb. Riese, too, became a place of pilgrimage; people wanted to see the place where the child who was to " renew all things in Christ " had been born. The pilgrimages which took place during the centenary year were an expression of the love and veneration in the hearts of all for Pius X.

THE EXHUMATION OF THE REMAINS

On February 12th, 1943, the Process for Beatification was introduced. This was followed by the Apostolic Process, which was concluded on September 3rd, 1950, with the declaration of his heroic virtues. The Cause of the Beatification had then entered its decisive stages. With great excitement all awaited the exhumation of the remains. In what condition would they find the body of the holy Pope, which in so short a time had become the object of veneration for the whole Catholic world?

When Pius X departed this life on August 20th, 1914, the world stood at the beginning of the dreadful war which he had prophesied, but when the sarcophagus was opened a still more murderous and extensive war had ravaged the earth. An unknown hand had written on the leaden coffin which contained the body of Pius X the prayer: " Save Rome; save Italy; save the world." We do not know who was responsible for the writing of these words, but they were the first thing seen by the Beatification Tribunal when they opened the sarcophagus to examine the remains on May 19th, 1944.

Opening the coffin they found the body intact, clothed in the papal insignia as it had been buried thirty years before. Under the taut skin which covered the face the outline of the skull was clearly recognizable. The hollows of the eyes appeared dark but not empty; they were covered by eyelids much wrinkled and sunk. The hair was white and covered the top of the head completely. The pectoral cross and pastoral ring shone brilliantly. In his last testament Pius X had specially requested that his body should not be touched and that the traditional embalming should not be done. In spite of this the body was excellently preserved. No part of the skeleton was uncovered, no bones were exposed. While the body was rigid, the arms, elbows and shoulders were quite flexible. The hands were beautiful and slender and the nails on the fingers were perfectly preserved.

A solemn silence prevailed throughout the whole proceeding; it was as though honour were being paid to the bodies of the martyrs, as in the catacombs in early Christian times. The body was then taken to the Chapel of the Holy Cross in the Basilica, where it remained from May 19th to July 2nd, 1944, and was the object of veneration for the whole Roman faithful. Pius XII went in person to venerate it.

TWO MIRACLES PROPOSED FOR THE BEATIFICATION

With the recognition of the heroic virtues of the Servant of God the Process for the Beatification reached its conclusion. But it was necessary to wait until God Himself confirmed the judgment of His Vicar on earth. The Process of Beatification tells of many graces and favours which had been received during his lifetime by the blessing of Pius X. As many are recorded as taking place through his intercession after his death. Of these, two were recognized, after a strict scientific examination, as being genuine miracles approved by the Church.

SUDDEN HEALING OF OSTEOSARCOMA OF THE HIP

The subject of the first of these miracles was a Sister of the Convent of the Visitation in Dôle, France, by the name of Marie Françoise Deperras. She was suddenly healed from an osteosarcoma of the hip—an illness much feared by the doctors.

As the illness had been declared incurable from the very first diagnosis the Sister prepared herself for death. The end seemed imminent as the pains were unbearable. The nurse of the convent, Sister Germaine, received a relic of Pius X, and persuaded the other Sisters of the Community to join in a Novena to the great Pope, to obtain through his intercession the healing of the sick Sister. The relic was fastened with a pin to the clothing of the patient while the Community joined in fervent prayer for her recovery. Nine days passed and nothing happened. Her condition became even worse, but her confidence in Pius X was very strong. Instead of despair, the worsening of her condition only incited the Sisters to greater confidence and they started a second Novena for the same intention. Though on December 6th her condition seemed hopeless, on the morning of the 7th she felt as if new life were streaming through her veins. She suddenly felt better and all pain vanished. She sat up in bed feeling in perfect health. Imagination? No, a first class miracle.

The doctor, who had left her a few hours before, had advised the Sisters to give her great care and attention as death was likely to come at any moment. When summoned, he was absolutely dumbfounded and could do nothing but confirm complete restoration to health and admit that he was faced with a fact wholly inexplicable in the light of human science. Besides this doctor, Henri Sullerot, the surgeon René Jennessau, and the practitioner, Félix Bourgeat, with whom Sullerot had repeatedly discussed the case and who had frequently visited the sick Sister, both admitted that the cure was inexplicable from a clinico-pathological point of view. All three doctors felt certain that the healing had a supernatural cause. Sister Marie Françoise rose from her bed and immediately took up her place in community life, completely healed. On March 21st, 1950, experts from the Sacred Congregation of Rites declared after a careful examination of all the data of the case that it was a sudden, complete and lasting cure which could only be explained in terms of the supernatural.

THE SUDDEN HEALING OF A MALIGNANT TUMOUR

The second miracle approved by all the doctors and specialists consulted, and recognized by the Sacred Congregation of Rites after the usual and detailed examination, took place in Italy. Sister Benedetta Maria of the Convent of St. Clare in Boves, in the Province of Cuneo, suffered from a dangerous abdominal growth—cancer. Before she was attacked by this she had already suffered from a dangerous illness of the stomach, and this new affliction rendered her condition serious. Her death was expected at any moment.

But in the Convent of Boves the Sisters were aware that the Process for the Beatification of Pius X was in progress and they resolved to beg his intercession. In February, 1938, the Community started a novena for this intention. The doctor, Dr. Abrate, would have liked to attempt an operation, though he admitted that he could not hope for much success. The patient and her Sisters firmly resisted this plan, since even the doctor had doubts about it. In the meantime the novena was continued.

One day Sister Benedetta was overwhelmed with devotion

to Pius X, and she swallowed a relic—a small part of his clothing. Miraculous medicine!

At that very instant the pain ceased, and the growth, which had become the size of an orange, vanished at a stroke. The Sisters were at that moment in choir, and could not believe their eyes when they saw Sister Benedetta enter the chapel fully dressed and unassisted. As soon as they left the chapel all the nuns together started asking questions excitedly, and the Sister could not get a chance to tell her story. She answered every one of the torrent of questions with the same expression: " Healed by Pius X! Healed by Pius X! "

Very soon the doctor came on the scene and wanted to know what all the excitement was about. When he was told the facts one by one, in anything but chronological order, he shook his head in amazement. " Doctor," said the Mother Superior, " you still have a little faith left." "But," replied the physician, " here we don't need faith; we are standing before an irrefutable fact." The doctor waited for some time in order to assure himself that the cure was permanent, before giving his certificate. Then he dictated his certificate to the Sisters and thanked and praised God Whose power had been manifested before his eyes. The very day that the cure had taken place, Sister Benedetta took up her duty once more as portress, and told everyone who came to the gate of the wonderful favour she had received at the intercession of Pius X.

The hour for the glorification of the servant of God was at hand. On February 11th, 1951, Pius XII acknowledged, by his authority as Vicar of Christ, the two miracles, and on March 4th following he declared that the Beatification of the Servant of God could be prepared without hesitation.

RAISED TO THE RANK OF THE BEATI

On June 3rd, 1951, in a most solemn ceremony, Pius X was raised to the honour of the altar. Providence arranged that this event should take place on the anniversary of the Baptism of the son of the poor Cursore of Riese. None of those who on June 3rd, 1835, accompanied him to the Church of Riese even suspected that 116 years later the Holy Father, amidst a vast crowd of pilgrims from all over the world, would venerate that child under the title of "Blessed." On the broad steps of St. Peter's, before the gilt shrine which contained the remains, Pius XII venerated the new Beatus. "Heavenly joy fills my heart," he said, and in a masterly way he painted the life of his great predecessor, stressing his eminent virtues, his shining example and his incomparable achievements. The long awaited wish of the faithful was fulfilled. All the bells of Rome chimed in festive manner, ringing out the song of praise and jubilation inscribed on the obelisk in the centre of the square of St. Peter's:

CHRISTUS VINCIT, CHRISTUS REGNAT, CHRISTUS IMPERAT

INDEX

INDEX

Ratti, Don Achilli, future Pope Pius XI, 100; Mgr., 218.

René Bazin, 129.

Rheims, 221.

Riese, 1, 3, 25, 52, 95, 97, 99, 129, 144; 180; the humble cottage there remains unchanged, a symbol of glorified poverty, 198; the poor Cursore of, 238.

Rodrigo, Don, 78.

Romanello, Don, Antonio, 54.

Romanin-Jacur, Leone, of Salzano, 93.

Rome, 51, 52, 170.

Rosa, Mgr. G. B., 9.

Rossi, Mgr., 133.

Rouen, Ecclesiastical Council, 162.

Salzano advances in every respect under its pastor's care, 41, 80, 95, 144, 158, 182, 206.

Sacred Congregation of Rites, 236-7.

St. Mark's Cathedral, Venice, has excellent choir, 115, 116.

Sanminiatelli, Card., 208.

Sanson, Margherita, mother of Pope, 1, 4; overjoyed with son's free place at Padua, "haven of peace," 7-8, 15; 53; welcomes patriarch-son home, 96.

Sarto, Giovanni Battista, father of Pope Pius X, 1; 4; consents to clerical life for son, 5; hears from Mgr. Casagrande that Giuseppe is granted free place in Padua seminary, 7-8.

—— Giuseppe, birth, 1; baptismal name, 1, 2, 3; receives Confirmation, early studies, "Bepi," pet name, 4, 5; gets free place in Padua seminary, 7-8; leaves Padua a priest; disturbing news of home, and father soon dies, 9; loses two true friends, Don Tito Fuzarini and Don Pietro Jacuzzi; at home, 10; visits home of his married sister, Teresa, at "The Two Swords" inn, and the villa of Countess Marina Loredan-Gradenigo, 11; still so depressed he had to collect aid, and was generously helped by Riese; begins study of Theology, 1854, 11; Bishop of Treviso, Mgr. Farina, reports him "a veritable angel" next year, 11; permitted to have long walks with his friend, Pietro Zamburlini, later Bishop of Udine, 12; declines to drive in pony and trap with married sister, 13; first two Minor Orders at Treviso, 1855, second two, same

year, 1857, Priesthood, 1858, mother, sisters and brother present, 13; "constant example of sincerity, piety and conduct," 13-14.

Ordained by Mgr. Antonio Farina in Cathedral of Castelfranco Veneto, 1858, 14; his First Mass at Riese parish church next day, 14; curate of Tombolo (1858-67), 15; untiring labour, 17, 18; Eucharist centre of his life, 19; constant interest in the poor, 20; toiled for every necessary reform, 21; known as "curate of curates," 23; helped his mother as necessary, 24; his ceaseless charity reproved by Don Constantine, 25; divides his last bushel of grain with a beggar, 27; preaches panegyric on St. Antony of Padua, 28; appointed pastor of Salzano, 28; is called "Giuseppe Santo," 29; Salzanese not pleased with promotion of curate of Tombolo, 30; first sermon at Salzano, 31; urges teaching of the Catechism, 33; unwittingly attracted neighbours to his church, 33; ceaseless activities at Salzano, and local Jew aids him, 34; his charity at Salzano reaches limits of human heroism, 35; fights cholera of 1873, 38; checks destructive fire, 41.

Salzano completely reformed, 41; Bishop Zinelli lauds his untiring parish priest, 41; summoned to the Curia of Treviso and appointed Canon, to live in the Seminary, 42; creeps quietly out of Salzano, 43; diocesan chancellor, 44; did not change his garb, 45; multiplied his activities here, 46; still surpassingly generous, 47; rigid but exceedingly just in discipline, 48; provost of Cathedral, 48; Vicar Capitular, 49; demotes relative, 50; office of Pro Vicar-General added to his other responsibilities, 50; his marvellous work under Mgr. Apollonio and Mgr. Callegari (1880-1884) recalled, 51; appointed Bishop of Mantua by Bishop Apollonio (1884,) 52; visits mother at Riese, and accepts very reluctantly, 52; consecrated Bishop, November, 1884, by Card. Lucido Maria Parocchi, 53; 54; shortage of priests; appeals for worthy support for Seminary, and restores it to the highest efficiency, concerning himself deeply with ordinations, 58, 59, 60,

M. H. GILL AND SON LIMITED, PRINTERS, DUBLIN.